Changing Careers For Dummies®

P9-AES-920

Cheat Sheet

Ten Signs That You Are Ready for a New Career

You may need to consider changing careers if any of the following are true about you:

- You get depressed every Sunday night at the thought of going back to work on Monday.
- You spend more time recovering from work than having fun.
- You watch the clock all day long.
- You spend more time checking your personal e-mail than working.
- You take frequent mental health days.
- You have a resignation letter drafted and waiting.
- You complain about your job to anyone who listens.
- You are bored silly at work.
- You are consistently late for work.
- You hope to win the lottery to solve your life's problems.

If you want to feel fulfilled, satisfied, and excited again, get your frustrations out of your system in Chapter 2. Then start exploring your future in Chapter 3.

Six Unique Work Arrangements

When changing careers, you may find that one of the following non-traditional work arrangements suits you better than working 9:00 to 5:00, five days a week:

- **Compressed workweek:** Work 40 hours in three or four days, instead of the typical five days.
- **Job share:** Partner with someone else to split the workload, and the pay, of one job.
- **Contract work:** Contract with a company through an employment agency to work for the duration of a specific project.
- **Telecommute:** Set yourself up with the equipment you need to perform your job from home.
- **Freelance:** Develop a working relationship with several companies so that you can choose the projects you want to work on.
- **Run a home-based business:** Launch a business that you run from your home.

Chapter 4 provides more details about these and other work arrangement options.

Discovering What You Want to Do When You Grow Up

To discover career interests, begin to do the following:

- Listen for passion in your own voice when you talk about something.
- Catalog the tools you love to use.
- Notice the problems you like to help your friends solve.
- Look for fascinations you've had since you were a kid.
- Recognize which personal experiences spark a sense of passion within you.

Chapter 6 tells you how to track down even the most elusive passions with these methods.

For Dummies: Bestselling Book Series for Beginners

Changing Careers For Dummies®

Cheat Sheet

Five Unusual Skills to Practice During Your Career Change

Doing the following can help you ease the transition between careers:

- **Value the ways you procrastinate.** By noticing where you hesitate or when you avoid situations, you uncover clues about what doesn't work for you in your career and your life.

- **Find your truth with a reality check.** Asking yourself probing questions helps you to step out of a comfortable, but possibly unsatisfying, rut and into a career and a life that meet your needs.

- **Listen to your cravings.** Pay attention to what you desire and you can discover what is truly important to you.

- **Sort out the essence of what you want.** By focusing on the feeling that you want to experience, you have a greater likelihood of succeeding because you aren't locked into achieving a specific outcome.

- **Distinguish deal-breakers from trade-offs.** You need to recognize when an element of a job is a deal-breaker that no amount of negotiating can resolve. Separating deal-breakers from trade-offs allows you to turn away from career opportunities that are bound to lead to frustration and angst.

Four Ways to Enhance Your Skills

Use the following ideas to beef-up the skills you need to succeed in your next career:

- **Get course credit for prior work experience.** Some education programs allow you to convert your experience into academic credits so that you can skip a prerequisite or decrease the number of courses you must take to finish a degree.

- **Take a teleclass.** This new form of education allows people from all over the world to participate in a class at the same time. All you do is pick up the phone in your home or office to join in.

- **Participate in company-sponsored training.** Many companies provide some sort of education benefit, including reimbursing you for college expenses, paying for you to attend a seminar, or sending you to a conference.

- **Sign up for online classes.** A broad variety of courses and degree programs are offered online, which makes it possible for you to go to school without leaving home.

Web Sites for Investigating Your Career Ideas

The following Web sites can help you find out what you need to know about your next career:

- **About.com** (www.about.com): Research jobs, industries, and career-change topics.

- **Review.com** (www.review.com): Read unique explanations of 100 interesting careers.

- **Wetfeet.com** (www.wetfeet.com): Explore your favorite industries and careers.

- **Salary.com** (www.salary.com): Conduct your compensation research.

- **Occupational Outlook Handbook** (http://stats.bls.gov/ocohome.htm): Check out potential careers.

Hungry Minds™

Copyright © 2001 Hungry Minds, Inc. All rights reserved.

Cheat Sheet $2.95 value. Item 5376-3.

For more information about Hungry Minds, call 1-800-762-2974.

Hungry Minds, the Hungry Minds logo, For Dummies, the For Dummies Bestselling Book Series logo and all related trade dress are trademarks or registered trademarks of Hungry Minds, Inc. All other trademarks are the property of their respective owners.

For Dummies: Bestselling Book Series for Beginners

Praise for Changing Careers For Dummies

"If it's a life-changing job search you're weighing, that is to say, a career change, you can do no better than to read this book. It's one of the best I've ever read on career change. Carol has really done her homework, and offers very many helpful ideas to guide you on your way."

> — Richard N. Bolles, author *What Color is Your Parachute? A Practical Manual for Job-Hunters and Career-Changers*

"Carol McClelland's book has lots of solid tips for people who need a new direction."

> — Dave Murphy, Career Search Editor, *San Francisco Chronicle*

"This book is like a Swiss Army Knife. Giving people the tools required for the success in the new world of work."

> — Richard J. Leider, founder, The Inventor Group; author *Whistle While You Work, The Power of Purpose*, and the best-selling *Repacking Your Bags*

"If you want a career that taps your true talents and allows you to answer to your highest calling, make *Changing Careers For Dummies* your constant companion for the duration of your career change."

> — Frank McKinney, author of *Make it BIG, 49 Secrets to Building a Life of Extreme Success*

"Dr. McClelland has triumphed in creating a valuable resource for those among us who feel overwhelmed by changing careers. Her step-by-step approach spins the yarn for creating a modern tapestry of career opportunities. An organizational expert, she not only provides the basic pattern for meaningful career change, but she also coaches career changers to make the current and future career search productive. Thorough, organized, and replete with common sense, this book is just right for those who need guidance to stay on track and incorporate passion into their career journey."

> — Robert Chope, PhD, Professor of Counseling at San Francisco State University, author of *Dancing Naked: Breaking Through the Emotional Limits that Keep You From the Job You Want*

"This is a very useful, no-nonsense guide to doing that difficult thing — changing the whole way that you make your living, feel useful, and gain your identity in our modern world. I would recommend it."

— William Bridges, William Bridges & Associates, author of *Job Shift: How to Prosper in a Workplace without Jobs*

"Carol McClelland's *Changing Careers For Dummies* is almost as good as having a career counselor by your side. The practical checklists, targeted inquiries, and brainstorming exercises provide inspiration as you weave together your life themes, create your own definition of success, and implement career change."

— Deb Koen, Columnist, *The Wall Street Journal's* CareerJournal.com, co-author, *Career Choice Change & Challenge*, vice-president, Career Development Services

"In this era of rapid cultural change, one of the greatest needs is for an honest map for the journey of transforming what you do and how you do it. Carol McClelland has given us a very good map indeed, one that should prove invaluable to anyone standing at the brink — or caught in the midst — of these brave and necessary transitions."

— Sherry Ruth Anderson, PhD, co-author, *The Cultural Creatives*

"Finally, Carol has released a book with the information that has helped myself and so many of my colleagues with job transitions. This book is a must for anyone who wants a career they feel passionate about."

— Dr. T. Lafeber, President, Lafeber Company

"Great book for getting focused and on track to create your perfect career. Carol McClelland transforms what can be a scary and difficult transition into an easy, exciting, and empowering process."

— Donna Fisher, Donna Fisher Presents

"Carol's work represents a remarkably holistic guide for constructing a new chapter. A welcome addition to the field!"

— Pamela McLean & Fredric Hudson, PhD, authors of *Life Launch: A Passionate Guide to the Rest of Your Life & Adult Years*

TM

References for the Rest of Us!™

...FOR DUMMIES

BESTSELLING BOOK SERIES

Do you find that traditional reference books are overloaded with technical details and advice you'll never use? Do you postpone important life decisions because you just don't want to deal with them? Then our *For Dummies*® business and general reference book series is for you.

For Dummies business and general reference books are written for those frustrated and hard-working souls who know they aren't dumb, but find that the myriad of personal and business issues and the accompanying horror stories make them feel helpless. *For Dummies* books use a lighthearted approach, a down-to-earth style, and even cartoons and humorous icons to dispel fears and build confidence. Lighthearted but not lightweight, these books are perfect survival guides to solve your everyday personal and business problems.

> "More than a publishing phenomenon, 'Dummies' is a sign of the times."
>
> — The New York Times

> "A world of detailed and authoritative information is packed into them..."
>
> — U.S. News and World Report

> "...you won't go wrong buying them."
>
> — Walter Mossberg, Wall Street Journal, on For Dummies books

Already, millions of satisfied readers agree. They have made For Dummies the #1 introductory level computer book series and a best-selling business book series. They have written asking for more. So, if you're looking for the best and easiest way to learn about business and other general reference topics, look to For Dummies to give you a helping hand.

Hungry Minds™

6/01

Changing Careers FOR DUMMIES®

by Carol L. McClelland, PhD

Foreword by Richard N. Bolles

Hungry Minds™

Best-Selling Books • Digital Downloads • e-Books • Answer Networks • e-Newsletters • Branded Web Sites • e-Learning

New York, NY ◆ Cleveland, OH ◆ Indianapolis, IN

650
.14
MCCLELL
2001

Changing Careers For Dummies®

Published by:
Hungry Minds, Inc.
909 Third Avenue
New York, NY 10022
www.hungryminds.com
www.dummies.com

Library Resource Center
Renton Technical College
3000 N.E. 4th St.
Renton, WA 98056

Copyright © 2001 Hungry Minds, Inc. All rights reserved. No part of this book, including interior design, cover design, and icons, may be reproduced or transmitted in any form, by any means (electronic, photocopying, recording, or otherwise) without the prior written permission of the publisher.

Library of Congress Control Number: 2001089322

ISBN: 0-7645-5376-3

Printed in the United States of America

10 9 8 7 6 5 4 3

1B/TQ/QR/QS/IN

Distributed in the United States by Hungry Minds, Inc.

Distributed by CDG Books Canada Inc. for Canada; by Transworld Publishers Limited in the United Kingdom; by IDG Norge Books for Norway; by IDG Sweden Books for Sweden; by IDG Books Australia Publishing Corporation Pty. Ltd. for Australia and New Zealand; by TransQuest Publishers Pte Ltd. for Singapore, Malaysia, Thailand, Indonesia, and Hong Kong; by Gotop Information Inc. for Taiwan; by ICG Muse, Inc. for Japan; by Intersoft for South Africa; by Eyrolles for France; by International Thomson Publishing for Germany, Austria and Switzerland; by Distribuidora Cuspide for Argentina; by LR International for Brazil; by Galileo Libros for Chile; by Ediciones ZETA S.C.R. Ltda. for Peru; by WS Computer Publishing Corporation, Inc., for the Philippines; by Contemporanea de Ediciones for Venezuela; by Express Computer Distributors for the Caribbean and West Indies; by Micronesia Media Distributor, Inc. for Micronesia; by Chips Computadoras S.A. de C.V. for Mexico; by Editorial Norma de Panama S.A. for Panama; by American Bookshops for Finland.

For general information on Hungry Minds' products and services please contact our Customer Care department; within the U.S. at 800-762-2974, outside the U.S. at 317-572-3993 or fax 317-572-4002.

For sales inquiries and resellers information, including discounts, premium and bulk quantity sales and foreign language translations please contact our Customer Care department at 800-434-3422, fax 317-572-4002 or write to Hungry Minds, Inc., Attn: Customer Care department, 10475 Crosspoint Boulevard, Indianapolis, IN 46256.

For information on licensing foreign or domestic rights, please contact our Sub-Rights Customer Care department at 212-884-5000.

For information on using Hungry Minds' products and services in the classroom or for ordering examination copies, please contact our Educational Sales department at 800-434-2086 or fax 317-572-4005.

Please contact our Public Relations department at 212-884-5163 for press review copies or 212-884-5000 for author interviews and other publicity information or fax 212-884-5400.

For authorization to photocopy items for corporate, personal, or educational use, please contact Copyright Clearance Center, 222 Rosewood Drive, Danvers, MA 01923, or fax 978-750-4470.

LIMIT OF LIABILITY/DISCLAIMER OF WARRANTY: THE PUBLISHER AND AUTHOR HAVE USED THEIR BEST EFFORTS IN PREPARING THIS BOOK. THE PUBLISHER AND AUTHOR MAKE NO REPRESENTATIONS OR WARRANTIES WITH RESPECT TO THE ACCURACY OR COMPLETENESS OF THE CONTENTS OF THIS BOOK AND SPECIFICALLY DISCLAIM ANY IMPLIED WARRANTIES OF MERCHANTABILITY OR FITNESS FOR A PARTICULAR PURPOSE. THERE ARE NO WARRANTIES WHICH EXTEND BEYOND THE DESCRIPTIONS CONTAINED IN THIS PARAGRAPH. NO WARRANTY MAY BE CREATED OR EXTENDED BY SALES REPRESENTATIVES OR WRITTEN SALES MATERIALS. THE ACCURACY AND COMPLETENESS OF THE INFORMATION PROVIDED HEREIN AND THE OPINIONS STATED HEREIN ARE NOT GUARANTEED OR WARRANTED TO PRODUCE ANY PARTICULAR RESULTS, AND THE ADVICE AND STRATEGIES CONTAINED HEREIN MAY NOT BE SUITABLE FOR EVERY INDIVIDUAL. NEITHER THE PUBLISHER NOR AUTHOR SHALL BE LIABLE FOR ANY LOSS OF PROFIT OR ANY OTHER COMMERCIAL DAMAGES, INCLUDING BUT NOT LIMITED TO SPECIAL, INCIDENTAL, CONSEQUENTIAL, OR OTHER DAMAGES.

Trademarks: For Dummies, Dummies Man, A Reference for the Rest of Us!, The Dummies Way, Dummies Daily, and related trade dress are registered trademarks or trademarks of Hungry Minds, Inc. in the United States and other countries, and may not be used without written permission. All other trademarks are the property of their respective owners. Hungry Minds, Inc. is not associated with any product or vendor mentioned in this book.

Hungry Minds™ is a trademark of Hungry Minds, Inc.

About the Author

As a pioneering career-change consultant, **Carol L. McClelland, PhD,** founder of Transition Dynamics, has helped thousands of clients, students, and readers discover more fulfilling careers and lives.

Carol believes a good career is satisfying and supports you in living the life you want to live. She guides people from all walks of life to create careers based on their unique dreams of how they want to live. With her support, her clients start their own businesses, enter the corporate world, find niches in non-profits, return to school, or recreate their own position within the same company. To find out more about her career change programs, visit www.getrollingagain.com.

Carol's unique understanding of the emotional aspects of changing careers grew from her professional and personal experiences. She became interested in transitions in 1983 while completing her Ph.D. in Industrial/Organizational Psychology at Purdue University. As an organizational consultant within a major insurance company, Carol facilitated various corporate transitions and mentored new employees while dealing with her grief surrounding her father's death and a period of severe burnout that led to her own career change.

Carol shares her ideas about the emotional side of career changes and other life changes in *The Seasons of Change: Using Nature's Wisdom to Grow through Life's Inevitable Ups and Downs* (Conari Press, 1998). To find out more her retreats and programs on this topic, visit www.seasonsofchange.com.

In addition to teaching career-related courses at Purdue University and San Jose State University, Carol presents at conferences and meetings and is a guest on radio talk shows nationwide.

Dedication

To my mother, Margaret McClelland, for teaching me, early in life, to focus on what I enjoy. Thanks for the joy, laughter, and love we've always shared. I am truly blessed.

Author's Acknowledgments

I gained the expertise I share in this book by working with clients as they experienced the bumps and triumphs of changing careers. I am honored to have worked with so many interesting, talented individuals.

To the colleagues, clients, and friends who have responded to a quick question here and there: Thank you for sharing your insights so freely.

With great respect I acknowledge the following people: Sherry Ruth Anderson and Paul Ray for their research on Cultural Creatives; Karen Hanen, Deb Koen, and Matt Griffin for their knowledge of the new flexible workplace; Terry Karp and Mark Guterman for their work on values; Howard Gardner, Clifford Morris, and Branton Shearer for details about Multiple Intelligences; Janice Summers for her perspective as a recruiter; Karen Csejtey for her entrepreneurial experience; and Lance Kasari and my brother, Thomas McClelland, for their views of the scientific world.

I'm also indebted to the following people: Carol Susan Roth, my agent, for calling me when the opportunity to write this book came to her attention; my editors Karen Doran for bringing this book in and Holly McGuire for seeing it through to publication; Mary Goodwin and Marilyn Maze for masterfully editing the manuscript; and Tracy Boggier, Melisa Duffy, Lindsay MacGregor, and Kevin Thorton for the work they and their teams have done to bring this book to career changers everywhere.

Although I love to write, the entire process can be overwhelming at times. For support that I have received I extend my heartfelt gratitude to Sunrise, my golden retriever and constant writing buddy, my family, Conscious Connections, White Spirit community, Connie Allen, Marie Capizzi, Jennifer Lamb, the Kasari family, Carol McDonald, Jennifer Reynolds, Janice Summers, Henry Wolgemuth, and Diandra Wood.

Kent, your ability to keep me laughing, the time we spend in nature, and our easy closeness have enriched my life immeasurably. I thank you for your constant support during the six months I've been writing. Here's to using the power of two to co-create the life we want to share. I love you.

Publisher's Acknowledgments

We're proud of this book; please send us your comments through our Online Registration Form located at www.hungryminds.com

Some of the people who helped bring this book to market include the following:

Acquisitions, Editorial, and Media Development

Project Editor: Mary Goodwin

Acquisitions Editor: Karen Doren

Technical Editor: Marilyn Maze

Editorial Manager: Pam Mourouzis

Editorial Assistant: Jennifer Young

Cover Photos: © Phil Banko/Stone

Production

Project Coordinator: Maridee V. Ennis

Layout and Graphics: Brian Drumm, Joyce Haughey, Jackie Nicholas, Jill Piscitelli, Betty Schulte, Brian Torwelle, Julie Tripetti

Proofreaders: John Greenough, Charles Spencer, TECHBOOKS Production Services

Indexer: TECHBOOKS Production Services

Hungry Minds Consumer Reference Group

Business: Kathleen A. Welton, Vice President and Publisher; Kevin Thornton, Acquisitions Manager

Cooking/Gardening: Jennifer Feldman, Associate Vice President and Publisher

Education/Reference: Diane Graves Steele, Vice President and Publisher

Lifestyles/Pets: Kathleen Nebenhaus, Vice President and Publisher; Tracy Boggier, Managing Editor

Travel: Michael Spring, Vice President and Publisher; Suzanne Jannetta, Editorial Director; Brice Gosnell, Publishing Director

Hungry Minds Consumer Editorial Services: Kathleen Nebenhaus, Vice President and Publisher; Kristin A. Cocks, Editorial Director; Cindy Kitchel, Editorial Director

Hungry Minds Consumer Production: Debbie Stailey, Production Director

Contents at a Glance

Foreword .... *xxiii*

Introduction *1*

Part 1: Setting the Stage for Your Career Change 7
Chapter 1: The World of Work: It Ain't What It Used to Be! 9
Chapter 2: Evaluating Your Current Situation 17
Chapter 3: Exploring Personal Needs and Home Realities 29
Chapter 4: Expanding Your Notion of What's Possible at Work 43
Chapter 5: What to Do in the Meantime 69

Part 11: Searching for Hidden Treasure — Your Passion ... 75
Chapter 6: Uncovering Clues to Your Passion 77
Chapter 7: Thinking Outside the Box 95

Part 111: Career Areas to Stimulate Your Thinking 109
Chapter 8: If You Thrive on Words 111
Chapter 9: If You Think in a Logical, Organized Fashion 129
Chapter 10: If You Connect Well with Others 153
Chapter 11: If You Have a Good Eye 169
Chapter 12: If You Want Your Work to Be Physical 183
Chapter 13: If You Have an Ear for the Sound of Music 195
Chapter 14: If You Love Nature and Its Creatures 205

Part 1V: Weaving It All Together 221
Chapter 15: Preparing Your Game Plan 223
Chapter 16: Testing the Waters of a Potential Career 235
Chapter 17: Getting All the Pieces to Fit 247
Chapter 18: Strengthening the Skills You Need 255
Chapter 19: Taking the Steps to Get Your Job 271
Chapter 20: Taking the Steps to Start Your Business 285

Part V: The Part of Tens 297
Chapter 21: Ten Tips for Staying Sane During Your Career Change 299
Chapter 22: Ten Keys to Keeping Yourself Inspired and Motivated 309

Index 319

Cartoons at a Glance

By Rich Tennant

page 7

page 221

page 109

page 75

page 297

Cartoon Information:
Fax: 978-546-7747
E-Mail: richtennant@the5thwave.com
World Wide Web: www.the5thwave.com

Table of Contents

Foreword..xxiii

Introduction 1

About This Book..1
How This Book Is Organized...2
Part I: Setting the Stage for Your Career Change....................2
Part II: Searching for Hidden Treasure — Your Passion...............3
Part III: Career Areas to Stimulate Your Thinking 3
Part IV: Weaving It All Together...3
Part V: The Part of Tens 4
Icons Used in This Book...4
Ask the Author..5

Part 1: Setting the Stage for Your Career Change 7

Chapter 1: The World of Work: It Ain't What It Used to Be!.........9

Lifetime Employment with One Company: A Pipe Dream for Most.........10
The Corporate World: More a Web Than a Ladder 11
The Cornucopia of Career Choices.......................................12
The One-Size-Fits-All Definition of Success: It No Longer Fits.......13
Onsite Work: No Longer a Necessity 15
9-to-5: Not the Only Option Any More...................................16

Chapter 2: Evaluating Your Current Situation 17

Looking at You and Your Life..18
Who and how you are 18
How you live..20
Your definition of success 21
Sizing Up Your Current Work Arrangement 21
How you work...22
Your pay and benefits 22
Where you work...23
Who you work with 24
Examining the Work You Do Now...26
Listening to Your Inner Cravings...27
Spotting Your Hottest Issues 28

Chapter 3: Exploring Personal Needs and Home Realities **29**

　Wouldn't It Be Great If 29
　Discovering How You Influence Your Work 30
　　Your personality or temperament...30
　　Your values..32
　　Your health..32
　　Your hobbies and interests 33
　Considering Your Location 35
　Looking at the Impact of
　　Family on Your Work...37
　　Your partner..37
　　Your children 37
　　Your parents and grandparents...38
　　Your support network...39
　　Your pets 39
　Writing Down Your Hottest Requests..40

Chapter 4: Expanding Your Notion of What's Possible at Work **43**

　Keeping Your Mind, and Options, Open...44
　Working the Way You Want to Work 45
　　Your work schedule 45
　　Your contract 48
　Working Where You Want to Work...50
　　The kind of company 50
　　The company size 50
　　The company culture...53
　　The purpose of the company..54
　　The company's reach...54
　　The location 56
　　The work area 57
　　The dress code 58
　Getting Paid on Your Terms 60
　　The amount 60
　　Payment options...61
　　Benefits 61
　Working with the Right People 63
　　Your coworkers...64
　　Other players 64
　　Your manager 65
　Recording Your Hottest Desires...66

Chapter 5: What to Do in the Meantime **69**

　When You Feel You Must Stay . . . for Now 69
　When You Can't Stay, but Must Have Money Coming In 71
　When You Don't Have to Stay for the Money 72

Part II: Searching for Hidden Treasure — Your Passion 75

Chapter 6: Uncovering Clues to Your Passion 77

Skills That Make Time Fly 77
    Finding your innate areas of intelligence 78
    Knowing what's as easy as breathing 81
    Thinking about skills you have but don't enjoy 81
    Singling out your favorite skills and intelligences 81
Topics That Make You Sizzle with Excitement 82
    Subjects that always draw your attention 82
    Subjects that make you want to help others 84
    Subjects that make you want to add your two cents 85
    Subjects that leave you forever searching for solutions 85
    Subjects that constantly call you to find out more 86
    Fascinations that you can trace to childhood 86
    Life-changing events that sparked a mission 86
    Listing your favorite topics of interest 87
Internal Drivers That Guide You to Excel 88
Processes That Make You Come Alive 88
Tools, Equipment, and Raw Materials That Make Your Work Play 89
Industries That Light Your Fire 90
People You Like to Help 91
Things That Make Work Meaningful 92
Recording Your Hottest Passions and Interests 92

Chapter 7: Thinking Outside the Box 95

Putting Your Deck Together 95
Dealing Yourself a Hand to Brainstorm New Careers 96
Sifting Out Your Most Intriguing Career Ideas 101
    Discovering what you love about each idea 103
    Uncovering the pros and cons of each idea 103
    Weaving themes together 104
    Isolating your key elements 104
    Marking your hottest career ideas 105
Expanding Your Career Horizons Even More 106

Part III: Career Areas to Stimulate Your Thinking 109

Chapter 8: If You Thrive on Words 111

Writing 112
    Technical writing 112
    Reporting information 113
    Writing opinions 114
    Sales writing 115
    Writing for various audiences 116

Working with Other People's Words.................................117
    Editing...117
    Managing information.....................................118
    Translating...119
    Transcribing...120
Using the Spoken Word to Inform or Entertain 121
    Newscasting or reporting...............................122
    Teaching 123
Using Words to Convince 124
    Law...124
    Marketing..125
    Public relations...126
    Sales 127

Chapter 9: If You Think in a Logical, Organized Fashion 129

Working in the Sciences 130
    Biology and medicine 130
    Chemistry..132
    Mathematics..133
    Physics..134
Engineering and Computer Science 135
    Civil engineering..136
    Mechanical engineering................................136
    Electrical engineering...................................137
    Industrial engineering...................................138
    Computer engineering...................................139
    Software engineering....................................140
Working with Money 141
    Keeping the books..142
    Making loans..143
    Managing money..144
    Investing...144
    Analyzing financial research..........................145
Organizing People, Data, and Things........................146
    Event planning...147
    Collecting..148
    Buying 149
    Investigating..150

Chapter 10: If You Connect Well with Others. 153

Helping Others Heal Physically................................154
    Nursing care..154
    Rehabilitation..155
    Holistic medicine...156
Helping Others Make the Most of Life.......................157
    Counseling..158
    Childcare..159

Helping Others Enjoy Their Leisure Time 160
    Recreation 161
    Travel 162
    Hospitality 163
Helping Others in a Business or Public Setting...........................164
    Staffing 164
    Supporting employees 165
    Managing businesses 166
    Keeping the public safe 167

Chapter 11: If You Have a Good Eye **169**
Working on a Two-Dimensional "Canvas" 169
    Graphic design 170
    Photography 171
Working on a Three-Dimensional "Canvas" 172
    Self-expressive art 173
    Fashion design 174
Creating Environments 175
    Architecture 176
    Construction 176
    Interior design 177
Mapping and Navigating the World 178
    Surveying..178
    Urban planning 179
    Piloting..180

Chapter 12: If You Want Your Work to Be Physical **183**
Doing Precision Work 183
    Metal working 184
    Jewelry work...184
    Dentistry...185
Working with Your Hands..186
    Equipment repair..187
    Culinary work 188
Working with Your Body..189
    Construction 189
    Training and coaching 190
    Firefighting 191
Creating with Your Body 192
    Acting...192
    Dancing...193

Chapter 13: If You Have an Ear for the Sound of Music **195**
Making Music...195
    Playing an instrument...196
    Teaching music...197
    Music therapy...197

Enhancing and Appreciating Sound and Music.............................199
Live performance 199
Recording 200
Producing 201
Using Your Voice 202
Singing 202
Voiceover 203

Chapter 14: If You Love Nature and Its Creatures 205
Working with Plants 206
Botany..206
Growing plants 207
Designing landscapes 208
Managing forests 209
Working with Animals 210
Zoology...210
Training animals 211
Caring for animals 212
Healing animals...213
Managing wildlife...213
Nurturing Nature and the Earth 215
Working with land and water 215
Ecology 216
Working with the weather and air 217
Waste management 218

Part IV: Weaving It All Together......................................221

Chapter 15: Preparing Your Game Plan 223
Staying Focused and Up-to-Date on Your Goals.......................223
Familiarizing Yourself with a Career................................224
Using online career and industry profiles.......................224
Using offline resources 226
Contacting professional associations............................227
Gathering salary information....................................228
Asking the Right Questions about a Career..........................229
Making Contacts..231
Priming the pump...231
Setting up additional informational interviews..................232
Staying objective in your quest 233

Chapter 16: Testing the Waters of a Potential Career. 235
Immersing Yourself 236
Taking a class 236
Imagining being on the job......................................237
Trying on the lifestyle...237

Connecting with Others in the Career..............................238
   Observing someone at work in the career........................238
   Hanging out in the environment...................................239
   Talking to people outside the field..............................240
   Observing the lifestyle..240
Finding a Community of Like-Minded People...................241
   Attending a meeting of professionals 241
   Subscribing to a newsletter 243
   Participating in an online community 243
Getting Your Feet Wet...244
Drawing Conclusions from Your Research 245

Chapter 17: Getting All the Pieces to Fit **247**
Overlaying Your Must-Haves with Your Vision.................247
When the Pieces Fit Together..248
When the Pieces Appear to Clash 249
   Finding the essence of what you want........................249
   Having a brainstorming blitz 249
   Spotting creative solutions 250
Reconciling True Differences..251
Formulating One Sentence That Says It All.....................251
Shifting Gears Midstream...253
Setting Your Sights on Your Target Career.......................253
   Making a realistic timeline 254
   Trusting your gut..254

Chapter 18: Strengthening the Skills You Need................ **255**
Knowing What You Need to Know 255
Discovering How You Learn Best...................................256
   Finding the most workable format 257
   Rooting out the best location 257
Getting Informal Training...258
Training on the Job...259
   Finding a related project in your current job 260
   Enjoying company-financed training 260
   Attending conferences...261
   Taking a short-term job 261
Getting a Degree 262
   Clarifying your goal..262
   Finding potential programs.......................................263
   Choosing the right program for you 265
   Getting financial assistance 266
   Going to school..267
   Sticking with it 268

Chapter 19: Taking the Steps to Get Your Job 271

Launching Your Search 272
  Refocusing your resume 272
  Alerting your network 273
  Searching online and off 274
Following Up on a Lead 275
  Landing the interview 276
  Preparing for the interview 276
  Asking the hard questions..277
  Getting a feel for the place 278
  Waiting with patience...278
Evaluating Your Options 279
  Making a list of your options 279
  Distinguishing deal-breakers from trade-offs...........280
Receiving an Offer..281
  Understanding the offer fully...................................281
  Giving your final answer..282
  Giving notice 282
  Updating your network...283
Feeling at Home in Your New Career 283

Chapter 20: Taking the Steps to Start Your Business 285

Verifying That You Have What It Takes 285
  Looking at key personality traits.............................285
  Possessing the right technical knowledge 286
  Having the practical business skills.........................286
  Exploring potential funding options 287
  Getting emotional support.......................................288
Exploring Your Idea..288
  Defining your product or service 288
  Talking to potential customers 289
  Checking out your competition.................................289
  Scouting your location options 290
Getting Real about Your Business...................................290
Taking Action with Your Business...................................292
  Creating your business identity 292
  Establishing your work space...................................293
  Developing sustainable
    marketing strategies...293
Feeling at Home in Your Own Business............................294
  Expecting everything to take longer than you expect....294
  Learning from each experience 295
  Finding the balance in your new life.........................295

Part V: The Part of Tens *297*

Chapter 21: Ten Tips for Staying Sane During Your Career Change . 299
  Committing One Way or the Other 299
  Gathering Your Resources 300
  Creating a Thinking Spot 301
  Giving Yourself Time to Think 301
  Creating Some Distance from Your Current Situation 302
  Letting Go of Old Strategies and Answers 303
  Getting out of a Rut..303
  Finding the Open Doors 305
  Creating a Plan, Then Acting on It 306
  Acknowledging the Transition in Your New Career.................307

**Chapter 22: Ten Keys to Keeping Yourself Inspired
and Motivated** **309**
  Scanning the News for Fascinating Careers.........................309
  Giving Yourself an Afternoon Off in a Bookstore 310
  Doing a Data Dump 311
  Starting with What Feels Easy 312
  Letting Yourself Dream Big 313
  Going on Vacation 313
  Projecting into the Future of Your Current Career 315
  Deciding How to Celebrate 316
  Talking with People Who Love Their Work.............................317
  Buddying Up 318

Index..*319*

Foreword

• •

Most forewords are written to urge you to read the book. But I know you are going to like this book, so you need no urging there.

What I want to urge in this foreword is something else, and that is the importance of career change, and more particularly, the importance of considering a career change in your own life.

Experts tell us that the average person goes through the job hunt eight times. I have observed that each time we go through a job hunt, we face a crossroads: Should we do a mechanical job search, or should we do a life-changing job search?

The mechanical job search is basically a matching process. It is so mechanical, even the Internet can do it for us. Your resume. All the employers' job openings. Is there a match? The site's "robot" will give you the news by morning. That's the mechanical job search.

The life-changing job search is different. If the mechanical job search starts with the labor market as "the given," the life-changing job search starts with you as "the given." The mechanical job search assumes that you're going to go on doing basically what you were doing before, but the life-changing job search assumes that all bets are off. You have certain transferable skills. They can be used anywhere. So, where would you most like to work? What would you most like to do for the rest of your life? Dream, dream, dream. More often than you can imagine, those dreams can be turned into reality!

A life-changing job search is, of course, just another phrase for "career-change." But I call it life-changing, because it involves so much more than just changing your career. In fact, there are four things that inevitably get weighed in a life-changing job search.

The first is the center of your life, which involves a reconsideration of what you want your life to revolve around. If it's currently work, do you want it to be family instead; or if it's currently making money, do you want it to be God instead? That sort of thing.

The second is the constants in your life. What about you has remained constant through all these years? Your skills, your values, your friends, what? Do an inventory, and then put these in their order of importance.

The third is the context of your life. What gives you perspective about your life? How do you measure how well you're doing in life? For many, this context of their life is God. If that's not yours, what is?

The fourth (and final) one is alternatives. You need to ask yourself how many alternative ways you have of describing what you most enjoy doing. How many alternative ways do you have of describing your target organizations or plans? How many alternative ways do you have of searching for that? A life-changing job search is a search for alternatives, so as to have more freedom.

If it's a life-changing job search you're weighing, that is to say, a career-change, plus, you can do no better than to read this book. It's one of the best I've ever read on career change. Carol has really done her homework, and she offers very many helpful ideas to guide you on your way.

— Richard N. Bolles, author of *What Color Is Your Parachute? A Practical Manual for Job-Hunters And Career-Changers (2002 Edition)*

Introduction

●●

*W*hether you change careers by choice or because of circumstances beyond your control, you stand on the brink of an awesome experience.

Thanks to advances in technology and added flexibility in the workplace, more employment options exist today than in any other time in history. Take advantage of this opportunity to create a new career for yourself that not only taps your favorite talents, but also lets you live the life you want to live.

Although you may have concerns about your career change, approach this time with as open a mind as possible. Give yourself the gift of exploration as you step forward to discover previously unexplored options and solutions.

If you want or need to make a career change, don't let a shaky economy or a personal situation stop you from looking to the future. The first stages of a career change involve imagining, thinking, exploring, and planning. You can embark on these steps now — without disrupting your current employment situation. After you know your new direction, you can decide when to make your move.

About This Book

You may find this book helpful in your quest to find a new career if you identify with any of the following statements:

- ✔ "I dread getting up in the morning to go to work, but I have no idea how to make a change."
- ✔ "I think I'm going to be laid off soon, and I want to plan ahead."
- ✔ "I want a career that allows me to meet my financial obligations while also giving me more time with my children and family."
- ✔ "My job isn't so bad, but I want to do work that is more meaningful and contributes to my community in some way."
- ✔ "I've worked very hard for years, and now I want a career I thoroughly enjoy."

The information, worksheets, and examples in this book can help you do the following:

- ✔ Update your view of the new world of work.
- ✔ Deepen your sense of your personal style and lifestyle needs.
- ✔ Define what you need in your work environment.
- ✔ Transform your passions and interests into viable career options.
- ✔ Explore numerous career ideas.
- ✔ Blend your ideal career with the realities of your life.
- ✔ Build the skills you need to be a success.
- ✔ Launch your plans for the future, whether you want to find a new job or start your own business.

Remember that the ideas in this book can help you plot your career change regardless of the state of the economy or your industry.

How This Book Is Organized

I divide *Changing Careers For Dummies* into five parts. A quick review of the Table of Contents and the following description of the parts gives you a solid overview of the entire book. If you want information about a particular topic, the Index can also help you locate it.

You can begin reading *Changing Careers For Dummies* at any chapter, and you don't have to read the book from cover to cover in order to get some valuable ideas for your next career. If you want to jump in, the best place to start is Chapter 2, where you check in with your current situation. After you define your hot spots, move to the chapter that seems most relevant to you. When you have a clear understanding of what you need in your life and your work, use Chapter 7 and the chapters in Part III to develop viable ideas to pursue.

Part 1: Setting the Stage for Your Career Change

The chapters in Part I help you explore what is and isn't working in your current career so that you can determine what you need and want for yourself and your family in your next career.

Part II: Searching for Hidden Treasure — Your Passion

Use the extensive checklists, worksheets, and brainstorming techniques in this part to discover your passions and interests, which become the basis for career ideas that you can explore.

Part III: Career Areas to Stimulate Your Thinking

The chapters in this part describe career ideas that may intrigue you if you have a certain skill, talent, or interest. For each career area, I provide the following information:

- ✔ A list of skills and talents that can help you determine if the careers in a particular section are of interest to you

- ✔ A description of the career area that spells out what the career entails and what it takes to be in the career

- ✔ Out-of-the-box angles that point to non-traditional work arrangements, niches in demand, and tips for entering the field

- ✔ Related jobs and specialties that show you professional alternatives

- ✔ Where-to-go-from-here information that links you to the primary professional association for the career area so that you can further your exploration

As you read about each career area, use the diverse information as a springboard to brainstorm ways to parlay your talents into careers that satisfy you and fit your life.

Part IV: Weaving It All Together

After you have a career idea or two that you want to pursue, Part IV helps you blend your ideas with what you know you need for your life to run smoothly. Through exploration and experimentation, you refine your ideas until you have enough confidence in your direction to take action. Depending on your situation, your next step may be to focus on getting more training, launching your job search, or starting your own business.

Part V: The Part of Tens

Changing careers can be a roller coaster of emotions because you are between two lives. You can't go back, and yet you don't know enough to fast-forward to your new life. The chapters in this part provide some quick tips on how to navigate the inevitable ups and downs of your journey, and also a couple of ways to help keep yourself motivated.

Icons Used in This Book

Throughout the book, icons appear in the margins to alert you to special information.

Whenever you see this icon, a question or idea triggers you to think about a particular aspect of your past, present, or future to help you uncover what you need or want in your next career.

Writing your thoughts down helps you see your situation more clearly. Start a journal so that you have all your ideas in one place.

This icon suggests ways that you can move beyond the traditional in your new career. Whenever you see this icon, stretch your mind to consider new possibilities or be outrageous as you brainstorm new options.

Sometimes you can fall into a pattern of making decisions based on what has been true in the past. When you see this icon, remind yourself to dig deep within to verify that your thoughts are aligned with your desires.

Anything next to this icon is to be avoided if at all possible.

This is an important truth that is worth repeating. Taking note of these ideas can help you make progress with your career change.

The paragraph next to this icon always includes a helpful hint to keep your career change moving forward as smoothly as possible.

Ask the Author

If you have questions or comments to share with me directly, e-mail me at carolmc@getrollingagain.com.

If you'd like to receive insightful and inspiring messages from me to keep you rolling during your career change, subscribe to my Get Rolling Again eNewsletter on my Web site at www.getrollingagain.com.

Part I

Setting the Stage for Your Career Change

The 5th Wave   By Rich Tennant

THOUGH SUCCESSFUL IN HIS FIELD, BOZO THE SURGEON ALWAYS FELT HIS TRUE CALLING LAY OUTSIDE THE OPERATING ROOM.

In this part . . .

The world of work has changed dramatically over the last few decades. Before you set out to determine what you want, update the way you think about work, your career path, and what's possible.

This part also helps you make sense of where you are now, in your career and in your life, so that you can determine which work arrangements can support the way you want to live.

Chapter 1

The World of Work: It Ain't What It Used to Be!

In This Chapter

▶ Looking at shifting trends

▶ Building a new understanding of how work works

Think back for a moment to when you left high school or college to start your first job. You no doubt had dreams about how your career would look and how your life would play out. Most likely your career goals were consistent with your expectations at the time, molded by your parent's beliefs about work, your observations of how their work affected your life, the economic climate of your hometown, and your own personal aspirations.

Fast forward to today.

Times have changed. Your career and life may or may not resemble your initial dreams and expectations. You may find that you are not content with what you've achieved. You may be frustrated by your work environment, the work you do, or the impact your work life has on your home life. You want more, or at least something different when it comes to your work.

Although you may have updated your expectations about the world of work over the years, the beliefs you took hold of growing up have deep roots. So deep, in fact, that they may still impact how you define success for yourself and what you believe is possible in your work.

Bringing all your beliefs about the world of work into alignment with today's realities frees you up to explore new options. As you read the scenarios in this chapter, note any beliefs that may play a role, consciously or not, in your current career situation.

Lifetime Employment with One Company: A Pipe Dream for Most

In the past, you had a very good chance of working for the same company throughout your career. No matter how bored or frustrated you became with your job or the company, you were unlikely to leave. The security of a steady paycheck and the knowledge that you would be taken care of in your golden years kept you coming to work.

Given recent changes in the economy, the way companies function, and people's increased desire for meaningful and fulfilling work, it's now unusual to work for the same company for the duration of your career.

If you read or listen to the news, you know that layoffs, mergers, buyouts, downsizing, and corporate restructuring are common these days. In an effort to stay afloat financially and maintain a competitive edge, companies do what they must when they must. The loyalty and security assumed in the past can no longer be taken for granted. Companies often cut ties with their employees without much notice.

In addition, it's now common for people to purposely leave a company to take a different job within the same field or to enter an entirely different career. You may decide that you need more variety, challenge, security, or fulfillment than your current career provides, or you may want to enhance key skills for a future career direction. For these reasons, you may be the one to initiate the end of your employment.

As you make your decision to leave, you may wrestle with some undercurrents of guilt about switching your loyalties. You may worry that you could tarnish your resume because people around you still see long-term employment at one company as a benchmark of career success. These feelings, which may be persistent, are carryovers from the old game rules. In the current world of work, you must take charge of your career and make the decisions that position you for the future you want.

A good rule is to stay in a job at least two to three years when you can. If you are in a volatile industry, such as a dot-com company, you may change jobs even more frequently due to economic realities. If the company you work for is about to go under, and you've only been there six months, don't wait! Start your search sooner rather than later.

If you've been in the same position in the same company for five years or more, you may be inadvertently telling potential employers that you are stuck. Enhance your viability in the job market by proactively incorporating challenges and variety into your current role.

Library Resource Center
Renton Technical College
3000 N.E. 4th St.
Renton, WA 98056

The United States Department of Labor estimates that you may have three to six careers in your lifetime, and that the next generation will have six to ten. And it's possible that you may hold several positions within each of these careers. Looking at these numbers, you probably won't make all of these changes at one company. Judiciously moving from company to company and from career to career gives you a golden opportunity to refine your skills and fulfill your professional goals.

Although you may feel a bit overwhelmed by the future at the moment, the more familiar you are with how to change your career, the more excited you can be about the opportunities opening before you. Prepare yourself for the ride of your life.

The Corporate World: More a Web Than a Ladder

In the past, when you got your first job, you knew with some certainty that you'd step up a rung of the corporate ladder every few years. You could expect to start out as a clerk and end up a manager during your tenure at the company because those who had come before you had done just that. In fact, in many cases, the career path was so well defined that you could plot your next moves with relative ease. You could fully expect your career to change based on promotion and transfer opportunities presented by the company. You could expect that the longer you stayed with the company, the more prestige you'd have, the longer your vacations, and the sweeter your benefits.

Times have certainly changed in the world of work. In most cases, when you start work you no longer have the luxury of seeing a clear career path stretched out before you. An obvious progression from one position to the next usually doesn't exist — at least not one that lasts for very long. Even if a career path seems apparent when you take a job, it will, in all likelihood, be modified, long before you have a chance to make your move, by changes within the corporation.

The fast moving modern economy doesn't permit companies to keep static, predictable structures any longer. Companies must move with the economic tides, ready to restructure at a moment's notice to meet the changing demands of their industry, technology, and customers. Although you may have a good sense of the next steps in your career, the fluid nature of corporations, resulting from reorganizations, downsizing, mergers, start ups, flatter hierarchies, globalization, and relocation, means that you can no longer follow a predetermined path to the top. You must be observant, alert, and ready to change with the times.

Library Resource Center
Renton Technical College
3000 N.E. 4th St.
Renton, WA 98056

Although the uncertainty can be a bit unnerving at times, the increasingly flexible nature of the work world means that you have new opportunities to write your own ticket! Rather than follow a set career path, you can take the reins of your own career.

You have more power than ever to decide where you are going and how you want to get there. The next rung of the corporate ladder isn't the only option any more. You can expand your horizons to fit your vision in the following ways:

- ✔ You can make a lateral move by taking a job at a similar level to expand your experience in a new field.

- ✔ You can consider downshifting to a position that would have once been considered "a step down" to allow you the time and flexibility to create the lifestyle you desire.

- ✔ You can look beyond your current employer to other companies that are better positioned to help you add a new skill to your repertoire.

- ✔ You can move in and out of the corporate structure as your skills and interests provide you with new opportunities to work in various capacities as a consultant, contractor, or part-time employee.

What was once a straightforward, linear career path within one company has become a multifaceted web of opportunities among companies. As you think of changing careers, broaden your scope of vision to include the vast array of options that are now available to everyone.

The Cornucopia of Career Choices

In the "good old days" of yesteryear, your career choices were pretty much laid out for you. You expected either to follow in your father's or mother's footsteps or to pursue a traditional career path based on what you were good at in school or what would provide a secure future. In the past, women and minorities found it difficult to break into many fields, which further restricted their career opportunities.

Your career choices are no longer so confined. The following factors have spawned new industries, roles, jobs, and specialties, creating an infinite number of employment opportunities:

- ✔ Technological advances
- ✔ Expansive growth in certain industries
- ✔ Widespread innovation
- ✔ Increased consumer consumption

> ✔ The evolution of more personalized customer service
>
> ✔ An increased focus on quality
>
> ✔ Diversity awareness
>
> ✔ Increased regulations, litigation, and legislation

With more access to education than ever before, women and minorities can pursue career options that where once out of their reach. With this background, women and minorities entering new fields and roles make historical firsts with some regularity these days.

With the sheer number of career choices available, you can't afford to wade aimlessly through the vast array of options to find the best career. The sketchy results you get from such a search can leave you feeling frustrated, hopeless, and resigned to the feeling that you'd better stay where you are, doing what you know, even if you aren't very happy.

If you constantly scan your surroundings for a job that you *could* do, stop. The I-could-do-that chorus means that you are looking outside yourself for the answer. Although you may get sporadic clues about your interests with this habit, you have more success when you look to what you enjoy and build a career from there.

You must narrow your focus before you start your search for a career change. By starting your job search with a direction in mind, you make more progress, faster. With any career change, it's the little successes along the way that keep you moving toward your ultimate goal. Chapter 6 provides a step-by-step plan to uncover your passions.

The One-Size-Fits-All Definition of Success: It No Longer Fits

The definition of a successful job and career used to be pretty uniform: Most people wanted a good, steady job in a stable company that provided them with enough income to buy a house, have a car, go on family vacations, put the kids through college, keep up with the Jonses, and eventually retire.

Times have changed; the definition of success has become, for many people, more personal. Although everyone agrees that having enough money to buy clothes and groceries and keep a roof overhead constitutes the most basic form of success, your personal definition of success may extend beyond these goals.

For some, the defining features of success are status and financial achievements that translate into having luxury cars, lavish homes, the latest electronic gadgets, fashionable clothes, and outstanding vacations. Others find this seemingly comfortable lifestyle falls short. Whether they've "made it" and then discovered that this lifestyle wasn't as fulfilling as they had once imagined, or they've experienced a major life event that has shifted their perspective, some people find themselves searching for a different kind of success — one based more on the quality of life and work than the quantity of dollars and cents.

The elements that enhance a person's quality of life and work are often unique to that person. However, many people, maybe yourself included, find that the following factors have become integral to their work and life satisfaction:

- **Having more family time.** You want to spend time with your children. You don't want to just hear about their first steps and first words from the day care provider; you want to experience these events yourself. You want to be home when your children get out of school to offer support as they learn to navigate the world. You want time to play together as a family.

- **Sharing time with your partner.** You want time to enjoy and nurture your relationship. You don't want to limit your relationship to the weekends that you carve out of a hectic schedule. You want to celebrate your love for each other by having the time and opportunity to relax together and enjoy each other's company.

- **Having the flexibility to travel, explore a hobby, or go back to school.** You want to have a life beyond work. You want to grow and expand who you are for reasons of personal fulfillment or to position yourself for future career moves.

- **Making a difference in the community.** You want work that has a positive impact on those who live in your community and beyond. You want work that has meaning — not just the opportunity to design, build, or distribute another widget, but the opportunity to give people something that enhances and improves their lives.

- **Being authentic and true to yourself.** You want work that allows you to express yourself and your beliefs. You want work that taps your skills and passions and aligns with your personal style. You don't want to have one identity at work and another at home; you want to be the same person in all areas of your life.

- **Having a balanced life.** You want to have a life that brings you more sanity than stress. You don't want life to pass you by in a blur. You want time to enjoy your work, your home, and your health. You want time to breathe between activities.

As strange as it may sound to those who grew up with the traditional definition of success, cutting back hours and making less money is a success for some because it allows them to create and enjoy the kind of lifestyle they desire. For others, the heavy workload and fine salary that are more consistent with the traditional definition of success provide a feeling of security, financial flexibility, and fulfillment. Both definitions of success and all the variations in between are equally valid.

At times, the old cultural norms and family expectations bubble to the surface. Even if you feel clear that your definition of success is not all about money and material goods, on the rough days, you may question whether you have chosen to do the right thing for yourself and your family. You may wonder if pulling back from your career to spend time with your children or to pursue a non-work related interest is in fact a sign of success. Although it may be hard to do, stick to your vision of success. This may mean taking a firm stand with friends and family members who don't understand your choices because they have different views of success.

When it comes right down to it, how you define success for yourself is up to you. Chapter 3 helps you explore the lifestyle that matches your definition of success.

Onsite Work: No Longer a Necessity

It used to be that everyone at a company arrived at the same location and stayed there for their entire workday. If you weren't in the building, people knew you weren't working. No one questioned this reality.

Where you actually do your work has become a question worth asking in recent years, as advances in communication technology, increased traffic, and shifts in people's values have made it both possible and essential for companies to address this issue.

Flex-place options allow you to work productively from locations other than the official workplace. Some flex-place innovations include the following:

- ✔ **Telecommuting:** New technological devices, such as cable modems, cell phones, faxes, and shared databases, allow people to work where they live — whether that's in the next town or thousands of miles away from the office. Typically, when logistics allow, employees are encouraged to come into the office on a regular basis.

- ✔ **Satellite offices:** In congested urban areas, some companies set up offices on popular but problematic commute routes so that their employees can stop in when bad traffic prevents them from reaching the office. Often, employees can choose to work in a satellite office a few days a week to shorten their commutes. Wasting less time sitting in backed-up traffic is a win-win for employees and employers alike.

- ✔ **On the road:** Although always part of the traveling salesman's life, working on the road has taken on a whole new meaning. Now people can work out of their cars, from a hotel room, on an airplane, or on a beach, as long as their computer batteries hold out and they can find a way to get online to connect with their company.

- ✔ **Virtual companies:** Actually an extension of telecommuting, this option allows people who live in various locations across the country or around the world to work together without sharing the same physical space. In fact, a virtual company may exist on paper without having a central office of any kind.

Even if you think your employer or potential employer doesn't offer flex-place options, don't discount the possibility. Sometimes companies agree to unusual arrangements if presented with compelling reasons for experimenting with something new. You just never know unless you ask. In Chapter 4 I describe a number of flex-place options in more detail.

9-to-5: Not the Only Option Any More

The majority of employees used to clock in and out at the same time day in and day out, year in and year out. Whether you worked the 9-to-5 shift or a different shift, your schedule was set. Most likely, you worked a five-day, 40-hour workweek, 50 weeks out of the year. So entrenched were you in this tradition, you didn't even think to ask for any accommodations.

A fixed schedule no longer works for everyone. To be productive and happy, employees are requesting more flexibility in how they structure their days. To address their employees' needs, companies experiment with the way time works at work.

Flex-time options typically fall into the following four categories:

- ✔ Modifying daily work hours — from 10:00 a.m. to 6:00 p.m., for example.

- ✔ Changing how the workweek looks by decreasing the number of days worked and increasing the number of hours worked each day.

- ✔ Transforming the concept of time off, allowing the employee to have more choice about taking time off.

- ✔ Focusing on getting the job done without tracking the hours or days you spend at work.

Becoming aware of flex-time options opens up new work arrangements that you may not have considered before. Chapter 4 gives more information about flex-time options.

Chapter 2

Evaluating Your Current Situation

• •

In This Chapter

▶ Checking in with yourself and your life

▶ Assessing your current work situation

▶ Evaluating the work you do

▶ Listening to your cravings

▶ Getting a sense of what comes next

• •

Did you know that you are sitting on a gold mine? The very same job that frustrates you or bores you to tears holds a number of valuable clues about your future career. In the same vein, the points of stress in your life can, with a little thought, prove to be enlightening, as well.

This chapter helps you assess where you are now. To make this process as easy for you as possible, I provide a series of worksheets to help you check in with the following:

✔ Yourself and your lifestyle

✔ Your work environment

✔ The work you do

These worksheets help you think about areas of your life or work more deeply than you may have before. As you fill out the worksheets, take your time. Let images, feelings, and memories float into your awareness. The depth and richness of your experience allows you to make more accurate assessments of your current situation.

Each worksheet consists of a list of elements in the left-hand column that are relevant to the topic at hand, a space for rating that element, and an area for indicating why you answered the way you did. When you rate each element, put an "X" into the appropriate box according to the following:

✔ **Good:** This element enhances your life or work.

✔ **Okay:** This element could be better or it could be worse. It either fluctuates or is generally mediocre.

✔ **Not So Good:** This element in some way diminishes your quality of life or your enjoyment of your work.

After you make your rating, note the reasons that you rated each element the way you did in the "Why?" column using the following guidelines:

✔ If you marked an element "Good," explain what's working.

✔ If you marked an element "Okay" or "Not So Good," indicate what's not working in this area of your work or life.

If you see any elements that aren't listed but are relevant to you, add them in the blanks at the bottom of each table and follow the preceding process.

If you are not working, use your last job as your frame of reference for this chapter. If you've been at home raising your children, recovering from an illness, or caring for a relative, think of your current experiences as your "job" in the following worksheets.

In the course of answering the questions in this chapter, you may uncover an issue that is deeper than you can resolve by changing your career. Although this doesn't mean that you can't or won't make a career change, it may mean that you need to address the issue first by reaching out to a professional counselor for support.

Looking at You and Your Life

Because you are reading this book to create a new career, you may question why I start out by asking about your personal life. The way I've always looked at it, a career works best when it fits with your life. The more you know about how you want to live, the more you know about your new career.

Who and how you are

If you have been working too hard, or have been totally focused on how frustrated you are with work, you may have lost track of yourself in the process.

To make clear decisions about your future career, you must reach in to find the true you again. Looking at your life through different lenses can help you see yourself more clearly.

Think about the last time you really let go of work. Perhaps you took a long weekend or an extended vacation. Now, think about how you feel at the end of the day or after a week at work. How similar or dissimilar are these two pictures? Ask yourself the following questions:

- ✔ How do you feel when you are relaxed and enjoying life?
- ✔ How do you feel when you put your work before yourself?

How would you like to feel about yourself on a regular basis? Imagine for a moment that you could put aside the bills, the appointments, the rushed schedule, and the conflicting needs of those around you and focus on yourself and your needs. Ask yourself the following questions:

- ✔ Who would you be?
- ✔ How would you feel?
- ✔ How would you be different? The same?

With these images and feelings in mind, rate the following elements of how and who you are in Worksheet 2-1.

Elements of Who and How You Are	Good	Okay	Not So Good	Why?
Your State of Health				
Having Time for Yourself				
Exploring Your Interests and Hobbies				
Reaching for Your Dreams				
Understanding Your Own Personality and Style				
Living in Alignment with Your Values				
Balancing Your Needs and Those of Others				

Worksheet 2-1: Evaluating various facets of your life and work.

How you live

Before you can focus clearly on the future, you must take a close look at your current life. If some aspects of your life work well, you want to keep those aspects intact. If certain areas of your life are not satisfying, you can find ways to alleviate the problems by making different decisions about your future.

Put your career and time at work on the back burner for a moment and think about your personal life. Ask yourself the following questions:

✔ How do you live your life? What do you like about it? What could be better?

✔ How do you spend your time with others?

✔ With whom do you like to interact?

✔ What do you do for fun?

✔ How is your financial situation?

✔ How happy are you with where you live?

Now, rate the following elements about how you live in Worksheet 2-2.

Elements of How You Live	Good	Okay	Not So Good	Why?
Your Social Life				
Your Leisure Time and Activities				
Your Relationship with Your Children				
Your Relationship with Your Partner				
Your Interactions with Your Family				
Your Financial Situation				
Where You Live				

Worksheet 2-2: Assessing how you live.

Your definition of success

Growing up, you probably created a way of defining success for yourself, based on your family experience, media messages, and your peers' views on the topic. Understanding how you see success provides important clues about the best career for you.

Think about and then write down the answers to the following questions about your personal definition of success:

- ✔ **When you first started working, how did you define success?** What were you striving to achieve? What made you feel successful?

- ✔ **What makes you feel successful now?** How has your definition of success changed since you first started working?

Read the answers you just wrote down. Is your definition of success primarily career-related, or are you looking at life success — how successful you are as a person? If you value your home life, but base your sense of success solely on your career achievements, the mixed messages you carry within yourself may create conflict, frustration, and feelings of failure.

Bringing your definition of success into alignment with your true values and current goals helps you move forward and create what you want.

Sizing Up Your Current Work Arrangement

It's Sunday night. In ten hours, you get up and go to work. On a scale from 1 to 10, how would you rate the intensity of your Sunday Night Blues?

1	2	3	4	5	6	7	8	9	10
Low								High	

What about the intensity of your Monday Morning Malaise?

1	2	3	4	5	6	7	8	9	10
Low								High	

Although these two questions serve as a quick barometer of how you feel about your work, looking at each element of your work arrangement gives you more in-depth data to work with as you think about your next career.

How you work

The way you work impacts how you live. By thinking through the pros and cons of how you work, you gain insights about what you eventually need to live the life you want.

Think about your work and your life over the last month. Ask yourself the following questions:

- ✔ Have you lived the life you want with the way your work is currently set up?
- ✔ Have you missed any opportunities due to the way you work?
- ✔ How has your schedule worked for you?
- ✔ What about the contract you have with your employer — whether you work full-time or part-time?

Worksheet 2-3 lets you clarify how you feel about how you work.

Elements of Your Time at Work	Good	Okay	Not So Good	Why?
Your Work Schedule				
Your Contract				
Your Vacation Time				
Your Sick Time				

Worksheet 2-3: Thinking about how you work.

Your pay and benefits

As a result of the work you do, you receive an income and possibly also benefits, which have some effect on what you can do in your life. The following questions help you evaluate this impact.

Think about the past year, both the high points and the low points. Ask yourself the following questions:

- ✔ What have you been able to do as a result of having the income you do?
- ✔ Did you use any of your benefits this year? How did they work for you?

■ ✔ Did your pay schedule meet your needs? Did the form of income you received have any effect on your lifestyle? For example, did you receive a salary, commission, overtime, or stock options?

■ ✔ What did you miss out on as a result of your income or benefits?

Worksheet 2-4 gives you a space to jot down your thoughts about important issues regarding your pay and benefits.

Worksheet 2-4: Evaluating your pay and benefits.

Elements of Your Pay and Benefits	Good	Okay	Not So Good	Why?
Your Income				
Your Benefits				
How You Are Paid				

Where you work

For some people, the environment in which they work is more important than what they do. By looking at what does and doesn't work for you in your work environment, you gain valuable clues that help you evaluate the fit of future work environments.

In your mind's eye, think about your day at work — from the moment you leave your home to the time you return. Ask yourself the following questions:

■ ✔ What is your commute like?

■ ✔ How do you feel arriving at work?

■ ✔ How does your body respond when you enter the building?

■ ✔ How do you feel while you are at work?

■ ✔ What is your return commute like?

■ ✔ How do you feel when you get home from work?

The sensations and impressions you feel as you answer these questions give you insights about how specific elements of your work environment affect you on a daily basis.

Use Worksheet 2-5 to rate your happiness level with specific aspects of your current working environment.

Elements of Your Work Environment	Good	Okay	Not So Good	Why?
The Kind of Company				
The Size of Your Company				
The Industry You Are In				
Your Commute				
Your Company's Surroundings				
The Interior of Your Building				
Your Personal Work Space				
How You Have to Dress				

Worksheet 2-5: Judging your state of mind about your work surroundings.

Who you work with

At first glance, it may feel as though you have little choice about who you work with. However, you can choose a career that allows you to interact with the kinds of people you enjoy most, whether they are colleagues who share your interests or clients who receive your services.

To discover more about what does and doesn't work for you in your current work community, take an imaginary walk through the halls of your office. Think about the people you work with on a regular basis:

- ✔ Stop at each office or cubicle in your mind's eye to get a sense of your interactions with each person.
- ✔ Revisit the meetings you've attended this week.
- ✔ Take a mental look at your e-mail inbox. Whose names show up there?
- ✔ Who comes to mind when you scan your telephone log or messages?

Reaching toxic levels

If you want to change careers, there's a good chance that you aren't completely happy in your current job. Or you may be interested in changing your career because your relationship or living situation is falling apart. In either case, it's important to discern whether the situation is "just" frustrating or actually toxic, making it impossible for you to move toward improving your career. Ask yourself the following questions:

✔ Are you frantic or desperate to leave your current job, living situation, or relationship?

✔ Do you feel threatened physically or emotionally? In your job? In your life?

✔ Are you so worn out by the end of the day that you can't think straight?

✔ Do you find it difficult to make any progress on your career change while in your current job?

If you answer "yes" to any of these questions, you probably work or live in a toxic environment. It's no wonder that you are having a difficult time making progress with your career exploration. Just making it through the day probably takes all you've got.

If you are serious about making a career change, you must make some headway in minimizing the toxicity in your life. Before you do anything else, acknowledge to yourself that your situation is, in fact, toxic. The following list

can help you identify what contributes to this toxicity:

✔ **Toxic work environment:** For example, noise, physical toxins, undue risk, unethical behaviors, dangerous actions, or violence.

✔ **Toxic boss or coworkers:** Attacks, rages, fights, violent behavior, threats, demeaning attitudes, or harassment.

✔ **Toxic work:** You are bored, overwhelmed, in over your head, or over-burdened. You have conflicting responsibilities, impossible deadlines, or severely inadequate supplies or support.

✔ **Toxic personal life:** You have a bad relationship, dangerous living situation, intense grief, old traumas, major life transitions, physical abuse, or addictions in your life.

After you know your situation is toxic, you have two choices. You can minimize your exposure to the offensive people or environments in whatever ways you can, including changing your shift, getting off a project, or using more stringent safety measures. Or you can just get out! Although it may feel drastic, if the environment is toxic enough for you to consider this option, you won't make any progress until you cut your ties with the environment or person involved. See Chapter 5 for suggestions on how to get out of the frying pan so that you can think more clearly.

With your impressions fresh in your mind, rate the following categories of people you interact with at work in Worksheet 2-6. Your response to the question "Why?" may, in this case, be a person's name.

Elements of Who You Work With	Good	Okay	Not So Good	Why?
Your Coworkers				
Your Employees or Support Staff				
Your Manager				
The Management				
The Company Culture				
Your Customers or Clients				
Your Vendors				

Worksheet 2-6: Rating your satisfaction with the people in your worklife.

If one person at work (or anywhere else in your life) drives you crazy, turn it around. Try to isolate what about this person makes you nuts. Your exploration can help you discover more about your personal style and tendencies, which can shine light on the kind of relationships you may want to avoid or seek out in your future career.

Examining the Work You Do Now

Consider the tasks and functions you perform at work. Think about the tasks and projects you've worked on this year and ask yourself the following questions:

- How do you feel when you do your work?
- What bores you?
- What excites and motivates you?
- When do you feel engaged by your work?

Take some time to write down your thoughts in Worksheet 2-7 regarding the way you spend your work day.

Categories	Good	Okay	Not So Good	Why?
The Tasks You Do				
The Skills You Use				
The Topics You Address				
The Process You Follow				
The Meaning You Find in Your Work				

Worksheet 2-7: Assessing your work day.

Listening to Your Inner Cravings

Many people think cravings are a need for something they can't or shouldn't have. Cravings are also a window to your desires, a gateway to understanding your true needs. Knowing your desires and needs comes in handy when you build a new career. Ask yourself the following questions:

- ✔ When you are tired and worn out, what do you wish for?
- ✔ When you feel stretched beyond belief, what do you need most?
- ✔ If you could have anything right now, what would it be?
- ✔ When you daydream, what ideas or pictures float by?

Don't censor or downplay what comes up for you. Don't worry about how you can create these things. Instead, focus on what you hear inside your own head.

Pay attention to cravings related to your work. For example, you may wish for any of the following when you think about what you truly desire from your work:

- ✔ A job you don't have to take home at night.
- ✔ A job where you interact with people.
- ✔ A job that allows you to eat chocolate.
- ✔ A job that allows you to attend school or build a new business.

Notice if your cravings extend beyond your professional life into your personal life. As you move forward on your quest for a new career, you want to make sure that you incorporate your personal dreams along with your professional ones.

Jot down your cravings after you've truly listened to yourself. If you find it hard to tap into your cravings on the spot, watch your thoughts over the next week or so to see what cravings surface as you live your life.

Spotting Your Hottest Issues

Look over your current situation (the various sections in this chapter can help you evaluate what's going on in your work and life). Then take it deeper. Identify five factors that, if resolved, would allow you to love your life and your work more than you do now. Use Worksheet 2-8 to write these issues down.

	Your Hottest Issues
1	
2	
3	
4	
5	

Worksheet 2-8: Recording what matters most to you.

Chapter 3

Exploring Personal Needs and Home Realities

. . . .

In This Chapter

▶ Understanding what you bring to your work

▶ Looking at how your life impacts your career choices

▶ Discovering your family's role in your career decisions

. . . .

*I*s there anything about you or how you like to live that's absolutely non-negotiable? Anything you refuse to give up or sacrifice for your job or your career?

This chapter helps you identify what you need to be happy with yourself, your life, and your work and what your family needs to flourish. By having this information at your fingertips, you can immediately identify and side-step job opportunities that may force you to give up what you truly want.

Wouldn't It Be Great If . . .

If you could live any way or anywhere you wanted to, how would your life look? Set aside your family's needs, your financial responsibilities, and your work duties for a moment. Allow yourself to access your fondest dreams.

When life is rough, what do you daydream about? Perhaps you think about some of the following:

- ✔ Living part time in the mountains or the tropics

- ✔ Working from home more

- ✔ Traveling the world

- ✔ Taking up a particular sport or hobby

I'm not asking you to be practical here; I'm asking you to voice a dream. Possibly for the first time. By acknowledging your desires to yourself, you open the possibility of bringing them into reality.

Writing down your dreams is the first step toward making them a reality. In your journal, give shape to your ideals by finishing the phrase: "Wouldn't it be great if. . . ."

Discovering How You Influence Your Work

As you think about your new career, it's a given that you bring yourself to the party. In my opinion, who you are is non-negotiable. A career that forces or requires you to be someone you aren't is not the career for you. As an interim, short-term position to make ends meet, okay, if you must, but in the long run, that kind of job just drains the life right out of you.

In the following sections, you identify elements of yourself that are important to incorporate into your future career decisions.

Your personality or temperament

Who you are is comprised of any number of characteristics, traits, and qualities. Some are likely to be more important to you than others. In fact, some may be so important that they define you.

Is there any aspect of yourself that if you couldn't share it, you would feel unnecessarily limited, constrained, or restricted by your career? Think about past jobs to see if there was any part of yourself that you couldn't express on the job and how that made you feel.

The following list of keywords aids you in identifying those parts of your personality and temperament that are essential for you to incorporate into a potential career. In the following list, circle the five words that describe the aspects of who you are that you absolutely must express at work.

Abstract thinker	Detail-oriented	Friendly
Active	Diplomatic	Humorous
Adaptable	Disciplined	Imaginative
Analytical	Efficient	Intuitive
Communicative	Empathetic	Inventive
Concrete thinker	Enthusiastic	Investigative
Consistent	Expressive	Mediator
Deep thinker	Fair	Methodical

Motivator	Precise	Sensitive
Observant	Punctual	Spontaneous
Open-minded	Quick	Supportive
Organized	Reflective	Versatile
Perfectionist	Reserved	
Persuasive	Resourceful	

If you feel stumped, ask your friends and family members for their opinions about your integral traits. Because they don't live in your skin, they may have a better perspective on this than you do.

Write down your choices in Worksheet 3-1 and record any thoughts you have about how you want to express each trait in your work.

If you want to understand more about your personality and personal style, check out one or both of the following Web sites:

- ✐ **Kiersey Character Type Sorter (www.advisorteam.com/user/kcs. asp):** The free questionnaire at this site helps you discover your personality type by providing you with a four-letter code that identifies where you stand on four "personality dimensions." The site offers additional information on each personality type. After you get your four-letter code, read about your temperament and your character to gain insights about your preferences for work environments and management styles.

- ✐ **Enneagram (www.9types.com/):** At this site you find two free tests to help you determine your personality type based on the Enneagram system, an ancient system built on psychological research of high-functioning individuals. By understanding your type, you gain an appreciation of your personal style, your blind spots, and how you can interact more effectively with others.

Your Traits	Your Thoughts on Each Trait

Worksheet 3-1: Your key personality traits.

Your values

Values are those beliefs, ideas, and things that are most important to you. The more aware you are of your values, the better the chances of creating a career that fits you.

The following list of keywords helps you identify the values that are crucial for you to uphold in your career and life. Look over the list of values, which was developed by Terry Karp, MA, and Mark Guterman, MA, and circle the ten that are most important to you.

Record your top ten values in Worksheet 3-2. Next to each value, write a few words or a phrase to capture what each value means to you. Be as specific as you can. If you have a value that is not part of the list, add it to the list.

Accomplishment	Family	Nature
Adventure	Friendship	Obligation
Affiliation	Fun	Pleasure
Artistic expression	Harmony	Predictability
Authority	Health	Recognition
Autonomy	Helpful	Respect
Balance	High earnings	Responsibility
Beauty	Honesty	Risk-taking
Challenge	Humility	Self-discipline
Community	Independence	Self-restraint
Competence	Influence	Service
Competition	Integrity	Spirituality
Contribution	Justice	Stability
Control	Knowledge	Status
Cooperation	Leadership	Structure
Creativity	Learning	Team work
Curiosity	Love	Time freedom
Diversity	Loyalty	Trust
Duty	Meaning	Variety
Faith	Moderation	Wisdom

Your health

Working requires a certain degree of physical and mental well-being. If your health is compromised in any way, being productive and comfortable is a matter of making careful choices about your career.

Is there anything about your state of health that may or should impact your career choice? For example:

- A prior illness or physical condition that limits your activities in someway

- Sensitivities or allergies that impact the kinds of environments you can work in safely

Your Values	Your Thoughts on Each Value

Worksheet 3-2: Recording your core values.

 Use Worksheet 3-3 to stimulate your thinking. Check off the topics that are relevant to you and then describe how your health may impact your options at work.

Your hobbies and interests

For some, a personal passion is far more important than work. So important, in fact, that they don't want to convert their passion into a professional venture. If you fall into this category, you can create a career that allows you to do more of what you are passionate about in your life.

 Does your current career allow you to pursue your interests to the degree you'd like? For example:

- ✔ If you are a nature photographer, do you have the flexibility in your schedule to travel?

- ✔ If you love to water ski, can you get to the lake frequently enough to do what you love?

- ✔ If you like to quilt, do you have enough time after work to devote to your craft?

Seeing where you fit in

Do you sometimes feel like a fish out of water? Like you see the world from an entirely different perspective than those around you? If you experience these feelings, then you may be in a different cultural subgroup than your family, friends, coworkers, or community. Read the following descriptions to see where you feel most comfortable:

✔ If you feel that men and women have particular roles at home and at work, you are most likely part of the Traditionals subgroup, which consists of 48 million adults. You appreciate small town life, place a high value on family, church, and community, and find comfort in the familiar ways of your youth.

✔ If you think financial status, material possessions, and economic and technological advances are signs of success, you are one of 93 million people who are part of the dominant subculture, the Moderns. You compartmentalize your personal life and work life, enjoy shopping, and believe efficiency, profitability, and speed are the best ways to measure the success of something. The media and most environments you encounter share your values. Although you may be cynical about the future, you believe the solutions to the world's problems can be found in science and engineering.

✔ If you value authenticity, personal relationships, holistic health, self-awareness, and your own personal growth, you are part of the youngest subgroup, the Cultural Creatives. You volunteer, enjoy the arts, books, and radio, take experiential, learning vacations, search for innovative solutions to long-standing problems, and value time in nature and time for yourself. Although you may know a few people who share your values, you feel that you are essentially alone in your quest to live fully because the media does little to mirror your values. Yet, a full 50 million other people in the United States share your values. You are not alone!

If you grew up in a family or a community with a different set of values than you hold, you may feel conflicted about how to define your own success. Coming to terms with who you are and what you value is an important journey because it allows you to live authentically. As you pull your life and your work into alignment with your values, life begins to flow. After you experience this alignment and the growth it allows, you may find that you want to change your definition of success. See Chapter 2 for more information on forming your personal picture of success.

To find out more about these three cultural subgroups, read *The Cultural Creatives: How 50 Million People are Changing the World* (Harmony, 2000) written by Paul H. Ray, Ph.D. and Sherry Ruth Anderson, Ph.D. or visit their Web site at www.culturalcreatives.org.

Use Worksheet 3-4 to write down your interests and indicate any specific work arrangements that may allow you to enjoy them more fully.

Your Health	How Your Health Impacts Your Career Options
☐ Endurance	
☐ Ability to move or sit	
☐ Strength	
☐ Flexibility	
☐ Chronic pain	
☐ Past injuries	
☐ General health	
☐ Mental health factors	
☐ Sleep issues	
☐ Sensitivities or allergies	
☐ Particular body parts	

Worksheet 3-3: Examining your physical and mental health.

Your Interests	How Your Interests Impact Your Career Options

Worksheet 3-4: Thinking about your hobbies and interests.

If you want to explore ways to transform your hobby or interest into a career, check out Chapter 6, which is all about identifying your passions.

Considering Your Location

Sometimes the place you live has a huge impact on your career options. Although becoming more conscious about how your location influences or limits your career choices may be scary, in the end you have more power because you know the realities that you work under. For example, if you realize that the options in your current location are dismal, you may choose to relocate or to carefully create a multifaceted career that allows you to leverage off the idiosyncrasies of your area.

Any number of factors may influence the economy in your area and your career options. Start by thinking about the following issues:

✔ **Weather:** Are there any cyclical weather patterns that impact your work options? For example, your area may experience dramatic highs and lows in weather, such as extremely cold winters or fry-an-egg-on-the-sidewalk summers, that influence the economy of your community during those times. Or you may live in a temperate climate that encourages a well-balanced economy throughout the year.

✔ **Economy:** Are there any unique features of your local economy that define or limit your career options? For example, do any of the following characteristics seem to describe your area?

  • Limited variety of industries in the local area

  • Slow economy

  • Recreation or tourist economic base

  • Rural area

  • Small town

  • Seasonal economy

✔ **Cost of living:** Does the cost of living in your area change your career choices at all? For example, does your mortgage or the cost of fuel require that you make a such a large income that your career choices are limited?

✔ **Travel:** Does your commute or access to transportation influence your career choices? For example, would driving to a certain district increase your commute beyond reason, or are you far enough away from a decent airport that extensive business travel is out of the question?

✔ **Communications:** Does your local phone system or Internet access have an impact? For example, if you live in a rural area, are you stuck with a slow modem connection? Is it impossible to sign up for call waiting on your phone? Do these technological limitations impact your choice of career?

There may be other local factors you can think of that limit or enhance your career options. Use the space in Worksheet 3-5 to jot down the characteristics of your location that have an influence on your career options.

	Local Factors	How Your Location Impacts Your Career Options
Worksheet 3-5: Taking your environment into account.		

After you consider the various characteristics that define the area where you live, take a step back to look at the big picture for a moment. Think about why you live where you do. Is it:

✔ **By default:** Because you grew up or went to school there and ended up staying.

✔ **By circumstances:** Because your spouse relocated to the area, your elderly parent lives there, or your child needs to attend a school in the area.

✔ **By choice:** Because you absolutely love living where you do.

If you aren't happy with where you live, you may need to gain clarity on this issue before your career options can come into focus.

Looking at the Impact of Family on Your Work

Your family and pets share your personal life, and they also impact your career. Look at your relationships with the various members of your family and the support they require from you. Use this information to help you define what is non-negotiable for you when it comes to finding a career that blends with your personal life.

Your partner

Whether you are married or dating, your primary relationship requires a certain amount of time and attention to flourish. Does your work allow you to nurture your relationship? For example:

Living and working on the road

Do you live in more than one place? Or would you, at some point, like to do any of the following:

- Have two homes
- Live in a RV and move whenever you desire
- Travel frequently
- Accompany your partner whenever he or she travels
- See your long distance partner more frequently and for longer periods of time

If you need this kind of flexibility to make the most of your desired lifestyle, consider a portable career, one that allows you to bring in an income from where ever you are. You may explore being a writer or editor, running an e-commerce site, or becoming a Web or graphic designer. Another option may be to create a career that capitalizes on the locations you visit. Perhaps you travel to an area with a unique craft or product that would sell well in your hometown.

- Do you spend enough uninterrupted private time with your partner?
- Do you have enough energy after work to enjoy each other's company?
- Do you get away together often enough?
- Do you get to have fun together?

Your children

If you have children, you no doubt already know how much their needs and your desires for them affect your work and life. If you could write your own ticket, what part would you play in your children's lives? For example:

- Do you spend the amount of time you'd like with them?
- How is your energy level when you see them?
- Do you take vacations together?
- Are you happy with the activities you share?

Time is fleeting. If you want to spend time with your kids, now is the time. Don't worry about how you can pull it off. Just use the questions in this section to start thinking about your true desires regarding your children. The clearer you are about your desires, the easier it is to find a way to make them happen.

Your parents and grandparents

Eldercare is more and more of an issue as Baby Boomers age, and their parents and grandparents live longer and longer lives.

Look down the road on this one. If you don't support these members of your family right now, count your blessings and enjoy the time you have with your parents or grandparents while they are thriving, knowing that you may be a caretaker at some point in the hopefully far distant future. Think about the following questions:

- How do you keep in contact? Is it as frequent as you'd like?
- How frequently do you want or need to visit?
- Do you or may you have any care-taking responsibilities?
- Do you or may you need to move any family members at some point in the future?
- Who else can share these responsibilities?

Your support network

Having a solid network of friends adds richness to life. Even when built on a good foundation, all friendships need care and feeding to survive. If your friends have moved away or moved on in a different direction, you may need to set aside time to meet new people and develop bonds with them. When thinking about your support network, consider the following questions:

- Do you have a network of friends you can count on?
- Do you spend time with them on a fairly regular basis?
- Do you keep in touch?
- Do you enjoy your friends?
- Are you making new friends?
- Are you accepting social invitations?

Your pets

Pets are great companions, and, if you have one or more, you know that they take some time and energy. Think about how your pets affect your work life:

- How long can you be away from home at any one time?
- Does having a pet impact your business travel?
- Does your pet have any health needs that impact your work?
- What kind of exercise does your pet need?
- Do you spend the time you'd like with your pet?

If want to have a partner, a child, a stronger support network, or a pet in the future, be sure to account for your desires in Worksheet 3-6. Spell out what about each relationship is non-negotiable when it comes to your future career. Be as specific as you can about how each relationship influences your work decisions.

Writing Down Your Hottest Requests

Take a couple of minutes to write down five factors that, if resolved, would allow you to love your life and your work more than you do now. (The various sections of this chapter can help you identify these factors.) These five factors, which you should enter into Worksheet 3-7, can help you evaluate potential opportunities to see if they are a good fit or would produce too much conflict to consider.

Be as up front as you possibly can be about what you want and need to feel fulfilled. Even if you don't or can't get all that you want, acknowledging and voicing what you truly want is one of the best ways to move your career in the direction you desire.

**Worksheet
3-6:**
Writing
down your
thoughts
about family
and work.

Your Family	How Your Family Impacts Your Career Options
Partner	
Children	
Parents/Grandparents	
Support Network	
Pets	

	Your Hottest Requests
Worksheet 3-7: Writing down your most important needs.	1
	2
	3
	4
	5

Chapter 4

Expanding Your Notion of What's Possible at Work

In This Chapter

▶ Visualizing your perfect work schedule

▶ Nailing down the best contract

▶ Determining where you work best

▶ Establishing how you want to get paid

▶ Identifying the kinds of people you enjoy working with

More work arrangements exist now than in any other time in history. You can work as a full-time employee or a sole proprietor. You can create a blend of employment and self-employment or merge in and out of each role as opportunities knock.

You need to figure out which arrangement is the best one for you. In the sections that follow, you have the opportunity to examine various options to see which ones work best for you and your family.

In Chapters 2 and 3 of this book, you can create lists of your hottest issues and requests to illuminate what is and isn't working in your life and work. If you haven't already done so, I recommend that you take a few minutes to fill out the worksheets in those chapters to help focus your thinking. If you have already filled them out, take a quick look at those lists to refresh your memory.

You want to create a career that helps you rework the aspects of your life and work that cause you frustration and angst, and to accentuate those parts that work for you. As you read this chapter, keep an eye out for any work arrangements and options that may help you address your hottest issues and requests.

Keeping Your Mind, and Options, Open

In recent years, companies have come up with a variety of innovative, cost-effective work arrangements to attract and retain talented employees, handle explosive growth, and weather unpredictable downturns. Understanding and remaining open to the options allows you to move into this fluid economy with more confidence and less fear.

Even if you feel that you have few options in your current situation, or you fear that the companies in your community won't subscribe to alternative work arrangements, keep your mind free to explore the wide range of options. After you get a better feel for the career you want and the work arrangements you desire, visit Work Options (www.workoptions.com), which provides resources for people who want to propose and negotiate flexible work situations.

If you feel drawn to work for yourself, answer the questions in this chapter as thoroughly as you can. Although your way of implementing these ideas may be a little different than what happens in corporate or governmental settings, the concepts themselves are still relevant to you and may stimulate new ways of thinking about your business structure. For additional thoughts on starting a business, see Chapter 20.

A number of the topics you read about in this chapter may strike a strong chord in you. You may find it easy to say, "Yes, that one works best for me." Other topics, however, may leave you saying, "Ho-hum" because they don't appear, on the surface, to matter that much to you.

Even if you don't seem to care one way or the other about a topic, think it through the best you can and take a stand. You never know what clarity and insight some additional thinking on the subject may bring you.

If you hear yourself saying, "I guess I could do that," stop yourself on the spot. The second those words form in your mind you are getting ready to settle, trying to force-fit yourself into something that could work but is not the best option for you. At this stage of the game, keep your focus on your ideal. Allow your mind to explore as many new options, new combinations, and new avenues as you can. Exploration brings to mind new solutions you haven't yet dreamed of.

As you fill out the worksheets in this chapter, you may discover elements that you feel you must have in your work and others that would be nice to have. For now, indicate any options that seem appealing. Chapter 17 helps you to delineate which elements are your must-haves.

Accentuating the positives

In your quest to find solutions to fix what is not working, you can forget those parts of your career that are positive. Take a moment to acknowledge the pieces of your work life that work well and make note of them in your journal. Perhaps you have a gifted boss, a work culture that allows employees to take care of personal emergencies when the need arises, or a great day care arrangement. Don't disregard these wonderful aspects of your life; integrate them into your picture of your next career.

Know that you may have some loose ends by the end of this section. You should expect some loose ends at this stage of the process, so don't worry. In fact, this is a good opportunity to practice sitting with your confusion and allowing the pieces of your puzzle to fall into place as they come to you.

Working the Way You Want to Work

The structure of your workday and workweek impacts how well your life and work blend together. Understanding what's now possible in the work world and gaining clarity about what works best for you puts you in a good position to make informed decisions about your future and to negotiate whatever you need to make your life work.

Your work schedule

If you think a 40-hour workweek is your only option, think again! Companies now offer a variety of work arrangements that allow them to find cost-effective solutions to problems created by fast-changing economic realities, while giving employees the opportunity to take on more flexible work schedules. Doing so helps employees ease the stress and strain of balancing work and home, which in the long run is good business for the company.

Before you attempt to pin down which schedule options appeal to you, use the questions in Worksheet 4-1 to help you define your ideal work schedule. Without calculating anything or trying to figure out the right label for what you want, answer the questions in the worksheet according to what works best for you and your body.

Your Scheduling Needs	
Your best starting time?	
Your best quitting time?	
Number of breaks?	
Lunch time?	
Maximum hours per week?	
Maximum hours per day?	
Which days do you want to work?	
What shift is best for you?	
Number of days per week?	
Any overtime?	
Preferred work pace?	
Need for flexibility to take care of personal appointments and emergencies?	
Ideal amount of paid time off for sick days and personal days?	
Ideal amount of vacation?	

Worksheet 4-1: Discovering your scheduling needs.

Take another look at Worksheet 4-1 with a different filter. Ask yourself how you may need to modify your ideal schedule to incorporate what works best for your family, pets, and social life. Note any conflicts or inconsistencies that arise. Don't worry about resolving these conflicts at this point; you don't have all the information you need to do so. Chapter 17 helps you sort out these conflicts and create workable solutions.

Given what you just discovered about your needs and desires, explore your options. As you review the options in Worksheet 4-2, put a check next to any that help you meet your needs and those of your family.

Your Scheduling Options	
☐ Flex-time	Working the standard number of hours, but starting work, with the manager's permission, at a specific time either earlier or later than the company's standard. Your quitting time shifts to account for your start time.
☐ Gliding schedule	Arriving at work at any time during a flexible band of time without manager's permission as long as you are at work during the required core hours.
☐ Variable day	Working any number of hours per day as long as you work a total of 40 hours by week's end.
☐ Completely flexible work schedule	Choosing when you work on a daily basis. As long as you get your work done, neither the company nor your manager care how many hours you work.
☐ Shortened workday	Reducing the hours you work each day to five, six, or seven hours.
☐ Shortened workweek	Working the same number of hours each day for four days a week instead of five.
☐ Compressed workweek	Working your 40 hours in less than the typical five days. Several schedules are used. For example: • Four 10-hour work days each week • Three 12-hour work days each week • Nine 9-hour work days over two weeks with the tenth day off
☐ Variable week	Working any days you please as long as you put in 80 hours over a two week period.
☐ Ad-hoc time off	Having the understanding with your company or manager that you can take off a prearranged amount of time to address family emergencies, medical appointments, children's events, or other issues that must be handed during regular business hours.

Worksheet 4-2: Taking charge of your work schedule.

Working in overdrive

You may find yourself snickering at the thought of having a career that allows you to work less than 40 hours per week. You would be happy if you could just get your workweek down to 50 hours. If so, you are not alone.

Between 17 and 25 percent of full-time employees work more than 50 hours per week. A full 10 percent say that they work over 70! It's a tough cycle to break, even if you know that it's hurting you.

Take a close, hard look at your values and the state of your life, if you do any of the following:

✔ Work such long hours that you don't see the light of day or your kids

✔ Forget to use your paid time off

✔ Forgo scheduled vacations at the last minute

✔ Can't stop even when your health begs you to

Ask yourself what you want out of life. Although it may take an extra dose of creativity and some patience, you can make choices that allow you to get a life — and a more balanced, fulfilling one at that.

Turn to Chapter 3 to take a close look at your lifestyle and values.

Even if it doesn't feel like the options in Worksheet 4-2 are possible, don't strike them from your mind just yet. With some proper prior planning and a well-written proposal, you can forge new trails in your company and community. If you want some assistance, visit Work Options (www.workoptions.com) which can take you through the step-by-step process of preparing your case.

Your contract

In addition to a wider variety of work schedules to choose from, the new world of work also offers a number of contract formats.

Read each option in Worksheet 4-3 and put a check mark next to any that appeal to you. Consider each of the possibilities, even if they seem out of reach to you at the moment.

Your Contract Possibilities	
☐ Full-time	Work 40 or more hours per week as a full-fledged employee of the company receiving full pay and benefits.
☐ Part-time	Work less than 40 hours a week by shortening your days or your workweek. Expect your pay to be commensurate with the hours you work and verify your workload is cut to match your reduced hours. Depending on the company's policies, you may or may not receive benefits.
☐ Job-share	Share a full-time job with another employee by splitting up the time worked each week, the pay, and the vacation time. You may act interchangeably and share the duties equally or split the duties according to each person's expertise.
☐ Phased-out retirement	Cut back your hours gradually upon retirement while continuing to perform the duties you have had.
☐ Temporary employee/ contractor	Work through a staffing firm or temporary agency, which place you in companies to work as long as they need you, whether it's for a couple of days or several months. You can expect the staffing firm to take care of your taxes and to offer you benefits of some sort. At the end of your stint, you may have the option to convert to a permanent status depending on the company's needs and your interest. This option allows you to check out a company and find out whether you want to work for them on a long-term basis.
☐ Independent consultant	Contract with a company to work for a specified length of time or on a specific project. You may be asked to sign up for another round if they like your work or the project is not yet completed. As an independent, you are required to handle your own taxes and provide your own benefits.
☐ Freelancer	Work independently doing projects for one or several companies at once. You may work very hard for several months and then have a few lighter months; it all depends on the jobs and clients you find and take on, over which you have total control.
☐ Self-employed	You have no contract at all – except to yourself! Run your own business to provide a product or service directly to your customers. Your tasks expand to include marketing, sales, accounting, fulfillment, and shipping, which means you wear and juggle many hats each and every day.

Worksheet 4-3: Considering your contract options.

Working Where You Want to Work

You spend anywhere from 40 to 60 percent of your waking hours at work. With all the time you spend working, you need to work in a place that aligns with who you are — at least you do if you want to be happy with your career. The worksheets in the following sections help you discern the kind of work place that best fits your professional and personal needs and wants.

Even if a question in one of the worksheets doesn't seem to matter to you one way or the other, force yourself to take a stand on the question anyway. Doing so ensures that you fully consider all of the issues that play a part in selecting a fulfilling career.

At the same time, only mark those choices that truly excite and intrigue you. "I could do that" is not a valid response; thinking this way leads you off the path of finding out what you really want to do.

The kind of company

When you think of working for a company, you probably think of large, pub-licly-held companies, without realizing all the other options that exist.

As you read about the culture inherent in each kind of company in Worksheet 4-4, check off the ones that appeal to you.

The company size

The size of a company impacts its inherent culture. Typically, the larger the company, the more layers of management and bureaucratic structure you must contend with to get your work done. In this kind of setting you probably work in a formal, more impersonal environment than someone working in a smaller company. Smaller companies often have a more casual feel to them, allowing more access to the top brass and more flexibility when you try something new.

Although a big company used to mean that your job was secure, shifts in the economic reality mean that your job could be lifted out from under you regardless of the company's size. Keep your skills up-to-date, your network in place, and a clear picture of where your career is headed. Sometimes the surprise departure from one company brings unexpected opportunities from other corners.

Company Form	
☐ Not-for-profit	Fulfills its mission by supporting a cause in a way that makes the company exempt from paying taxes. Because funding usually comes from grants and fund-raising efforts, employees may need to be creative to accomplish the company's goals.
☐ Education	Educates people of any age. Schools and academia have a culture that values learning and teaching above all else. The schedule matches the school year, which often means long interim breaks.
☐ Government	Provides services to citizens through government agencies based on programs established by legislation. The culture is fairly stable, although changes may occur when leadership changes.
☐ Public company	Strives to satisfy the stockholders and customers by providing successful services and products. All records are open to the public, which gives you a clearer understanding of how the company is doing before and after you start working there. Public companies tend to be mature and larger in size than other kinds of companies.
☐ Start-up, pre-IPO (Initial Public Offering)	Pushes to create a viable product, capture market share, and eventually go public. Start-ups by their very nature (being in the initial stages of building a business) tend to be very fast-paced with a fair amount of scrambling to stay ahead of the wave. Some have funding or venture capital support, which creates additional stability.
☐ Web-based	Works with or creates the latest Web technologies, so established rules or structures do not exist. Things are often being done for the first time, with experimenting and pushing the envelope to discover what works and what's next.
☐ Privately-held company	Owned by an individual or a small group of private investors and has no intention of going public. The company's culture and product lines are likely to be fairly stable. The degrees of flexibility, employee participation, and experimentation depend on the owners and their relationships with the staff.
☐ Family-owned	Owned and operated by one family that may have founded the business. Family dynamics and traditions are usually a part of the in-house politics.
☐ Partner-owned	Run by two people. Assessing the stability and sanity of their relationship gives you an idea of the culture of the company.
☐ Home-based	Run out of home. It's likely to be comfortable and casual, though may be somewhat cramped and prone to family related interruptions and crises.

Worksheet 4-4:
Forming ideas about the kind of company you'd like to work for.

As you read Worksheet 4-5, imagine yourself in each setting and check off the company sizes that seem to fit your needs. Use your prior experiences and what you know about yourself to make these decisions.

For more examples of companies of various sizes, consult Fortune's 100 Best Companies to Work For and Fortune's List of the Biggest Employers. You can find these on Fortune's Web site at www.fortune.com.

Small businesses have an unbelievably large impact on the economy. Twenty-five million small businesses in the United States make up 99.7 percent of the employers. These businesses employ over 50 percent of the people in the private work force and provide three-quarters of all new positions. When you start looking at potential employers, don't count small businesses out.

Company Size	
☐ Sole-proprietor	One person runs the show – you. You play the roles of Chief Executive Officer and Chief Bottle Washer and everything in between. Graphic designers, career counselors, and travel agents who work solo are examples.
☐ Partnership	Two individuals come together to form and run a business such as a restaurant, a retail store, or a consulting company.
☐ Micro business	Four or fewer employees run the business together. Typical examples are a gardening service, a cart-vending business, or a booth at a farmer's market.
☐ Small company	Fewer than 1,000 employees. Scitor, Fenwick & West, and David Weekley Homes are examples.
☐ Mid-size company	Between 1,000 and 10,000 employees. Examples are Genentech, Adobe Systems, and Pella.
☐ Large company	Between 10,000 and 100,000 employees. Hewlett Packard, Southwest Airlines, Deloitte & Touche, Merck, Four Seasons Hotels, and Wegmans Food Markets are examples.
☐ Gigantic company	Over 100,000 employees – for example, Walmart, FedEX, and McDonald's.

Worksheet 4-5: Considering the size of the company you want to work for.

The company culture

Although the company size has a hand in how your experience of work plays out, don't underestimate the power of the overall company culture to impact your life. Becoming aware of the variables that make up a company's culture gives you the knowledge that you need to ask your interviewers the questions that help you verify that their culture matches your career goals.

As a sole proprietor, you create your company culture from scratch. Allow the characteristics in the following list to give you insights about how you want to position your company culture for yourself, your clients, and your customers.

In the following list, circle the top ten characteristics you'd use to describe your ideal company culture.

Is ethical
Is honest
Gives back to the community
Is prestigious and well-known
Encourages the participation of family members at social events
Promotes cultural diversity
Focuses on quality
Is customer driven
Values creativity
Is fiscally responsible
Has sound business practices
Focuses on the bottom line
Is profit driven

Is based on cutting-edge technology
Focuses on wellness
Is respectful of employees
Encourages employees to keep reasonable work hours
Demonstrates flexibility
Is environmentally aware
Is socially responsible
Values the contribution of women and minorities
Allows me to be myself (clothing, lifestyle, values, and so on)
Is casual
Is highly professional
Is formal

Has a hierarchical structure
Is down-to-earth
Is informal
Promotes open communication
Is friendly
Emphasizes teamwork
Has a cooperative environment
Has high professional standards
Thrives on pressure
Competes aggressively
Challenges me
Is a fun place to work
Focuses on results
Is forward thinking
Is innovative
Stresses excellence

Record your top company culture characteristics in Worksheet 4-6. Next to each characteristic write a few words or a phrase to capture what each one means to you. Be as specific as you can. If you need a company culture characteristic that you don't see on the preceding list, add it.

Your Cultural Characteristics	Your Thoughts on Each Characteristic

Worksheet 4-6:
Picturing your perfect company culture.

The purpose of the company

A company that manufactures products differs significantly from one that conducts research. A company's purpose impacts its culture, the kinds of jobs it offers, its organizational structure, and its language. As you think about your options, you may realize that you feel at home in one company and like a fish out of water in another.

As you read Worksheet 4-7, notice how you may feel providing these products and services to customers. Use check marks to indicate any company purposes that match your interests. Even if you don't know the specifics of each kind of environment, pay attention to your initial response to the description. Those that seem interesting may be worth exploring further (see Chapter 15 for more information). Feel free to mark as many as work for you.

The company's reach

Each company reaches out to its customers, whether they are local clients who come into the shop or global customers whose main contact is over the Web. Think about the kinds of contact you wish to have with your customers. Do you want face-to-face conversations? Would you prefer phone contact? Even if you may not work directly with customers, this question is important because the reach of the business may impact the work pace, the hours of operations, the technology used, and the extent to which you travel.

Look at the options that I describe in Worksheet 4-8 to get a sense of which kind of experience works for you. Mark as many as you like.

Company Purpose	
☐ Provides a service	Clients are helped in an intangible way. For example, through financial counseling, therapy, consulting, staffing, or child care.
☐ Manufactures a product	Consumers can touch or hold in their hands what the company produces — for example, a car or computer, clothing, or furniture.
☐ Provides information	Provides data through reference materials, news, and statistics.
☐ Does research	Work done in research institutes, think tanks, and institutes of higher education creates new information and inventions.
☐ Entertains	People laugh and enjoy themselves as a result of the company's work.
☐ Sells	Goods reach consumers because they've been sold through wholesale and retail channels.

Worksheet 4-7:
Looking at the purpose of different types of companies.

Company Reach	
☐ Local	Business focuses on local clients and their needs, which means someone working in this business is likely to have face-to-face interactions with clients.
☐ Statewide	Business and operations are located in one state.
☐ Regional	Company serves a particular geographic region.
☐ National	Company focuses attention on one country. A company this large may have branches or departments across the country, which means you may have coworkers you only work with by phone or during brief visits.
☐ Global	Company has a presence throughout the world with their products and services as well as their operations. Note: Any Web-based company has a global scope. Most if not all interactions with clients are likely to be via e-mail and phone.

Worksheet 4-8:
Scoping out the reach of potential companies.

The location

Worksheet 4-9 talks about the factors that make a work location comfortable for you. Next to each factor, spell out in detail what you need within each category.

As you answer the questions in Worksheet 4-9, dig deep to identify the specific characteristics that seem most important for you to have in your work location.

If you want to run your own business, the decisions you make about your location depend on a number of additional factors including zoning, foot traffic, availability, and rents. If you think you want to work from home, your answers to the questions in Worksheet 4-9 can help you verify your desire. For more information on starting your own business, see Chapter 20.

Some companies, in addition to providing flex-time options, offer some flexibility in where employees do their work. Although originally motivated by the need to retain talented employees, some employers discover cost savings and increased productivity when they implement some of the following options. As you think about your situation, consider the following as possible solutions:

- **Telecommuting:** Work from home for part of your scheduled workweek. To insure adequate visibility at work, telecommuters often work from home two to three days a week and come into the office for meetings and face-to-face contact with coworkers and customers the other days.

- **Satellite offices:** Typically established along intense commute corridors, satellite offices allow employees to stop by to work if traffic is bad, or to eliminate their commutes some days by working there all day.

- **Office hotelling:** When office space is tight and expensive and the employee base is somewhat transient due to travel schedules or offsite projects, some companies choose a solution called *office hotelling* as a way to cut costs. When they expect to spend time in the office, employees call ahead to reserve office space. Upon arriving, the employee finds his assigned desk for the day, gathers his file cabinet on wheels, sets up shop, and gets to work.

- **Virtual office:** Various hi-tech communication channels make it possible for people in different parts of the country or the world to come together electronically to provide a product or service to customers. By using the Internet, fax, phone calls, and video conferencing to communicate among themselves and with clients, the employees and company save time and money because there is no need to commute, travel, or create and maintain a collective office space.

- **On the road:** You may not need to work in an office at all. You may work out of your car, from clients' sites specified by your employer, or from wherever you happen to be, whether in town, out of the country, in a building, or out in nature. If you choose this route, research the cutting-edge technology to make your life a bit easier.

Your Work Location	
Acceptable commute distance?	
Safety requirements?	
Ideal parking situation?	
Preference for surrounding neighborhood or area?	
Required amenities close by?	
Best source of food?	
Ideal exterior surroundings?	
Preferred feel of interior?	

Worksheet 4-9: Thinking about your work location.

The work area

Productivity is the name of the game when it comes to work. Do you know what characteristics you need in your personal work space to be efficient and productive? Although you may not always get what you want, if you know your requirements, you may turn away from a job with an office space that is definitely counterproductive to you. For example, if the thought of sitting in a cubicle five days a week makes your skin crawl, you may need to look beyond traditional companies or find ways to make yourself feel more at home in that environment.

Worksheet 4-10 lists elements of your personal workspace that can enhance or detract from your productivity. Check the ones that strike a chord in you and add any notes to clarify and specify your needs in more detail.

If you notice as you fill out Worksheet 4-10 that working in a closed building of any variety stresses you out, this section may offer valuable clues about your next career. Would you prefer to work outside? Do you need to move around at will? Would traveling to several locations throughout the week help? Whatever you do, listen to your body's response to your options.

Your Personal Workspace	
☐ Cubicle or office?	
☐ Door you can close?	
☐ Shared office?	
☐ Privacy requirements?	
☐ Lighting preferences?	
☐ Noise factors?	
☐ Animals in your office?	
☐ Foot traffic?	
☐ Windows?	
☐ View?	
☐ Office colors?	
☐ Feel of office?	
☐ Furniture needs?	
☐ Equipment requirements?	
☐ Supplies needed?	
☐ Storage space needs?	
☐ Workspace needs?	
☐ Meeting space preferences?	

Worksheet 4-10: Laying out your ideal work area.

The dress code

If your comfort or ability to express yourself are tantamount to your happiness, how you dress for work each day may prove to be very important to you. If not, you may consider skipping Worksheet 4-11. Before you settle into thinking that you must wear what you've always worn to work, think about what really makes you happy.

Hitting the road

Traveling for business can be exciting, disruptive, exhilarating, and exhausting all at once. If you want travel to be part of your career, take some time to think about how and how much you want to travel. Clearly visualizing your travel plans helps you make good decisions, when the time comes, about the fit between you and a prospective job. Consider your personal and family priorities as you set your intentions. Ask yourself the following questions:

- ✔ How often can I travel?
- ✔ How long do I want to be away at any one time?
- ✔ How far am I willing to travel on a single day trip?
- ✔ Do I have any limits on national destinations?
- ✔ Will I travel internationally?
- ✔ How do I like to travel?

Place a check mark in Worksheet 4-11 next to the dress code that makes you most comfortable. If several options appeal to you depending on your tasks for the day, choose the three that "suit" you best.

Worksheet 4-11: Getting dressed for work.

Your Dress Preferences	
☐ Uniform	Company-specified outfit.
☐ Professional	Formal attire, which may consist of a suit and tie for men and a suit and heels for women.
☐ Professional casual	Coordinated outfits, such as a pair of slacks and a matching shirt or pullover sweater.
☐ Self-expressive	Wardrobe that uses accessories, colors, and designs to add personal flair is encouraged.
☐ Comfortable	Jeans and t-shirts, for example.
☐ Ultra-comfortable	Work clothes, sweats, PJs, robe and slippers, or perhaps even nothing at all.

Getting Paid on Your Terms

Obviously, one of the key reasons you work is to make an income and have access to benefits that make your life easier and less stressful. As you consider changing careers, being aware of your income and benefit requirements puts you in a strong position to negotiate or create what you need in your next career.

The amount

One crucial number to know as you enter into your career change is the income you need to live the way you want to live. This is not necessarily the amount you live on now, but includes the money you need to do the things you've always wanted to do.

Use the following process to make a ballpark estimate of what it takes for you to live comfortably. As you come up with various career plans, return to this list to assess the financial feasibility of your plans:

1. **Calculate what it costs you to live.**

   Base your calculations on what it cost you to live last year. If you use a bookkeeping program, this number should be easy to find. If not, scan your check register and credit card statements to see how much you spent. You can also look at your total income last year and add in credit card charges that you made but couldn't pay off last year.

   If you are thinking of relocating, you may need to adjust your calculations for the cost of living in the new area. To get an idea of these costs, visit the Web site at www.jobfactory.com/salary.htm and click on the Relocation Calculator to determine the power of your salary in your new area.

2. **Add any major expenses you expect to incur in the next few years.**

   For example, think about any pending major purchases, like a car or a house, or other large cash outlays, like college tuition for yourself or your children.

3. **Add any debt you want to pay off.**

4. **Add any savings plan you want to integrate into your life.**

5. **Add any income required to enhance your life and fulfill your dreams in the next few years.**

For example, if you want a different day care situation, factor in the added cost. If you want to travel more frequently, include a travel budget. If you plan to have a child, estimate the additional costs for the first year or two.

Another useful number to have in your back pocket is the least amount of money you could live on for one year. I'm not suggesting that this number would be helpful for everyone. However, sometimes paring back your lifestyle can open up interesting options that give you the freedom to step into a new life. For example, knowing this number gives you added decision-making power if you ever decide you want to start a business (see Chapter 20), cut back your hours, return to school (see Chapter 18), or take a sabbatical to travel (see Chapter 5).

Payment options

Receiving pay for the work you do is no longer as simple as earning an hourly wage or an annual salary. Companies use a variety of methods to pay employees, temporary or contract workers, independent consultants, expert consultants, or freelancers. Some methods of payment are more consistent and predictable than others in terms of the dollar amount and the expected pay period.

As you read each description in Worksheet 4-12, put a check mark next to any form of payment you would consider in your next career.

For more information about payment options, visit www.salary.com and click on "Salary Advice" to check out the base salary and stock options sections.

Benefits

Although you can't, at this point, know for sure what benefits any future employer may offer, you can determine the benefits that are most important to you and your family. If you are considering self-employment or plan to work for short-term stints at various companies, this exercise proves extremely important, because you won't have a company providing your benefits. Instead, you must understand your needs thoroughly enough to search out ways to provide the benefits you need for yourself.

In Worksheet 4-13, put a check mark next to any benefits that you feel are relevant to your situation.

Your Payment Options	
☐ Hourly	Get a check for the hours you worked during the pay period.
☐ Salary	Get a check on a regular, dependable basis for a consistent amount each pay period.
☐ By project	Receive payment for work done on a project. May be paid at predetermined milestones as progress is made.
☐ Commission	Earn a percentage of everything you sell. Sometimes combined with a base salary.
☐ Royalties	Earn a percentage on the sale of something you wrote or created.
☐ Bonus	Receive an extra check as a reward after the completion of a big project, at the end of the year, after cost-savings goals are met, when statistical improvements are made in a product's quality, or for signing on with a new company.
☐ Stock options	Have the option to buy company stocks at a fixed price. Your eligibility for this may be influenced by your tenure in the company, your level, and the rules that govern the company's stock program. Do your research to understand how this complex payment option works in the company.
☐ Profit sharing	Share in the profits of the company. The amount you receive depends on how well the company did during the year.

Worksheet 4-12: Making the bacon.

Visit www.salary.com and click on the Salary Advice tab to read more about various benefits.

Your Benefits	
☐ Medical insurance	Covers visits to your doctor and catastrophic health problems.
☐ Dental insurance	Covers visits to your dentist.
☐ Eye care insurance	Covers visits to your eye doctor.
☐ Long-term and short-term disability	Provides replacement income if you should become incapacitated due to illness or accident. This benefit is most important if you have children or a mortgage.
☐ Severance package	Provides money that allows you to transition into your next job. Finding out whether you have this benefit during the hiring phase might seem awkward, but it's better to know how the system works before any sparks fly.
☐ Life insurance	Protects the financial well-being of your family in case of your death.
☐ Child care	Provides assistance to employees with children. Options vary by company from an onsite or near-site child care center that is run or supported by the company to financial subsidies, resources and referral systems, options for sick-child care, summer programs, and back-up care.
☐ Elder care	Includes a combination of resources, referrals, seminars, support groups, and long-term insurance for family members to help employees who must care for elderly or ill parents or grandparents. This benefit is gaining popularity as employees take on more and more care-taking responsibilities.
☐ Employee assistance program	Refers you to a counselor if you are wrestling with personal issues that are distracting you from your work. After a few appointments, you may be referred to a counselor who is covered through your medical insurance.
☐ Retirement	Establishes a retirement fund, such as a 401(k), that allows you to contribute pre-tax dollars to your nest egg. The company may match your contribution dollar for dollar. If you are close to retirement age and expect to be with the company when you retire, ask about other benefits, such as health insurance, that come to you upon retirement. Make sure to ask how long before you qualify to receive retirement benefits.
☐ Parking/commuting	Provides onsite parking, subsidized offsite parking, or tokens for commuters.
☐ Convenience or concierge services	Eliminates tasks from your "to do" list and frees up your time and your mind to work more productively. Independent contractors hired by your company provide a variety of services which may include dry cleaning, housecleaning, take-home meals, pet care, onsite chair massage, legal services, financial consulting, and social outings. Offerings are bound to become even more creative as time goes on as this is the hottest new way to retain employees. Although you generally pay for the services you use, the peace of mind and simplification of your life may make it worthwhile.
☐ Expense account	Gives you a per diem amount or charge card you use to handle expenses while you are away from the office. Depending on your work, you may be assigned a company car, as well.
☐ Community service	Allows you to take off work hours to volunteer through corporate volunteer programs or more informal arrangements.
☐ Health club	Gives you access to an onsite gym or a full or discounted membership to a nearby gym.

Worksheet 4-13: Thinking about benefits.

Working with the Right People

The people you interact with at work have a huge impact on how much you enjoy your job, whether they are your coworkers, those who come in-house to perform tasks, or your manager.

Your coworkers

Although you can't always choose your colleagues, you can determine the kinds of relationships that work best for you. After you know what you are looking for, if you spot a problem right off the bat in an interview, you know that job isn't for you.

If you want to work solo, the term co-worker may seem a little off base. In your situation, your co-workers are your colleagues, professionals in your trade association, or people you team up with to work on a particular project.

Think about two of your favorite coworkers over the years. What elements of your working relationship made it work so well? Next, think about two of your least favorite coworkers. What was it about these relationships that made it so hard? To get the full picture in both cases, think of their personalities, style of communication, work style and pace, strengths and weaknesses, and how you socialized with them during and after work hours.

After making some notes in your journal about these four relationships, identify the characteristics that are most important to you. Record the most important characteristics of the first column of Worksheet 4-14 and then describe why you included them in your list.

In an interviewing situation, it may be hard to evaluate your coworkers. You may not meet all of them, or if you do, the interaction may be so superficial that you can't make a true assessment of the fit. If you are switching jobs or careers within the same company, your prospective coworkers may play a bigger role in your decision making process because you may have already had an opportunity to interact with them. In either case, trust your intuitive gut sense of your prospective coworkers. Chapter 19 talks more about evaluating a position based on the information you gain during an interview.

Other players

In this day and age, the people who make up your work team may not be employed by the same company you are. Understanding the working relationship that these people have within a company helps you decide whether you could work with them effectively.

The following roles are relevant whether you work in a large company or on your own:

✔ **Expert consultants:** Hired to use their expertise to resolve specific problems or situations. Often their role and the work they do is dictated by the proposal they themselves created to land the job. Whether they are self-employed or employed by a consulting firm, they may work on other projects for other companies while working on a project for your company.

- ✔ **Freelancers:** Complete their piece of the project independently and may submit their work electronically, although they may interact with others to discover what they need to know to get the job done. They typically work on a number of projects for different customers at once.

- ✔ **Independent consultants:** Come into the company for the duration of a project as needed to provide a key skill or piece of knowledge that no one within the company has.

- ✔ **Temporary employees/contract employees:** Fill in on a short-term basis when a regular employee is out or there's a project crunch and no one within the organization can handle it.

- ✔ **Vendors:** Provide your company with key materials for projects and may offer support for the piece they supply.

- ✔ **Virtual assistants:** Work from their own offices to provide you with the support you need to get your work done. Great for entrepreneurs and small business owners who don't have the space or financial where-withal to employ a full-time assistant. For more information about virtual assistants, visit www.assistu.com.

Your manager

You may talk with your prospective manager during your interview. By knowing the management style that allows you to be most productive, you can ask direct, carefully worded questions to discern whether each prospective manager is someone you can work with productively.

	Key Characteristics	Why Is This Important to You?
1.		
2.		
3.		
4.		
5.		
6.		
7.		
8.		
9.		
10.		

Worksheet 4-14: Picturing your ideal coworker.

If you are your own boss or are planning to be, Worksheet 4-15 requires you to create a split personality for a moment. Answer the questions as accurately as you can as an employee, thinking all the while about how you can better manage yourself.

Use Worksheet 4-15 to record what your manager can do to make you more productive and fulfilled. Begin by putting a check mark next to all of the qualities and traits that your perfect manager would have and then go back and circle the five that are most important to you.

Recording Your Hottest Desires

After you identify the various aspects of what you want (see the preceding sections in this chapter), you can build a profile of your ideal work situation.

In Worksheet 4-16, indicate your ideal preference for each element that you experience at work. Be as explicit as possible and factor in your needs and priorities and those of your family. Don't worry if you see obvious inconsistencies or conflicts. You can sort those out in Chapter 17.

If your ideal profile looks like a stable, 8-to-5 job with a guaranteed two-week vacation, I encourage you to take another look at this chapter to see how you may expand your options a bit. The days of the secure, career-for-life are numbered. Even if you had a stable career up until now, don't expect the next ten years to look like the past. You must build some flexibility into your picture. If you don't, the current economic realities and trends may do it for you.

My Best Manager . . .
☐ Tells me what's truly important about a project
☐ Appreciates me and my work
☐ Shares credit for a job well done
☐ Emphasizes results over methods
☐ Communicates expectations clearly
☐ Gives clear instructions
☐ Sets realistic deadlines
☐ Communicates openly about upcoming problems or changes in projects, the staff, or the company structure
☐ Pitches in when the staff is in a bind
☐ Reflects my strengths back to me so I can see them too
☐ Recognizes my contribution
☐ Tells me how I'm doing
☐ Gives me constructive feedback
☐ Treats me with respect
☐ Hires competent coworkers and deals with incompetent ones
☐ Shows compassion and patience if I'm going through a rough time
☐ Trusts me enough to let me do the job the way I believe it needs to be done
☐ Lets me learn and grow from my mistakes
☐ Considers my ideas and those of others
☐ Answers my questions
☐ Speaks truthfully
☐ Laughs with me and sees the lighter side of things
☐ Models what I need to know to do my job well
☐ Keeps promises
☐ Shares the information I need to be effective
☐ Gives me training, resources, and space to do my job
☐ Mentors me
☐ Helps me grow in my career
☐ Helps me see the big picture
☐ Makes fair decisions

Worksheet 4-15: Visualizing the perfect manager.

	Your Hotlist of Work Wishes
Your work schedule	
Your contract	
Kind of company	
Company size	
Company culture	
Company purpose	
Company reach	
Company location	
Your work area	
The dress code	
Amount of pay	
Pay options	
Benefits	
Your coworkers	
Other players	
Your manager	

Worksheet 4-16:
What you wish you had at work.

Chapter 5

What to Do in the Meantime

In This Chapter

▶ Staying sane if you have to stay in your current career for now

▶ Exploring interim plans if you must leave

You know that you want to change careers, but unfortunately, a new career doesn't happen overnight. It takes some time to come up with your options, decide what you want, and then make it happen.

In the meantime, you may be faced with the necessity of working at a job that you've grown to hate in a career that got tired long ago. Even if you wanted or needed to leave immediately, you know that you can't because you don't have the money. If you do have the financial security to leave, then you face different, but equally difficult, pressures associated with the looming unknowns of an unstructured future.

This chapter shows you various ways to ease the discomfort that you may feel in your current position or in your transition from one career to another.

In order to make sound decisions about your next career, you need to be in a position to think rationally. Don't let desperation with your current situation rush you into pursuing another unsatisfying career.

When You Feel You Must Stay . . . for Now

You know that you want to leave. You also know that now is not the time to make your move. Family, personal finances, or the economy may motivate you to stay where you are for a while. But because you aren't particularly happy in your current position, you know that something has got to give, or else.

With some creative thought, you can find a way to make your situation work for a while, giving yourself time and energy that you can devote to getting out of a bad career. Read over the following list to see if any of these ideas open the way to an as-yet-unseen temporary solution:

- ✔ **Take a vacation:** Use your accrued vacation time to get out of town for a while. A change of scenery may be just what you need to clear your head. The longer you can get away, the better.

- ✔ **Go on a retreat:** Arrange to spend some quiet time alone either at home or in a beautiful setting. Ask people in your life to refrain from contacting you during your retreat so that you can have an extended block of time with and by yourself.

- ✔ **Take a leave:** A letter from your doctor or therapist may open the door for you to take a leave, which could give you the time and space you need to regain your perspective. Talk with your human resources department to discover what medical or stress leaves are available to you.

- ✔ **Renegotiate your responsibilities:** Make a list of all the tasks you handle at work and at home. With as much honesty as you can muster, identify any tasks you no longer care to handle yourself. Work with your manager and members of your family to restructure your responsibilities and ease the constant pressure you have felt day in and day out.

- ✔ **Downshift to individual contributor:** If you are a manager, consider stepping into a role of individual contributor so that you spend your time working again, rather than dealing with the stresses of supervising others. Think through your options, come up with a plan or two, and talk with your manager to see what you can negotiate.

- ✔ **Reinvent your job:** Take a good look at your job to identify any new projects or responsibilities you could add to bring more fulfillment, variety, or challenge to your current job.

- ✔ **Transfer within your company:** Look around the company for an open position that may be less stressful, allow you more peace of mind, and give you more time to focus on your long-term plans.

You may hesitate to ask your employer for the things you need. If you truly must stay for a while in an unsatisfying job or career, you have to find a way to make the situation bearable. You have to get over this fear and ask questions that may be, at first, tough to ask. Clients of mine have negotiated the following outcomes by asking what they assumed would be pointless questions:

- ✔ Cut back their hours while keeping their benefits and privileges

- ✔ Took an extended leave — with full pay!

- ✔ Added two weeks to their vacation

- ✔ Worked from home several days a week

When you are clear about what you need, it never hurts to ask!

Treating yourself

Sometimes listening to the cravings inside you can relieve quite a bit of pressure from your day. Small treats like the following can make a huge difference to your outlook:

✔ If you crave quiet time alone, try putting a "Do Not Disturb" sign on your bedroom door for 30 minutes each morning.

✔ If you want to get away, but you can't afford the time or money for a full-fledged vacation, try spending a night at a local bed & breakfast or campground.

✔ If all you want is to get caught up on your sleep, take an afternoon nap this weekend.

✔ If you want to escape the drama playing out in your own life, grab a novel and a blanket and curl up to read about someone else's life for a while.

✔ If waiting for the phone to ring is driving you crazy, switch on the answering machine and get out of the house. Take a walk, focusing on the details of your surroundings.

✔ If you feel isolated, but don't know who to connect with, begin going to the corner café everyday around the same time. You may run into someone you know or meet someone new.

When You Can't Stay, but Must Have Money Coming In

Under certain circumstances, you may need to leave your current job before you can make any progress with your career change. If things are bad enough in your current position, your first goal may be to give notice as soon as possible. This is especially true if you are absolutely burned out by your work, or if your work environment is toxic in some way. (See the sidebar in Chapter 2 for more information.)

Even if you must leave your current job, you probably need money coming in during your career change to survive. One of the following options may provide the answer:

✔ **Get a job in an unrelated field:** Even if the job is doing something that you aren't interested in pursuing long-term, you can make money. You may find that doing something completely different gives you renewed energy and vision. Just make sure that this interim job doesn't sap your strength for following up on your long-term career aspirations.

✔ **Sign up with a temp agency:** Contact a temporary agency so that they can place you in a job. Although work may come in short bursts, at least you have money coming in. Letting someone else find a job for you also frees up your time for investigating your career options.

✔ **Take another job in the same field:** Although it may not be your first choice, using the skills from your career to land a similar job in a different environment may be a viable option. Thinking of this new job as an interim position can help you keep your attention focused on your long-range planning.

✔ **Find a stepping-stone job:** If you have some idea of the field you ultimately want to enter, use this transition time as an opportunity to gain valuable work experience. Search for a position that allows you to apply your established skills in a new industry or setting that is relevant to your future career.

✔ **Use creative financing:** Take a good look at your finances. Can you see any creative ways to use your funds to support your transition? For example, your savings, a credit line on your home, or a loan could pave the way for you to:

- Take a relevant, but lower-paying position.

- Go to school to improve your standing in your new field.

- Take a couple of months off.

The option you choose may depend on how far along you are in your thinking about your new career. The more focused you are about your direction, the more you can use your interim position as a vehicle to explore a potential field.

When You Don't Have to Stay for the Money

Lucky you! You can afford to leave your current position, and you don't have to start investigating a new career immediately. If you are physically and emotionally burned out, but you are in a good financial position, your best option may be to take some time off.

A gift of time, whether it's in the form of a vacation or a year off, can be life-changing. The clarity you gain and the self-understanding you acquire can help you align with your deeper truths and purpose, which makes creating a new career that much easier. Investing in yourself in this way can produce returns that pay off for the rest of your life.

Although you may be tempted to call this option impossible, remember the value of ideal thinking. You never know what's possible until you explore your options. Give yourself the opportunity to read over these ideas for making your time off powerfully productive:

✔ **Structuring a sabbatical:** Creating time away from your career for study, rest, or travel can produce a great payoff. Listen to your cravings and then come up with a plan that matches your needs. Being clear about your overriding goal for the time you've gifted yourself helps you stay focused and guides you as you choose between various activities and options.

✔ **Avoiding panic:** Although you may be tempted to worry about your future, give yourself permission to take a certain amount of time off before you even begin to think about your career. Position your time off so that you know you have the funds you need to cover your expenses for that period of time. If it allows you to relax more deeply, go a step further to create a back-up plan in case it takes longer than you anticipate to identify your next career.

✔ **Staying sane without a job:** After being in a structured work environment for a length of time, you may struggle with what to do with yourself when you don't have to be at work all the time. Use a few classes or regularly-scheduled group events to build a bit of structure into your life. Create some structure while giving yourself a lot of flexibility to follow your needs and desires of the moment.

✔ **Fielding the big question — "What do you do?":** One of the hardest parts of not working for an extended period of time is explaining your decision to others, whether they are former coworkers, friends, or family members, who just don't understand the concept. Remain clear that you are making the best decision for yourself; then, no matter what they say, you are grounded and content with yourself. Having a short, but sweet, statement in your back pocket is always a good strategy, too. Modify one of the following to suit your own situation:

  • "I'm taking some time off to explore my options."

  • "I'm doing fine. In fact, I'm having the time of my life!"

  • "There's no need for you to be concerned. I'm right on track."

✔ **Using your time wisely:** After giving yourself this block of time, don't fritter it away with busy work. Each day, ask yourself what you feel like doing and then follow through on it. If you want to rest, do that. If you want to read all day, do that. During your time off, reduce the number of have-to's you force yourself to accomplish each day.

> ✔ **Allowing new aspects of yourself to surface:** Use your unstructured time to explore who you are. Without the trappings and constraints of work, you may discover new sides of yourself you never knew existed. Do the things you've always wanted to do: read books, go to talks, travel, walk in nature, enjoy a new hobby. Although non-career related discoveries may seem counter-productive in the moment, anything you find out about yourself allows you to bring more clarity to your career decisions when the time comes. Who knows; your exploration may uncover an entirely new professional outlet.

Give yourself this gift of some time off. Whether you can afford to take off several months or a full year, you, your work, and your life may be transformed by your experience. At first you may say to yourself, "I can't possibly do that! I've got responsibilities to meet and people who need me." However, if you endure the stress and strain of a bad job, you may not meet your responsibilities all that well, anyway. Regardless of anything else you do or feel you must do, your biggest responsibility is to yourself — without you nothing in your life works or matters much.

Part II

Searching for Hidden Treasure — Your Passion

The 5th Wave   By Rich Tennant

"I know he'd be happier in a job he didn't have to take home with him at night."

In this part . . .

Are you still searching for the answer to the age-old question: What am I going to do when I grow up? This part guides you through a brainstorming process to identify your passions and interests and transform them into a list of viable career ideas.

Chapter 6

Uncovering Clues to Your Passion

In This Chapter
▶ Identifying your talents
▶ Discovering what fascinates you
▶ Figuring out what gives meaning to your work

*I*n this chapter you build a list of your passions and interests. I recommend that you read one section at a time and let the list build as you answer each question. The longer your list, the more options you have when you pull them together to create your new career ideas. (See Chapter 7 for more information on building your list of career ideas.)

If you get an idea right off the bat that you want to run with, stop. I encourage you to stick with the process to create as detailed a list as you can. The depth and richness of your entire list makes the worksheets in Chapter 7 as effective as possible.

Skills That Make Time Fly

Surely you have experienced a time when you were so intrigued and involved with what you were doing that you completely lost track of the time. Time flew by, stood still, or seemed to warp in some unusual way. The skills and activities that create that feeling provide valuable clues to discovering a career that you love.

Unfortunately, it can sometimes prove difficult after such an experience to retrace your steps and say for sure what was so intriguing. Use the following questions as triggers to help you uncover or rediscover the skills and activities that bring you this pleasure and satisfaction.

Finding your innate areas of intelligence

Each person possesses natural talent or intelligence in one or more areas. The trick is to figure out in what ways you are naturally gifted.

In school, good verbal and mathematical skills are regarded as signs of intelligence, while other forms of talent are not. After working with talented youngsters and people with brain damage, Howard Gardner, author of *Frames of Mind: The Theory of Multiple Intelligences,* published by Basic Books, realized that just because someone has limited abilities in one area doesn't mean that she has limited abilities in other areas; Gardner created a different way to define intelligence, one that encompasses nine different talents.

 Each person's unique Multiple Intelligence profile points to viable career options. In the following lists, which are based on seven of the most common intelligences, circle any and all items that you know you enjoy. I group the items so that similar skills are close together. If you find that a skill you have is not listed, add it!

Do you think in words?

Circle any of the following words that resonate well with you.

Vocabulary
Grammar
Figures of speech
Mnemonics
Creating words
Meaning of words
Derivation of words
Word puzzles
Journal or diary
   keeping
Taking notes
Creative writing
Creating vivid
   descriptions

Writing poetry
Complex writing
Editing
Reading with great
   comprehension
Poetry appreciation
Dramatic reading
Making presentations
Verbal debate
Impromptu speaking
Storytelling
Humor or jokes
Memory for names,
   dates, and details

Memorizing
Mediation
Diplomacy
Negotiating
Persuasion
Playing devil's advocate
Explaining
Teaching using
   language
Sensing layers of
   conversation
Foreign languages
Translating
Interpreting

Do you think in a logical, organized fashion?

Circle any of the following words that resonate well with you.

Outlining
Graphic organizers
   (flow charts and
   diagrams)
Counting
Estimating
Quantifying

Straight-forward
   calculations
Complex calculations
Doing calculations in
   your head
Using abstract symbols
Using formulas
Programming

Identifying numeric
   patterns
Deciphering codes
Discerning
   relationships and
   connections among
   information
Recognizing patterns

Problem solving
Reasoning
Critical thinking
Processing logic
   questions rapidly
Seeing cause and effect
Event planning

Project planning
Organizing
Scheduling
Prioritizing
Dividing up tasks
Research
Decision making

Investigating
Strategizing
Analyzing
Comparing
Explaining
Categorizing
Creating spreadsheets

Do you connect well with others?

Circle any of the following words that resonate well with you.

Giving feedback
Receiving feedback
Coaching
Verbal communication
Nonverbal
   communication
Empathizing
Sensing others' motives
Ability to discern
   perspectives of
   others
Sensitive to others'
   moods
Determining who is
   best to do the job
Cooperating
Collaborating
Getting along well with
   others

Building relationships
Networking
Putting people at ease
Finding common
   ground
Creating and
   maintaining synergy
Building consensus
Understanding group
   process
Facilitating group
   discussion
Recognizing cultural
   values and norms
Clarifying vision
Setting goals
Helping others
   brainstorm

Helping others see
   possibility
Giving advice
Building others'
   self-esteem
Motivating others
Comforting others
Acknowledging others
Trusted confidant
Extracting information
   from others
Interviewing
Providing customer
   service
Managing
Leading
Role playing

Do you have a good eye?

Circle any of the following words that resonate well with you.

Visualizing
Imaginative
Forming mental images
Recreating experience
   in mind
Color schemes
Sense of aesthetics,
   beauty, or balance
Arranging objects (such
   as furniture)
Creating patterns, and
   designs
Painting
Drawing
Sculpture

Pictures or
   photography
Cartooning
Designing graphic
   representations
Manipulating images
Sense of direction
Map reading
Mapmaking
Finding the best route
Navigating
Creating charts and
   diagrams
Working with charts
   and diagrams

Accurate perception
   from different angles
Spatial reasoning
Thinking in 3-D
Recognizing spatial
   depth and dimension
Spatial implications
Abstract spatial
   imagery
Building
Assembling
Making models
Taking things apart and
   putting back
   together

Do you have a good sense of your body?

Circle any of the following words that resonate well with you.

Movement to music
Folk or creative dance
Expressive or creative dance
Choreography
Using your body to express yourself
Expressive gestures
Body language
Drama
Mime
Mimicking
Role-playing
Creating with your hands on a large scale

Creating with your hands on a medium scale
Precision work with your hands
Handling objects skillfully
Sign language
Finger dexterity
Physical exercise
Sports and games
Using your body in complicated ways to accomplish goals
Eye-hand coordination
Eye-foot coordination

Martial arts
Mind-body connection
Internal body map
Natural sense of how your body moves
Aware of body sensations when active in other ways
Quick response time
Good sense of timing
Flexibility
Agility
Endurance
Balance

Do you have an ear for music?

Circle any of the following words that resonate well with you.

Good singing voice
Singing a melody
Remembering a melody
Remembering lyrics
Harmonizing
Blending
Keeping time

Pick up a beat easily
Vocal sounds or tones
Perfect pitch
Relative pitch
Sensing qualities of a tone
Tonal patterns

Intervals
Composing
Arranging
Improvising
Actively listening to music

Do you appreciate nature and its creatures?

Circle any of the following words that resonate well with you.

Picking up nuances between large numbers of similar objects
Discriminating among living things
Discerning patterns of life
Examining things in nature
Sensitive to formations in nature

Observing natural phenomena
Using scientific equipment to observe nature
Keeping detailed records of observations
Creating hierarchy makes sense
Classifying things into hierarchies
Pattern recognition

Collecting
Organizing collections
Labeling collections
Understanding animal behavior
Aware of animal needs
Characteristics of animals
Interacting with living creatures
Plant care
Plant identification

Knowing what's as easy as breathing

One skill you may overlook is the skill that is so easy and natural for you that you assume everyone can and does use it in their work.

If you are a whiz at editing, speaking, playing an instrument, facilitating groups, or working with animals, and you have a tendency to discount your natural abilities, take a closer look. You may find a clue to your future in a skill that you always assumed everyone brought to the party.

If you have difficulty deciding how this exercise applies to you, ask a few trusted friends and family members what they see as a natural part of you that you take for granted. Write down any additional skills you come up with.

Thinking about skills you have but don't enjoy

Although it's tempting to think that you should do whatever you are good at, doing something you don't enjoy is a drain whether you excel at the skill or not. Do yourself a favor and cross out any skills on the previous lists that you don't enjoy.

The skills you'd rather not pursue in the long run may, however, prove to be helpful in the short run as you move into a new field or industry. Put these skills on the back burner until you begin plotting how to transition into your new field or position.

Singling out your favorite skills and intelligences

Review the circles you made in the preceding sections a second time. Where do you have the highest concentration of check marks? These areas are your natural strengths, and they correlate to specific natural intelligences including the following:

- ✔ Thinking in words correlates to a Verbal/Linguistic Intelligence.
- ✔ Thinking in a logical, organized fashion correlates to a Mathematical/Logical Intelligence.
- ✔ Connecting well with others correlates to an Interpersonal Intelligence.
- ✔ Having a good eye correlates to a Visual Intelligence.

> ✔ Having a good sense of your body correlates to a Body/Kinesthetic Intelligence.
>
> ✔ Having an ear for music correlates to a Musical Intelligence.
>
> ✔ Appreciating nature and its creatures correlates to a Naturalist Intelligence.

Review all the skills you identified, including the items you circled in the preceding sections and anything you listed in the section "Knowing what's as easy as breathing."

Identify and make a list of the 14 skills you most want in your career. Feel free to group similar items.

If you would like more clarity about your Multiple Intelligence profile, look at the Multiple Intelligence Developmental Assessment Scale available on the Web at `www.angelfire.com/oh/themidas/sample.html`.

Topics That Make You Sizzle with Excitement

Your expertise and interest in a certain area brings with it a particular language, focus, and sense of humor that defines your work.

Because you may be looking beyond your current profession to take an entirely new direction, the questions in this section tap your interests in your professional life and your personal life.

Don't be concerned if a particular exercise doesn't produce any ideas. Think about it a bit and then move on. I include a variety of questions because I want to trigger your imagination from several angles in order to help you create as thorough a list of interests as possible.

Subjects that always draw your attention

When you read the paper, listen to the news, visit a bookstore, or talk with people, what topics grab your attention? These topics provide valuable clues about your passions, which may ultimately point you in the direction of a particular career. Don't be concerned with how that's going to happen, just know that identifying your interests may open doors to career ideas that fascinate and delight you.

In the following list, I include several topics to get you started, but please don't feel limited to this list. Place a check next to any and all topics that intrigue, interest, or fascinate you. If additional topics or subtopics come to mind as you read the list, catch them! Don't let them escape or fade away — write them down.

If you don't feel inspired or interested in much of anything these days, the "muscle" that helps you know you are interested in a conversation, drawn to a flavor of ice cream, or pulled to read a book may have atrophied. Using it again reawakens that internal quickening that happens when you enjoy something. Expand your horizons by experimenting — for example, by taking classes, going to museums, visiting the library, or doing things you used to love. Keep your senses open for signs that you are enjoying yourself.

In the following list, circle any words that resonate well with you or add your own topics to it.

Animals	Electronics	Nature
Antiques	Entertainment	Nutrition
Archaeology	Ethnicity	Outdoors
Architecture	Environment	Paranormal
Art History	Fitness	Peace
Arts	Flowers	Performing arts
Astrology	Food	Personal finance
Astronomy	Furniture	Personal growth
Aviation	Future	Pets
Bird watching	Games	Philosophy
Boating	Gardening	Photography
Books	Genealogy	Politics
Business	Health	Pop culture
Cars	History	Psychology
Celebrities	Home	Recreation
Children	Humor	Relationships
Clothing	Internet	Religion
Collectibles	Investing	Sexuality
Comics	Jewelry	Spirituality
Computers	Languages	Sports
Cooking	Literature	Technology
Crafts	Magazines	Television
Criminology	Medicine	Theater
Dance	Movies	Travel
Death and grief	Music	Weather
Education	Myths	Women's issues

Your voice tells the story

To discover the topics that you feel passionate about, listen to yourself talk. Your voice is a great tool for judging how excited you are about a particular topic. As you listen, notice the general intensity with which you speak, including the following:

✔ **The speed of your words:** The faster you talk, the more excited you are.

✔ **The insistence in your voice:** If you try to convince, persuade, or educate someone on a topic, you are probably a proponent of the cause you're speaking about.

✔ **The duration of your monologues:** If you talk non-stop for any length of time, you are fascinated by the topic.

If you have a hard time hearing changes in your own voice, recruit your friends to point out to you, in the moment, when you are speaking dynamically. Develop an agreed upon hand signal or code word, so that they can signal you without interrupting your flow.

Subjects that make you want to help others

Often the ways in which you want to help others can give you additional clues to your passions.

When each of the following groups calls upon you, what topic do they typically ask you to help them with? Which topics do you enjoy helping them with?

✔ Your coworkers

✔ Your manager

✔ Your friends

✔ Your family members

✔ Your pets

✔ The organizations you volunteer with

Write down any additional topic areas that come to mind when you answer these questions.

Subjects that make you want to add your two cents

Focus on your own behavior. Under what circumstances do you willingly offer your point of view and share your expertise? What subjects make you want to do the following:

- ✔ Share what you know with strangers, acquaintances, or peers, whether they ask for your two cents or not?

- ✔ Form a response in your head, even when you have no intention of letting it leave your mouth?

Add these topics to your list.

Subjects that leave you forever searching for solutions

Do you ever see something that's not working and spend time rolling it around in your mind to find a better, more efficient, more effective, more elegant way to resolve it?

Do you ever find yourself doing the following:

- ✔ Rearranging your office or someone else's in your mind to enhance productivity?

- ✔ Restructuring the roads to eliminate traffic congestion?

- ✔ Experimenting with different ingredients to create a better recipe?

- ✔ Redesigning the dash of your car so that you can adjust the controls more safely?

What topics or areas of expertise do you tap when you search for these solutions? The following topics correspond to the previous list of solutions:

- ✔ Organization and workflow

- ✔ Transportation and traffic flow

- ✔ Cooking

- ✔ Ergonomics and design

Be sure to add any new ideas to your list.

Subjects that constantly call you to find out more

Take a look at your bookshelf, your bookmarks on your Web browser, and the classes you've taken recently, and answer the following questions:

- ✔ What are you drawn to find out more about?
- ✔ What topics draw you deeper and deeper?
- ✔ What subjects are you interested in exploring in the future?

If you come up with more topics of interest, add them to your list.

Fascinations that you can trace to childhood

Take a trip down memory lane. Memories of your childhood dreams and college aspirations may hold rich clues to your interests. For example:

- ✔ Was there something you always wanted to be when you grew up?
- ✔ Do you recall being fascinated by anything in particular in your youth?

Did you have any favorite books or movies? If you can, experience them again to rediscover what intrigued you in those days gone by. Take a closer look at the contents to see if your favorites hold a metaphor for your life and your life's work.

Include topics from your youth in your growing list of topics that interest you.

Life-changing events that sparked a mission

Sometimes the hardest knocks in life have a silver lining; sometimes because these experiences propel you into the satisfying work of preventing others from experiencing what you did or supporting them as they go through a similar journey.

For example, my work in transition consulting took shape as a direct response to my father's death several months after I finished my Ph.D. People's response to my grief showed me how little people and companies understood change and how to help individuals in the midst of major life transitions. Helping others make sense of their own journeys through the ups and downs of life has been a passion of mine personally and professionally ever since.

My commitment to helping people discover work that allows them to live the life they want also has direct ties to my personal experience. About three years into my stint in the corporate world, I became very ill with a fatigue problem. One day I heard myself say that I didn't want to get better because I didn't want to work as hard as I had been working. Then I realized I didn't mind hard work — I just didn't want to be in the work environment I was in. In that moment, I started my own career change to create a business that allowed me the flexibility to take care of my body and my personal needs.

Here are other examples:

- A husband went to great lengths to inform his wife of the state of their affairs the day before he was to go into surgery. Unfortunately, he never made it to surgery. On his way home from running an errand, he was killed in an accident caused by a drunk driver. After remarrying and rebuilding her life, his widow, inspired by her first husband's foresight, went on to start an estate organization business, called Exit Stage Right, to help people get their important papers organized in one place so that if disaster struck, they or someone else would have everything they needed at their fingertips. You can read more about her work on the Web at www.exitstageright.com.

- A single mother who struggled through the end of her painful marriage while raising her children used her experiences to create a workshop and write a book for newly divorced mothers. You can read more about her work at www.sheilaellison.com/.

- A couple who retired from jobs in the publishing industry realized that they felt too young to withdraw from the world, so they launched a Web site (www.2young2retire.com) as a forum for people over 50 to explore what's next in life and to redefine the concept of retirement.

Is there any way that you can use lemons to make lemonade for yourself? Add these ideas to your list of topics.

Listing your favorite topics of interest

After you read the preceding sections, create a list of 14 topics that you'd most like to include in your work. Please note that you are not abandoning any interests here. If you have an interest that you know is more of a hobby than a focus for your work, don't put it on the list.

Internal Drivers That Guide You to Excel

Your personality, values, and skills guide your actions no matter what you do — whether you mow the lawn, figure out a problem at work, entertain guests, plan a trip, work on a hobby, or think about a new career.

There are hundreds of ways to do a project, and you bring something that's uniquely yours to the experience. Something that adds value beyond getting the work itself done. Something that gives you a special quality or way of perceiving the world.

The trick is to identify what guides your actions.

Begin by coming up with an example of each of the following:

- ✔ A hobby-related project
- ✔ A work task or project
- ✔ A project around the house

As you look at these three seemingly unrelated projects, think about how you approach each one. Is there something you look for, strive for, or attempt to create in each scenario? Do you strive for efficiency, accuracy, elegance, simplicity, quality, conciseness, or timeliness? Do you want to create comfort, beauty, a sense of fun, or harmony?

Write down the six most important values that guide your work.

Processes That Make You Come Alive

If you have a difficult time narrowing down your topics of interest, you may be more attached to the process you engage in than the topic you address.

Take a look at your life and the projects you are drawn to. Can you think of any process or set of steps you do regardless of the topic or task at hand? Some examples follow to get you thinking. Feel free to add your own.

Building	Organizing	Turning something
Creating	Planning	around
Designing	Producing	Writing
Inventing	Researching	
Managing a project	Starting up a project	

What are your two favorite processes? Take a moment to write them down in your journal.

Tools, Equipment, and Raw Materials That Make Your Work Play

If you love the tactile experience of working with your hands, the tools, equipment, and raw materials you use may define the work you love.

The number of tools, equipment, and raw materials is infinite, so use the following lists as a starting point. Then personalize your list by looking around your home and office for other tangible things you enjoy using.

Tools and equipment:

Automotive repair tools

Camera and film

Camping gear

Carpentry hand tools and power tools

Clocks

Collectibles and antiques

Computers and peripherals

Cooking utensils and appliances

Craft equipment, such as scissors or a glue gun

Framing equipment or matting materials

Furniture

Gardening tools

Machinery

Medical testing equipment

Musical instruments

Office equipment

Paint brushes, canvases, and an easel

Sewing machine, pins, needles, and patterns

Sports equipment

Telescopes, microscopes, or binoculars

Vehicles

Writing tools

Raw materials:

Fabrics, threads, and notions

Food, spices, and condiments

Flowers and vases

Lumber and hardware

Pictures and photographs

Plants and soil

Wrapping paper

Yarn, beads, sequins, and ribbons

Make a list of the tools, equipment, or raw materials you like to use in your work. Be as specific as possible. If tangible things don't float your boat, don't worry about it. Just do the best you can and move on. After you create your list, if you find that you have more than ten items listed, circle the ten that you most want to use in your work.

Industries That Light Your Fire

Each company falls within a particular industry. By identifying industries that interest you, you effectively narrow your search for a new career.

Circle the six industries in the following list you are most interested in working within. Cross out any you absolutely know you aren't interested in. Leave the remaining industries as they are.

Accounting
Advertising or public relations
Aerospace or defense
Agricultural production
Air transportation
Amusement and recreation services
Apparel or textile products
Cable or pay television services
Chemical manufacturing
Child care services
Commercial banking
Computer or data processing
Computer hardware
Computer software
Construction
Consulting
Consumer electronics
Consumer products
Department, clothing, and accessory stores
Drug manufacturing

Eating and drinking establishments
Education
Electronic equipment manufacturing
Energy or utilities
Enterprise software
Entertainment or sports
Food processing
Grocery stores
Government
Health care
Heavy manufacturing
Hotels and lodging
Human resources
Insurance
Internet and new media
Investment banking
Journalism or publishing
Law
Management
Mining or quarrying
Motion pictures
Motor vehicle manufacturing and dealers

Mutual funds and brokerage
Networking and peripherals
Non-profit or government
Pharmaceuticals or biotechnology
Printing or publishing
Public utilities
Radio or television broadcasting
Real estate
Retail
Securities and commodities
Semiconductors
Social services
Steel manufacturing
Telecommunications
Transportation
Trucking or warehousing
Venture capital
Wholesale trade

Understanding the attributes of an industry helps you get a feel for whether that industry and its occupations are a good fit for you. Turn to Chapter 15 for more information on researching an industry.

People You Like to Help

Looking at your past and your interests, what characteristics describe your favorite client or customer? Focus your attention on the client groups that interest you and energize you in some way.

Check off any characteristics in Worksheet 6-1 that help you define your target client group and specify the subgroups you are most interested in working with.

Do not choose characteristics just because you have a lot of prior experience with that kind of population, unless, of course, you still love working with them.

Characteristic	Define Your Target Client Group
☐ Age	
☐ Gender	
☐ Certain belief system	
☐ Cultural/ethnic background	
☐ Geographic area	
☐ Sexual orientation	
☐ Life stage	
☐ Education level	
☐ Income level	
☐ Problem or life situation	
☐ Shared interest	
☐ Particular talent	
☐ Lifestyle	

Worksheet 6-1: Looking for the people you like to help.

Things That Make Work Meaningful

When you think about meaningful work, what do you long for? What phrase comes to mind when you hear the sentence, "Through my work and life I want to . . ." Use the following examples to stimulate your own thinking.

Make a difference
Be of service
Leave something for
   future generations

Solve a problem
Create beauty
Educate others
Invent something of use

Promote a cause
Give back to the
   community

What phrases run around most in your head? Jot them down in your journal.

Recording Your Hottest Passions and Interests

Create a list of your hottest passions and interests and record them in Worksheet 6-2. (Chapter 7 tells you how to turn this wish list into concrete career ideas.)

Review what you recorded so far in your journal and transfer that information to Worksheet 6-2. As you do this, take the opportunity to fine-tune your list by removing any duplicate ideas, adding anything that may be missing, and modifying the wording to make the items as accurate and informative as possible.

When considering a career change, you need to focus on your present wishes, rather than on what you have done in the past, or what you think you should do. To help you break free of these restrictive patterns of thinking, ask yourself the following questions:

- ✔ If you know that you'd be well taken care of financially no matter what career you chose, would you rethink any of your hottest passions or interests?

- ✔ Would you drop a skill in Worksheet 6-2 because it was practical or because you spent years in school to build it?

- ✔ Would you add in your artistic and aesthetic passions?

- ✔ Would you include a different target client group?

Make whatever changes you need to in Worksheet 6-2 to make the list as accurate as it can be.

Your Favorite Skills

1.	8.
2.	9.
3.	10.
4.	11.
5.	12.
6.	13.
7.	14.

Your Favorite Topics

1.	8.
2.	9.
3.	10.
4.	11.
5.	12.
6.	13.
7.	14.

Your Favorite Processes

1.
2.

Your Favorite Internal Drivers

1.	4.
2.	5.
3.	6.

Your Favorite Tools, Equipment, and Raw Materials

1.	6.
2.	7.
3.	8.
4.	9.
5.	10.

Your Favorite Industries

1.	4.
2.	5.
3.	6.

Your Target Client Group

1.	4.
2.	5.
3.	6.

Your Meaning In Work

Worksheet 6-2: Your passions and interests.

Chapter 7

Thinking Outside the Box

● ●

In This Chapter

▶ Finalizing your list of passions

▶ Brainstorming career ideas

▶ Narrowing your focus

● ●

As you think about your next career, you may use what you've done in the past as your guide to your next position. Although this linear approach may yield results, it may also limit you if you are at all frustrated with your current career. Focusing on only your recent past, rather than on your true career passions, can severely limit your opportunities.

The fun, non-linear creativity worksheets you find in this chapter help you use a broader range of passions and interests as the basis for brainstorming potential career ideas. Have fun filling out these worksheets. The more you play with this chapter, the more you can get out of it.

Use this chapter to expand your horizons. Think big. Be outrageous. Give all of the ideas you come up with equal weight in your brainstorming process. You have plenty of opportunities to evaluate and enhance the feasibility of your ideas.

Putting Your Deck Together

Before you begin brainstorming, take a good look at your list of Hottest Passions and Interests. (See Chapter 6 for more information on creating this list.) Verify that you thoroughly enjoy each element on your list. If you feel any sense of hesitation, dislike, or dread associated with an item — no matter what the reason — let that item go. You need to make your list as strong as you possibly can by deleting or modifying elements that don't quite work.

Now imagine that you have a deck of cards, and each card in the deck represents one of the skills, passions, and interests on your list. Imagine further that you can deal out the cards from this deck in various combinations representing different dream careers that combine your skills, passions, and interests. As you shuffle this deck in your mind, consider how many exciting combinations exist. The possibilities are endless.

Give every item on your list a number. To retain the richness and depth of your list, do not group or combine the items.

Dealing Yourself a Hand to Brainstorm New Careers

Although you may get some career ideas by scanning your entire deck (see the previous section for information on creating your deck), dealing yourself a hand allows you to see specific combinations more easily:

1. **Choose four numbers at random within the range of 1 and the largest number on your list.**

   Write the numbers you choose on the blanks provided in the first row of Worksheet 7-1.

2. **Refer to your list of Hottest Passions and Interests to discover what passions, interests, and skills correspond to each number.**

   Write the description in the boxes under the numbers in Worksheet 7-1.

3. **Brainstorm as many career, project, or business ideas as you can that include at least three of the elements in your hand.**

   Stretch your mind. Think creatively. At this stage, any idea is a good idea! Don't censure your flow of ideas. Keep in mind that you don't have to want to do the job to include it on your brainstorming list. Do what you can to fill in the ten career blanks provided in Worksheet 7-1. The following example gives you an idea of how to transform your hand into a series of career ideas.

If, after you work with your "hand" for a while, you realize that one word really doesn't fit with the others, choose another number at random and replace the unworkable item with the new one.

Repeat these three steps for Worksheets 7-2, 7-3, and 7-4. Avoid using the same number in different hands. Plan to spend about ten minutes per hand on your first pass; you can always come back later to finish your lists of career ideas for each hand. If you like, ask a friend or two to help you brainstorm additional career ideas. Don't fret if you don't reach ten careers; the worksheets are helpful even when you don't fill in all the blanks.

Don't worry about how much you know or don't know about what's out there. With what you know right now, you can create the ideas you need. In fact, you may surprise yourself with the ideas you come up with! Chapters 8 through 14 can help you expand your horizons even further.

An Example Hand			
#12 Enhancing graphic images	#14 Writing	#32 Aesthetically pleasing design	#6 Teaching
Career Ideas			

1. Graphic designer, using words and images
2. Web designer
3. Teaching others to do graphic design or Web design
4. Writing a how-to-book about graphic design or Web design
5. Producing a newspaper or newsletter
6. Teaching interior design
7. Enhancing photographs
8. Teaching people new enhancement techniques
9. Developing new image enhancement techniques
10. Illustrating a book of poems

Your First Hand

_____   # _____   # _____   # _____

Career Ideas

1. _____
2. _____
3. _____
4. _____
5. _____
6. _____
7. _____
8. _____
9. _____
10. _____

Worksheet 7-1:
Dealing your first hand.

Your Second Hand

_____   # _____   # _____   # _____

Career Ideas

1. _____
2. _____
3. _____
4. _____
5. _____
6. _____
7. _____
8. _____
9. _____
10. _____

Worksheet 7-2: Dealing your second hand.

Your Third Hand

_____   # _____   # _____   # _____

Career Ideas

1. _____
2. _____
3. _____
4. _____
5. _____
6. _____
7. _____
8. _____
9. _____
10. _____

**Worksheet
7-3:**
Dealing your
third hand.

Your Fourth Hand

# _____	# _____	# _____	# _____

Career Ideas

1. _____

2. _____

3. _____

4. _____

5. _____

6. _____

7. _____

8. _____

9. _____

10. _____

**Worksheet
7-4:**
Dealing your
fourth hand.

Sifting Out Your Most Intriguing Career Ideas

Go through the four worksheets in the preceding section and circle any careers or business ideas that appeal to you. Shoot for a total of ten ideas. Then copy them into the first column of Worksheet 7-5. If you can, group similar or related ideas together. Then read the following two sections to find out how to fill in the rest of this worksheet.

You don't have to be sold on the feasibility or practicality of your career ideas to include them in this list. You just need to feel interested, drawn to, or intrigued by the idea or some aspect of it.

Intriguing Career Ideas		
Career Idea	What You Love	Pros & Cons
1.		
2.		
3.		
4.		
5.		
6.		
7.		
8.		
9.		
10.		

Worksheet 7-5: Recording the ideas that interest you most.

You may end up doing one of the careers that you list in Worksheet 7-5. And then again, you may not! You may ultimately choose a career that combines several of these ideas. As you explore your intriguing career ideas, you may also be drawn in an entirely different direction. For now, don't stress yourself out by trying to figure out which direction is right. Instead, relax and use the questions in the following two sections to deepen your thinking about your ten intriguing career ideas.

Discovering what you love about each idea

Take a close look at your list of career ideas. The more clues you uncover about what intrigues you, the more your future direction comes into focus.

In the second column of Worksheet 7-5, write down a sentence or several phrases to describe what draws you to each career idea on your list. It may be one or more of the following:

- **A feeling:** It could be a feeling of freedom, independence, or responsibility.
- **The work format:** Which could include working alone, part-time possibilities, and travel.
- **The work itself:** Including tasks, topics, and roles.
- **The lifestyle:** These may be the vacation schedule, the ability to get home early, and more time with the kids.

Uncovering the pros and cons of each idea

Each career or business idea in Worksheet 7-5 has an upside and a downside to it. Based on what you know right now, what do you believe are the pros and cons of each career idea? Jot down the phrases that come to mind in the third column of Worksheet 7-5. Again, think about work arrangements, the impact on your lifestyle, and the work itself.

If you find the same issues surfacing again and again, don't despair — celebrate, instead! Repetitive clues are a gift because they illustrate what is really important to you. Look for and make note of any themes created by these repetitive clues. Do any phrases or ideas show up multiple times in your descriptions?

Asking your friends to take a look

Because your friends look at your life from a slightly different perspective than you do, they may see combinations and themes in your worksheets that you haven't seen yet. Invite them to look at your hands and your list of career ideas to see what they come up with. Don't feel pressured to accept what they say hook, line, and sinker. Just incorporate their ideas into your overall creative process and appreciate their different perspective.

Weaving themes together

The best career for you may be one that combines several themes from your list of intriguing career ideas in a unique way that few have ever thought of before. The following examples show how people have found success in their careers by combining a variety of talents into a single career:

- ✔ A writer who is also a counselor combines his skills to create a practice that helps clients break through their creative blocks.

- ✔ An artist with a post-graduate degree in forensics and physical anthropology combines her talents to help a law enforcement agency reconstruct a face for a recently discovered skull.

- ✔ A biologist with advanced programming skills has his pick of jobs as companies search for bioinformatics programmers to analyze the human genome for potential configurations that can lead to drug discoveries.

Take another look to see if your themes can be linked together to create any creative career options. Although this may take some thought, spending some time playing with your ideas can bring new options to light. As you look at your list of themes, daydream about how you can combine them. Don't get pulled down by the logistics or feasibility of your combinations — just explore possible combinations. Have fun with it!

Isolating your key elements

For some people, one element of their career or lifestyle is so important to them that it ends up being the cornerstone of their new career.

Thinking about your lifestyle, your style, and what you've written about your intriguing career ideas, do you see the key to making a decision about your career? Are there any features of your career that must be in place for your life to work? Use the questions in Worksheet 7-6 to help you sort this out.

Read through the questions and put one slash through the box if you resonate with the notion. Then look at all the statements with one slash, and choose the two or three that are the keys to your career decisions. In each of the corresponding boxes, make a slash in the opposite direction to create an "X."

As you proceed with your discovery process, keep your keys in mind. They can help you stay focused in attaining your goal of a new career.

Marking your hottest career ideas

After reading this section, take another look at Worksheet 7-5 and see what career ideas keep rising to the top of your list. In the worksheet, circle the ideas you want to explore in more detail.

	Keys to Your Career Decisions
	Is there a particular passion or interest you want to pursue in your work?
	Are you enthralled by a particular industry?
	Is there a certain company you want to work for?
	Is there a specific task or function that's the ticket?
	Is there a distinct topic you feel drawn to incorporate into your work?
	Do you thrive when you use a particular process?
	Is your work environment the most important factor for you?
	Are the people you work with a crucial piece to the puzzle?
	Is your work format the clincher?
	Is an aspect of your personal style/needs/desires the deciding factor?
	Must your work have definite meaning?
	Is there an aspect of your lifestyle that defines what you need?

Worksheet 7-6: "X" marks the spot of your career decisions.

Don't worry about finding a label

Although you may feel pressure to find a label for your new career right away, don't push too hard to find one. Don't feel that you are failing just because you don't have an official label for what you want to do. The absence of a name doesn't mean the opportunity doesn't exist. It may mean that your career idea is on the cutting edge.

When I helped my brother explore his career options after he graduated, we found that he had two themes running through the projects he had done over the years: programming, especially scientific programming, and converting complex 3-D data into easily understood images. Although we struggled and struggled with what title to give his dream job, he ultimately found a job posting that encompassed both of his passions. Ironically, the job title he has now gives little indication that those two skills are part of his job.

Expanding Your Career Horizons Even More

After people create their list of intriguing career ideas (see the preceding section), they often wonder if they are missing something. They question whether they know enough about what's "out there" to have made an adequate attempt at coming up with a list of career ideas.

As I mention in Chapter 1, the number of jobs that exist today is infinite and constantly growing. There is no way you can know or research all the options that exist. Instead of being overwhelmed with all the possibilities, shift your strategy to narrowing your options to high potential career areas so that when you begin your research, your explorations can be focused, thorough, and deep in the fields that count.

Sometimes looking at a variety of careers can trigger your thinking. To help you explore what is out there, the following seven chapters describe career ideas that correspond to the Multiple Intelligence charts in Chapter 6. Look at Chapter 6 to remind yourself of your strongest Multiple Intelligences. If you appear to have a strong:

- Verbal intelligence, read Chapter 8.
- Analytical intelligence, look at Chapter 9.
- Interpersonal intelligence, browse through Chapter 10.
- Visual intelligence, take a gander at Chapter 11.

> ✔ Body intelligence, flip to Chapter 12.
>
> ✔ Musical intelligence, turn to Chapter 13.
>
> ✔ Nature intelligence, having a keen understanding of living things and the earth, read Chapter 14.

At a minimum, read over the chapters that correspond to your top two or three Multiple Intelligences.

The subsections within each chapter begin with a short list of relevant Multiple Intelligence skills to help you determine at a glance whether the careers in that section may interest you.

As you read about the various careers in these chapters, you may find your thinking expands. You may find a new perspective on a career you have already been thinking about, or you may discover something entirely new. If you are attracted to a career or one of the out-of-the-box angles, make a note, mark the page, or write in your journal about the idea right away. Taking action the moment that you feel a spark of interest is essential because spontaneous connections can fade if left for a later time.

Although you may have a couple of promising career ideas, you are, in actuality, still in the middle of your creative process. Nothing is yet set in stone. Before you dive in and activate your job search, use Chapters 15, 16, and 17 to verify that your career ideas are in fact good matches for you. After confirming that they are viable options, then proceed by launching your job search in Chapter 19 or your business planning process in Chapter 20.

Creating a composite career

A composite career, a term introduced by William Bridges in his book *JobShift: How to Prosper in a Workplace Without Jobs*, published by Perseus Books, allows you to meet your personal, career, and financial goals by weaving several careers together to create a fulfilling professional life. The format of a composite career can be designed to meet your specific needs. For example, a composite career could be any of the following:

✔ A full-time job with occasional part-time projects on the side

✔ Two part-time jobs

✔ One part-time job and a business

✔ Two businesses

In addition to giving you added flexibility and variety in your work, you also gain a surprising sense of security with this arrangement. With multiple income sources, you are no longer dependent on one paycheck. If one income stream dries up, you are no longer a sitting duck. You can always rely on the other ones to tide you over. Consider how a composite career could change how you think about structuring your new career.

Part III

Career Areas to Stimulate Your Thinking

The 5th Wave

By Rich Tennant

"Maybe you'd like to be an artist? Here's a test you can take. Just draw this picture of Luca Signorelli's 'The Damned Cast into Hell' to see if you have talent."

In this part . . .

*I*f you have a seed of a career idea, use the chapters in this part to help you leverage your idea into any number of creative career options.

Rather than see these chapters as complete lists of possible careers, think of them as springboards that trigger you to think of your idea in entirely new ways. Use your answers to the Multiple Intelligence lists in Chapter 6 to determine which of the chapters in this part align with your interests. As you look at each chapter, scan the boxes, which contain skills and talents taken from the Multiple Intelligence lists, to find the careers areas that appeal to you.

Library Resource Center
Renton Technical College
3000 N.E. 4th St.
Renton, WA 98056

Chapter 8

If You Thrive on Words

• •

In This Chapter

▶ Checking out careers with a focus on the written word

▶ Finding careers that involve your ability to speak

▶ Tapping into careers with education potential

• •

*I*f you think in words and enjoy expressing your thoughts, feelings, and knowledge with words, check out the careers I discuss in this chapter.

This chapter consists of four sections, each devoted to a different career category. To determine whether the careers in a particular category may interest you, read the introductory paragraph and check out the skills highlighted in the box.

If you discover that you marked some of the skills when you filled out the Multiple Intelligences lists in Chapter 6, explore the section to discover more about careers that provide a good match for your skills. If you didn't mark any of the skills, but still find the category interesting, skim through the careers to see if anything catches your eye. If you aren't interested in the career area, skip right over it to look at another section.

Use the description of each career idea as a launch pad for exploration and creative thinking. Pay close attention to the out-of-the-box angles and the related jobs and specialties because ideas in these sections may help you expand how you think about your career ideas.

If an insight comes to you while you read, snag it! Get it in writing as soon as possible because spontaneous aha's have a way of fading fast if not acted upon in the moment.

Writing

Words are ubiquitous. Aside from words exchanged in personal correspondence, nearly every word you read each day has been crafted by a paid professional. Indeed, words are the currency of the Information Age and the Technology Age.

If you have any of the following skills or interests, one of the careers in this section may intrigue you.

Complex writing	Editing	Poetry appreciation
Creating vivid descriptions	Figures of speech	Vocabulary
Creating words	Grammar	Word puzzles
Creative writing	Journal or diary keeping	Writing poetry
Derivation of words	Meaning of words	

Technical writing

As a technical writer, you explain complex scientific information in a way that makes sense to readers, whether they are novices or experts. In addition to having good general writing skills and an interest and aptitude in science, you must be an especially clear thinker who can communicate complex technical information in a well-organized, easy-to-comprehend way.

Over the years, your training and work experience may lead you to specialize in a particular aspect of technical writing, but no matter where you focus your talent, staying current on scientific developments helps you excel at your work.

Out-of-the-box angles

As a technical writer, you have a number of avenues you can take: covering the scientific, health, or medical beat for a publication; creating pharmaceutical documentation, protocols, and instructions; developing biotech marketing materials; writing scientific textbooks; or drafting public health policies, for example.

Technical writing tends to take place on a cyclical, contract basis. Always keep your doors open, even when money is so tight that you must get another job to make ends meet. If you launch a business as a technical writer, you must show your clients that you mean business and are there to stay.

To guard against slow times, keep in contact with former satisfied clients so that they think of you when each new project comes up. It is much easier to sell to a repeat client than to find a new one.

Don't get dependent on just one major client. What happens if that business cuts back or goes under? You put your livelihood on the block right along with it.

Related jobs and specialties

Technical writer, medical writer, scientific writer, health journalist, legal analyst, specifications writer, manual writer, documentation specialist, technical speech writer, regulatory associate, annual report writer, technical editor.

Where to go from here

Society of Technical Communication, Inc. (STC): `www.stc-va.org`; 901 North Stuart Street, Suite 204, Arlington, VA 22203; 703-522-4114.

Reporting information

Use your way with words to inform and educate others on the issues of the day. Accurate, objective reporting is your primary goal.

Although each story is unique, the process you follow is similar. After investigating leads to find a story, you gather the facts, observe what you can, interview relevant, trustworthy sources for quotable material, and do background research. After you have the information you need, you organize it into a concise, well-written, engaging piece and submit the story in time to meet your deadline.

You can expect your life to revolve around deadlines and late-breaking news developments. To do well, you must be resourceful and persistent, take initiative, and stay confident in unfamiliar circumstances. Keeping your calm in the face of dangerous assignments and pressing deadlines is a crucial, daily part of your job.

Out-of-the-box angles

Watch for changes in trends in reporting as cable, Internet, satellite radio, and other new media establish their places in the communications world.

These days, researching a story means more than doing an interview. You must log onto your computer to find sources, access databases, and analyze the data that backs up facts for your story. In some cases, your analysis of a database may actually lead to a story. Do what you can to strengthen and develop your computer skills.

 Find out all you can about news photography. Editors and producers often ask entry-level reporters to take their own photographs in the field. Having a working knowledge of news photography enhances your employability.

Related jobs and specialties

Journalist, reporter, correspondent, news writer, investigative reporter, general assignment reporter, health reporter, foreign affairs reporter, social events reporter, sports reporter, political reporter, broadcast journalist (see the following section), radio writer, stringer, researcher, abstractor.

Where to go from here

Society of Professional Journalists: www.spj.org; Eugene South Pulliam National Journalism Center, 3909 North Meridian Street, Indianapolis, IN 46208; 317-927-8000; Fax: 317-920-4789.

Writing opinions

In sharing your opinions about current events or experiences with your audience, your intention may be to stir the pot to get people thinking about the topic from a different perspective. Or you may be interested in giving them a preview of a movie, play, restaurant, art exhibit, or travel destination.

To excel at writing opinions, you must have a good grasp of the genre so that you can make valid assessments and valuable comparisons. Incorporating your personal perspective and experience to add color and interest to your pieces differentiates this style of writing from pure journalism (see the preceding section).

Out-of-the-box angles

One way to expand your reach is to syndicate your columns so that they appear in more than one publication. With a little legwork, you can self-syndicate your column by approaching publications on your own, as long as their markets don't overlap. After you gain experience, you can go directly to one of the major syndicates to gain access to publications throughout the country.

Because it may be difficult, especially starting out, to make a living writing opinions, you can build this work into your composite career. (See the sidebar in Chapter 7 for more information about composite careers.)

Related jobs and specialties

Columnist, critic, reviewer, commentator, news analyst, newspaper critic, travel writer, editorial writer, book or movie reviewer.

Where to go from here

American Society of Journalist and Authors: www.asja.org; 1501 Broadway, Suite 302, New York, NY 10036; 212-997-0947; Fax: 212-768-7414.

Sales writing

Your purpose for writing is usually to convince someone to buy a product or service, give a donation or a grant, or hire your client. Such writing tends to be catchy, persuasive, and concise. It takes practice, and lots of it, to produce such results in a fast-paced, deadline-oriented environment.

Out-of-the-box angles

When you first start out, take any writing job that comes along, even if it is not your first choice. The experience you gain, the knowledge you accumulate about how the writing process works, and the samples you create pave the way for better jobs.

One untapped market in your area may be professionals who don't have an advertising staff on board. If you have advertising skills, you can make a big difference in the success of their businesses.

With the advent of new technologies, copywriters must expand their talents to include scriptwriting for infomercials, multimedia, and interactive media.

If you have any interest in working in the non-profit world, grant writing may be the answer. Because non-profits are funded primarily from grants and donations, they depend on your skills and expertise to survive.

Related jobs and specialties

Copywriter, advertising writer, resume writer, grant writer, public relations, publicity (see the section later in this chapter), advertising editor.

Where to go from here

American Marketing Association: www.ama.org; 250 South Wacker Drive, Suite 200, Chicago, IL 60606; 312-648-0536.

Writing for various audiences

If you are not inclined to be a technical writer, journalist, or copywriter, but you do want to write, don't despair. Plenty of other careers allow you to make a living as a writer.

Whether you focus on informational pieces or creative projects, you must dedicate yourself to honing your craft. Because writing broadcast copy, scripts, lyrics, speeches, jingles, plays, and jokes requires many different styles, take courses to master the nuances of the writing style you want to make your specialty, and then practice.

Out-of-the-box angles

To make a living as a freelance writer, you must be as persistent as you can be, always looking for possible angles and publications to submit your work to. You may need to put a lot of irons in the fire before the cash flows in consistently, but if you enjoy writing enough to make it your career, you may even enjoy the challenge.

Some surprisingly lucrative pocket markets for writers include greeting cards, newsletters, filler articles for publications, specialty cookbooks, and encyclopedia articles.

In addition to submitting pieces to newspapers and newsstand magazines, think outside the box: airline magazines, motor club magazines, newsletters on- and offline, trade magazines, alumni publications, and start-up magazines all need writers.

The writing profession has great potential for flex-place employment arrangements. Have laptop and Internet connection, can write and travel!

Related jobs and specialties

Non-fiction author, essayist, business scriptwriter, reference writer, speech writer, television scriptwriter, movie scriptwriter, creative writer, lyricist, playwright, short-story writer, gag writer, joke writer, monologist, storyteller, poet, novelist, humorist, writing instructor, writing tutor.

Where to go from here

National Writers Union: www.nwu.org; nwu@nwu.org; National Office East, 113 University Place, 6th Floor, New York, NY 10003; 212-254-0279.

Working with Other People's Words

After words have been written or spoken, another set of professionals swings into action to publish or produce pieces based on these words, organize them, retrieve information from them, translate them, or transcribe them.

If you have any of the following skills or interests, one of the careers in this section may intrigue you.

Editing	Grammar	Translating
Figures of speech	Interpreting	Vocabulary
Foreign languages	Reading with great comprehension	

Editing

As an editor, you read, query, and rewrite the words writers produce to create a more powerful final piece. You also sometimes manage the big picture, including how the articles and pictures come together to create a newspaper or magazine, or how the chapters hang together to produce a book. You use your knowledge of the publication's readership to determine what gets included and what gets cut.

You recommend changes to text, make corrections, modify the document length, plan the layout, and coordinate the activities of all involved in producing the final document. You must produce accurate, eye-catching results day in and day out under strict deadlines that vary by publication. To excel at your position, you must express yourself verbally and in writing in a clear, organized, and logical manner.

Out-of-the-box angles

Although the Internet and e-commerce may have an impact on the publishing industry, the full extent and form of the impact is yet to be determined. Stay tuned and stay alert, as your future may be defined by the changes that transpire in these arenas.

As more and more publications create an online presence, editors must work with media beyond words. Sound clips, video clips, and animated spots that would not be possible within a print publication can now be integrated rather easily into an online piece.

Niche-market publications, which target a product, region, profession, or industry that appeals to a specific group of readers and advertisers, are an area of rapid expansion in the publishing world. A sampling of niche publications includes *Beverage World, Chain Leader, Charleston Regional Business Journal, Gulf Mariner,* and *Runner's Gazette.*

Editors can make a good living working freelance. Consider building a specialty based on the type of documents you prefer to work with, such as trade non-fiction, technical manuals, or proposals, or the subject matter you enjoy, such as travel, business, or medicine.

Related jobs and specialties

Managing editor, assistant editor, associate editor, production editor, technical editor, advertising editor, news editor, sports editor, section editor, publications editor, assignment editor, acquisitions editor, development editor, manuscript editor, executive editor, editor in chief, publisher, copy editor, proofreader, copy marker, indexer, fact checker, dictionary editor, photography editor, art editor, program director.

Where to go from here

Editorial Freelance Association: www.the-efa.org; info@the-efa.org; 71 West 23rd Street, Suite 1910, New York, NY 10010; 212-929-5400; Fax: 212-929-5439.

Managing information

Revolutionary changes are underway in this profession. The knowledge that used to be managed by librarians within the four walls of a library has burst forth thanks to the many ways information and data are now being stored: on the World Wide Web and CD-ROMs, and in virtual libraries and remote databases, for example.

At first glance, it seems that the role of the librarian may be obsolete because people have all the access they need due to these technological advancements. But the world may need your information management and retrieval skills now more than ever; finding a piece of information in this ever-growing sea of data can be downright frustrating and fruitless without these skills.

Out-of-the-box angles

Rather than helping people locate the information that they want, you can devote your efforts to making sure that information is organized and labeled effectively at the front end, allowing users to access information as they need it. Information architecture, as this is called, is in great demand within the Internet world these days.

If you are interested in a great self-employment opportunity with flex-place potential, become an information broker. Information brokers search out, analyze, interpret, and synthesize information for clients such as marketing businesses, governmental agencies, medical institutions, law firms, investigators, politicians, and public relations firms.

Related jobs and specialties

Academic librarian, corporate librarian, public librarian, systems librarian, independent researcher, information broker, knowledge manager, information professional, corporate information officer, information architect, archivist, records manager, research analyst, database consultant, digital library manager, cybrarian, information literacy trainer, library technician, metadata specialist.

Where to go from here

American Library Association: www.ala.org; ala@ala.org; 50 East Huron Street, Chicago, IL, 60611; 800-545-2433; Fax: 312-440-9374.

Librarians in the 21st Century: http://istweb.syr.edu/21stcenlib/index.html.

Translating

You take documents in one language and translate them into another language, usually your native language, without changing the meaning of the text. To do the work effectively, you must have a good working knowledge of necessary computerized tools, such as terminology banks, spell checkers, and dictionaries.

Typically, translators know two or more languages, have good verbal and linguistic aptitude, have an understanding of the cultures of the pertinent countries, and are extremely attentive to the detail involved in translation.

If you simultaneously translate or interpret conversations, you must assimilate all that you hear and rapidly translate it into another language, often under politically tense circumstances. Obviously, your mental dexterity and endurance are key in this profession.

Out-of-the-box angles

With the globalization of the marketplace and the Internet, businesses must make their materials and products, both online and offline, accessible to people who speak other languages. As a result, translators are needed to prepare Web sites and software for localization and globalization purposes.

To enhance your chances of employment as an employee or a contractor, focus your training on the official languages of the United Nations, including French, Spanish, Arabic, Russian, and Chinese.

Knowing multiple languages can be a plus if you are interested in pursuing careers in embassies, diplomatic service, publishing, entertainment, and tourism.

Related jobs and specialties

Literary translator, textual translator, technical translator, liaison interpreter, consecutive interpreter, simultaneous interpreter, court interpreter, conference interpreter, sign language interpreter, legal terminologist, medical terminologist, reviser, interpreter, closed-caption writer.

Where to go from here

American Translators Association: www.atanet.org; ata@atanet.org; 225 Reinekers Lane, Suite 590, Alexandria, VA 22314; 703-683-6100; Fax: 703-683-6122.

Transcribing

You create a verbatim record of what transpires in meetings, during courtroom proceedings, or as a result of medical situations. To do this work effectively, you must be familiar with the profession-specific terminology used by your clients, whether it is legal or medical in nature. You must hear well and type what you hear accurately and precisely.

Other intriguing options

Linguistics: Use your understanding of language to enhance communication between people and cultures in areas of bilingualism, language rehabilitation, accent reduction, and language acquisition. For more information, contact the Linguistic Society of America: www.lsadc.org; 1325 18th NW, Suite 211, Washington D.C. 20036-6501.

On occasion, your work setting requires that you remain calm and focused on your tasks, even in highly-charged situations.

Out-of-the-box angles

Part-year assignments are available in this field. Signing up with a temporary agency is another employment option.

Replacing the stenographic machine in the courtroom is the electronic recording device, which allows you to make a complete tape recording of all proceedings, complete with a different track for each speaker. This machine eliminates the need for courtroom interruptions, allows for immediate playbacks, and provides judges with immediate access to the tapes if the need arises.

With the electronic recording device, as a transcriber, your training time is cut in half, and your work process is less cumbersome; you transcribe from taped material that can be replayed as necessary, rather than from phonetic shorthand records that require a multiple-step process to obtain the final product. Knowledge of this device may enhance your employability in some markets.

Related jobs and specialties

Court reporter, court stenographer, medical transcriptionist, legal secretary, litigation secretary, closed-caption writer, court recorder.

Where to go from here

American Association of Electronic Reporters and Transcribers, Inc.: www.aaert.org; info@aaert.org; 2715 North Third Street, Suite 207, Phoenix, AZ 85004; 800-233-5306.

Using the Spoken Word to Inform or Entertain

Some word-based careers focus on using the spoken word to educate, inform, inspire, motivate, and entertain an audience.

If you have any of the following skills or interests, one of the careers in this section may intrigue you.

Dramatic reading	Making presentations	Storytelling
Explaining	Memory for names, dates, and details	Taking notes
Humor or jokes	Mnemonics	Teaching using language

Newscasting or reporting

To make it in this profession, you must have, above all else, the voice, personality, confidence, and looks to attract a large, loyal following. Ratings run the show. To excel, you must also have a working awareness of the topics you cover because, on occasion, you must ad lib all or part of your show.

Your working conditions are one of a kind. Tight, unpredictable schedules punctuated with ongoing deadlines add to the stress of producing concise, top-notch stories about breaking news.

Out-of-the-box angles

A tight market is expected to get tighter. As markets consolidate, more and more shows are produced in one place and replayed in many markets. Digital technology and new alternative media make producing a show easier and quicker.

To enhance your employment possibilities, gain experience with the technical side of producing your own show. A show can do without a dedicated technician, but it can't do without the host! By producing your own show, you save your station money, making yourself more desirable in the market.

After you have a basic amount of experience under your belt, consider specializing to better your chances of employment. Some specialty areas to target are business news, health news, and consumer news.

Related jobs and specialties

Television news anchorperson, network reporter, newscaster, news anchor, weathercaster, traffic reporter, news correspondent, disc jockey, talk show host, radio host, announcer, sports announcer, master of ceremonies, voice-over talent (see Chapter 13), comedian, comic.

Where to go from here

National Association of Broadcasters: www.nab.org; nab@nab.org; 1771 North Street, NW, Washington, D.C. 20036; 202-429-5300; Fax: 202-775-3520.

Teaching

Gone are the days of teaching endless drills to promote rote memorization. As a teacher, you create projects, interactive discussions, and hands-on learning opportunities to help your students think and problem solve.

You must prepare your students to be active, successful members of the workforce after graduation. In addition to having a good grasp of the subjects you teach, you must evaluate your students' needs and communicate with each of them in a way that is motivating, effective, and matched to their abilities. Using your creativity to work around limited budgets and tight resources is a valuable talent.

Out-of-the-box angles

Many schools have difficulties hiring teachers who are qualified in math, science, and computer science. At the college level, the demand is for business, engineering, health sciences, and computer science instructors.

Being geographically mobile, bilingual, licensed in more than one subject, or a minority teacher increases your employment prospects.

Many states have launched financial incentive programs, such as covering moving expenses, initiating loan-forgiveness programs, awarding signing bonuses, and providing housing assistance to encourage more people to become teachers in anticipation of increased enrollment over the next several years.

Three out of ten college professors work on a part-time basis as adjunct faculty members. Some part-timers make teaching a component of a composite career, while others create full teaching careers by taking on part-time positions at more than one school.

Related jobs and specialties

Elementary school teacher, secondary school teacher, kindergarten teacher, public school teacher, private teacher, special education teacher, English-as-a-second-language teacher, substitute teacher, teaching assistant, teacher's aid, reading specialist, curriculum specialist, preschool teacher (see Chapter 10), college professor, school librarian (see the previous section), training specialist (see Chapter 10).

Where to go from here

American Federation of Teachers: www.aft.org; 555 New Jersey Avenue, NW, Washington, D.C. 20001.

Other intriguing options

Professional speaking: Your experience, expertise, or passion may put you in a prime position to launch a career educating, inspiring, and motivating large audiences as a professional speaker. Hone your skills, refine your talk, and dress for success, and you are on the road! For more information, contact the National Speakers Association: www.nsaspeaker. org; Information@nsaspeaker.org; 480-968-2552.

Using Words to Convince

If you have a strong command of the language, you may enjoy persuading others to follow your lead or agree with your point of view. Whether you make your convincing arguments in writing, in conversations, or during presentations, you may find the following careers to be exciting and challenging.

If you have any of the following skills or interests, one of the careers in this section may intrigue you.

Diplomacy	Memorizing	Playing devil's advocate
Impromptu speaking	Negotiation	Sensing layers of conversation
Mediation	Persuasion	Verbal debate

Law

In this profession, you interpret the existing laws to help your clients understand and successfully navigate whatever legal circumstances they face. Regardless of whether you serve as your clients' advocate, representing them in either a criminal or civil trial, or in the role of advisor, suggesting a proper course of action for a business-related situation or a personal matter, you take the relevant case law together with the facts of the case and distill it all into a convincing argument or strategy for your client.

Your ability to articulate your position clearly, perhaps modifying it in the moment to take advantage of changing circumstances in a trial or negotiation, is your key to success.

Out-of-the-box angles

Instead of starting your own private practice or working in a law firm, think about a law-related position within a corporation, the government, a non-profit organization, or a legal aid society.

Specialties abound in this field, including public interest, intellectual property, probate, estate, bankruptcy, divorce, international, and environmental law.

For some time, the number of graduates in this field has outstripped the available jobs. Don't let that stop you; just start thinking beyond the traditional box to include jobs that require legal know-how, such as legal analyst, title examiner, lobbyist (see the following sidebar), politician, corporate executive, or business developer.

Another relatively new option is to work through a temporary agency as a "lawyer for hire" on an as-needed basis, either until a full-time position becomes available or for the long term.

Related jobs and specialties

Trial lawyer, house counsel, district attorney, public defender, law professor, judge, judicial clerk, legal assistant, paralegal, lobbyist, mediator, politician.

Where to go from here

American Bar Association: www.abanet.org; Service Center, 541 North Fairbanks Court, Chicago, IL 60611; 312-988-5522.

Marketing

After a product is developed and manufactured, and before the sales people can sell it, the marketing group must make the target customers aware of the product. As a marketer, you create such an identifiable brand for the product that when customers have a need, they think of your product first and continue coming back for more.

Due to the multifaceted nature of this career area, a blend of strong communications skills, sharp analytical abilities, creativity, and interpersonal skills make you a good candidate for a marketing career.

Out-of-the-box angles

As more and more companies outsource their marketing needs, the possibility of working as an independent consultant increases.

You may find your niche within the marketing field in product development, market research, direct mail, advertising, or public relations (see the following section).

The Internet and the growing emphasis on the global market have opened up new frontiers in this field. Developing technologies mean new marketing methods and avenues surface all the time. Keep your eye on trade journals to see how this new frontier impacts career choices.

Related jobs and specialties

Marketing communications, brand manager, marketing assistant, promotions specialist (see Chapter 9), market research analyst (see Chapter 9), graphic designer (see Chapter 11).

Where to go from here

American Marketing Association: www.ama.org; info@ama.org; 311 South Wacker Drive, Suite 5800, Chicago, IL 60606; 800-AMA-1150; 312-542-9000; Fax: 312-542-9001.

Public relations

You make sure that the public sees your client or company in the best possible light. You attract the attention of the press with riveting press releases, unusual events, and breaking news, so that they run pieces that communicate your client's or employer's message. You work hard to make sure that the message is clear and carried consistently across the multitude of media channels.

When events or errors cause negative or damaging publicity, you use your communication skills to turn the situation around as quickly and seamlessly as possible.

Out-of-the-box angles

Some unique specialties to consider include the areas of entertainment, politics, special interest groups, and publishing.

After making a name for yourself, you can definitely spin this career into your own business.

Everyone in this career area started at the bottom and worked their way up. You are no exception. You have the best chance of getting hired if you have a background in journalism or have completed an internship.

Related jobs and specialties

Publicist, press agent, public affairs, media spokesperson, public relations consultant, press secretary, information officer, lobbyist, fund-raiser.

Where to go from here

Public Relations Society of America: www.prsa.org; 33 Irving Place, Union Square, New York, NY 10003; 212-995-2230; Fax: 212-995-0757.

Sales

For every product produced and every service offered, someone must make a sale before the company brings in any money for their efforts. No matter what the product or service, the sales process is essentially the same, although the timeline of events may vary.

Your knowledge of your client's needs and the product, and your ability to listen, explain, and create unique solutions to meet the client's needs, are what close the deal. Anything you can do to enhance your credibility is a plus, including working on your appearance, reliability, and efficiency.

Out-of-the-box angles

Think about your work style and your need for structure and contact with coworkers before you decide how you want to sell: in house, on the road, from your home office, door-to-door, or in a retail store, for example.

Whether you are employed with a base salary and commissions, or are an independent rep covering a particular territory with a commission-only pay structure, your contract creates the potential for an unlimited income. Imagine making more money than your manager does; it happens all the time in sales.

In addition to traditional sales, most companies now sell their products and services online, as well. Salespeople who are technically savvy may be at an advantage because they are a valuable asset to both sides of the business.

Related jobs and specialties

Account executive, insurance agent, real estate agent, financial services sales, manufacturer's sales rep, broker, wholesale sales rep, retail sales, services sales rep, telemarketing sales rep, demonstrator, sales manager.

Where to go from here

National Association of Sales Professionals: www.nasp.com; 8300 North Hayden Road, Suite 207, Scottsdale, AZ 85258; 480-951-4311.

Other intriguing options

Ombudsman: As an independent party, investigate and resolve complaints customers have with the government, business, university, hospital, or other private organizations. In most cases, you are the last resort for these parties. Your jurisdiction may be limited to certain kinds of problems that take place within a specified time period. Depending on the financial value associated with the complaint, your determinations and recommendations may be binding, meaning the organization must comply with your decisions. For more information, contact the International Ombudsman Institute: www. law.ualberta.ca/centres/ioi/index. htm.

Foreign service: Work overseas, using your communication skills, fluency in the host country's language, and your social skills, to serve as a liaison between the foreign host country and your home country. You handle any situations related to your compatriots or their businesses

in the host country, read and produce reports, and share your opinion of the state of the country, which officials use to guide decisions about international relations. For more information on working in American Foreign Service, contact the Executive Council on Foreign Diplomacy: 818 Connecticut Avenue, NW, 12th Floor, Washington D.C. 20006; 202-466-5199; Fax: 202 872 8696.

Lobbying: Use research, reports, grassroots interest, and persuasive conversation to convince legislators to vote in a way that favors the group that sponsors your efforts. To succeed, you must have access to the top players, which means that your life revolves around networking. If you establish a close relationship with a supportive legislator, you may help draft legislation for your cause. For more information, contact the American League of Lobbyists: www.alldc.org.

Chapter 9

If You Think in a Logical, Organized Fashion

In This Chapter

▶ Exploring your scientific and technical career options

▶ Transforming your way with numbers into viable financial careers

▶ Discovering ways to use your planning skills

Your ability to think in a logical and organized fashion can open the door to a variety of careers in the scientific world, technical venues, financial circles, and planning situations.

This chapter consists of four sections, each devoted to one of these career categories. As you read the introductory paragraph in each section and check out the skills I highlight in the corresponding box, notice if you marked some of the skills in the list when you filled out the Multiple Intelligences lists in Chapter 6. If so, read the section to discover careers that are a good match for your skills. If not, skim through the careers to see if anything catches your eye or skip to another section.

Use the career ideas I describe in this chapter to explore your own options. The out-of-the-box angles and the related jobs and specialties can aid your creative process as you think about your career ideas.

If you enjoy nature and want to use your scientific skills with plants, animals, or the earth's resources, take a look at Chapter 14.

Working in the Sciences

Whether you want to conduct research to further the theories of science, or take what others have discovered and use it to find solutions to practical problems, you may be intrigued by the pure science careers that I describe in this section.

If you have any of the following skills or interests, one of the careers in this section may be for you.

Analyzing	Explaining	Reasoning
Complex calculations	Graphic organizers (flow charts and diagrams)	Recognizing patterns
Counting	Identifying numeric patterns	Research
Critical thinking	Investigating	Seeing cause and effect
Deciphering codes	Outlining	Straight-forward calculations
Decision making	Problem solving	Strategizing
Discerning relationships and connections among information	Processing logic questions rapidly	Using abstract symbols
Doing calculations in head	Programming	Using formulas
Estimating	Quantifying	

Biology and medicine

As a biologist, you study life itself, from the smallest cell to the largest ecosystem. You apply your expertise to solving problems in health-related fields, agriculture, and environmental preservation. (See Chapter 14 for more information on environmental preservation.)

Whether you focus on research and development, applied research, product development, or manufacturing, your dedication, inquisitive nature, attention to detail, and stamina contribute to your success in this field. Whether you have a Ph.D. or work as a technician, your specialty in biochemistry, microbiology, or medical science defines your project focus. Regardless of your specialty, the increasingly complex instrumentation, research methods, and production techniques used in this field require that you have well-developed technical skills.

Out-of-the-box angles

Some research predicts a 25 percent increase in the biotech industry over the next decade. A growing demand for drugs, fueled by new international markets and the aging global population, means a promising future for pharmaceutical companies and the biologists, medical scientists, and technicians they hire.

The Human Genome Project continues to indicate the feasibility of designing drugs to interface directly with individual human cells. Although still in a pure research phase, growth in this industry may have a positive impact on biologists and technicians over time.

In this field, your work environment can vary dramatically depending on your employer. If you want a flexible, unstructured environment that rewards creativity, go for a job in a small company. If you feel more comfortable with structure and set processes, gravitate toward one of the bigger, more established firms. Just be sure that you know ahead of time that their mission and style fit your personal goals.

Related jobs and specialties

Biological scientist, research biologist, microbiologist, medical microbiologist, medical biologist, cell biologist, molecular biologist, geneticist, genomist, biological technologist, biological technician, bacteriology technician, microbiology technologist, biological laboratory technologist, aquatic biologist, marine biologist, limnologist, immunologist, anatomist, toxicologist, geneticist, parasitologist, embryologist, histologist, virologist, protozoologist, pharmacologist, cardiovascular technologist, clinical laboratory technician, pharmacy technician, surgical technologist, biological technician, health technologist, health technician (see Chapter 10), radiologic technologist, sonographer.

Where to go from here

The American Institute of Biological Sciences: www.aibs.org; AIBS Headquarters 1444 I Street NW, Suite 200, Washington, D.C. 20005; 202-628-1500, extension 253; Fax: 202-628-1509.

Chemistry

Your patience, ability to work alone or on an interdisciplinary team, and your attention to detail provide you with the foundation you need to be a chemist or chemistry technician.

How you apply your knowledge of the chemical world depends on what you want to produce. As a basic researcher, you investigate chemicals to understand how they function and to find compounds with certain characteristics. Or you can take the findings of other researchers and apply them in new ways to produce products and processes. Yet another option is to work in production or quality control in a manufacturing plant testing product samples and making sure that the products are sound and of good quality. In all likelihood, you perform one of these functions in a specialty area, such as analytical, organic, inorganic, or physical chemistry.

Out-of-the-box angles

The aging population and the growing desire for more benign personal products and cleaning methods have created an increased demand for chemists in the pharmaceutical and biotechnological industries. Other hot spots include makers of consumer products and the semiconductor industry.

If you prefer not to work in a large company, a recent trend gives you new options. Small, specialized consulting firms are springing up as large companies' decide to outsource their research and development functions.

If you want to work outside the lab, consider teaching, working for the federal government examining patents, acting as a technical consultant in your area of expertise, or being a sales representative for chemical products.

As the use of robotics to handle routine laboratory functions increases, technicians are called upon more frequently to operate highly sophisticated laboratory equipment. To excel, you must have extensive experience with computers and computer-interface equipment.

Related jobs and specialties

Chemist, toxicologist, food scientist, physical chemist, chemical engineer, hazardous waste manager, analytical chemist, production chemist, quality control chemist, biochemist, organic chemist, inorganic chemist, chemical analyst, food technologist, chemical laboratory analyst, chemical technician, chemical process technician, chemical research technician, formulation technician, industrial hygiene technologist, petroleum chemist, research chemist, mass spectrometer technician, chemical engineering technologist, geochemical technician, biochemistry technologist, master textile dyer, textile chemist, clinical chemist, pharmacological chemist, theoretical chemist, electrochemist, research chemist.

Where to go from here

American Chemical Society: www.acs.org; 1155 16th Street NW, Washington, D.C. 20036; 202-872-4600, 800-227-5558.

Mathematics

You use mathematical theory and computational techniques to find solutions to practical problems in financial and business settings, the social sciences, or the hard sciences. Because so much of your work uses computers, knowledge of computer programming is essential, as are good reasoning skills and the ability to discuss and explain your solutions to others who may not have the extensive background in mathematics that you do.

Out-of-the-box angles

Most employees using mathematics in their jobs do not have the word "mathematician," in their job titles. Look to engineering, computer science, statistics, physics, atmospheric science, and economics for additional careers that use math extensively.

One subfield that has gained importance recently is cryptanalysis, in which specialists create, analyze, and decipher encrypted information transmitted for military, financial, and legal enforcement purposes. The need for secure transfer of data over the Internet is another angle to this specialty.

Combining your mathematical talents and computer skills can be the ticket to finding employment outside the sciences. Explore your options in the investment and banking industries, educational services, research and testing, insurance companies, or utilities.

You can also apply your knowledge of mathematics and statistics to designing accurate surveys, evaluating the quality of products, analyzing scientific data, or making forecasts in a variety of subject areas, including biology, economics, psychology, marketing, education, engineering, or medicine.

Related jobs and specialties

Mathematician, theoretical mathematician, applied mathematician, actuary, statistician, math teacher, computer scientist (see the section later in this chapter), economist, market research analyst, demographer, statistical analyst, biostatistician, biometrician, epidemiologist, insurance actuary, atmospheric scientist.

Where to go from here

American Mathematical Society: www.ams.org; ams@ams.org; 201 Charles Street, Providence, RI 02904-2294; 800-321-4AMS; Fax: 401-331-3842.

American Statistical Association: http://amstat.org/index.html; amstat@amstat.org; 1929 Duke Street, Alexandria, VA 22314; 703-684-1221, 888-231-3473; Fax: 703-684-2037.

Physics

Your inquisitive nature, your ability to think through complex, abstract ideas, and your exceptional mathematical ability put you in a good position to become a physicist. Use your knowledge to conduct basic research to understand the laws of nature, or take applied research findings to solve practical real-life problems. Your solutions may lead to advancements in equipment, materials, and devices.

Only about 20 percent of physicists work in government labs. Most stay in a university setting or work in private companies in the semiconductor industry, aerospace and defense, computer hardware industry, or heavy manufacturing.

Out-of-the-box angles

Because physics is the broadest of all sciences, specializing in a subfield of physics, such as astronomy, elementary particle physics, acoustics, plasma, solid-state, optics, atomic, molecular, or space, increases your employment options. In some cases, your specialties may give you the background you need to combine two fields, such as biophysics, geophysics, and astrophysics, which further increases your employability.

If you plan to move into applied physics, be sure to take courses outside physics to broaden your knowledge so that you can accurately apply your scientific knowledge to relevant business issues. Economics, business management, or computer science are viable options.

Related jobs and specialties

Physicist, biophysicist, astrophysicist, astronomer, physics teacher, research scientist, medical physicist, acoustics physicist, health physicist, nuclear physicist, optics physicist, biophysicist, cosmologist, aerodynamicist, experimental physicist, remote sensing scientist, solid-state physicist, plasma physicist, nuclear technician.

Where to go from here

American Institute of Physics: www.aip.org; aipinfo@aip.org; One Physics Ellipse, College Park, MD 20740-3843, 301-209-3100; Fax: 301-209-0843.

Engineering and Computer Science

Careers in engineering allow you to use scientific findings to create viable products or find solutions to technical or structural problems. As a result, most of the work engineers and computer scientists do is quite practical and focused on solving specific problems.

If you have any of the following skills or interests, one of the careers in this section may intrigue you.

Analyzing	Graphic organizers (flow charts and diagrams)	Recognizing patterns
Complex calculations	Identifying numeric patterns	Research
Counting	Investigating	Seeing cause and effect
Critical thinking	Outlining	Straight-forward calculations
Deciphering codes	Problem solving	Strategizing
Decision making	Processing logic questions rapidly	Using abstract symbols
Discerning relationships and connections among information	Programming	Using formulas
Doing calculations in head	Quantifying	
Estimating	Reasoning	

Civil engineering

This career allows you to build large-scale projects from start to finish, sometimes spending up to ten years on one project. You start each project with preconstruction planning, which includes surveying, assessing needs, determining budgets, and designing. Then you coordinate all aspects of the actual construction, handling and making decisions about any problems on the spot. After the work is finished, you evaluate the project and maintain it. As you work to bring the project in on time, your patience may be tested as you encounter delays due to bureaucratic stalls, politics, and the weather.

Out-of-the-box angles

Rather than building new structures, many projects in the coming years may focus on rebuilding outdated parts of the infrastructure, such as roads, tunnels, bridges, the power grid, and public buildings.

If you want to build something new, civil engineers are needed in record numbers to design and build water treatment plants and sites to process hazardous waste. To take advantage of this trend, start bolstering your knowledge in these areas by taking classes or participating in projects that address related issues.

Related jobs and specialties

Civil engineer, environmental engineer, municipal engineer, construction project engineer, public works engineer, sanitation engineer, water management engineer, highway engineer, traffic engineer, bridge engineer, construction engineer, hydraulic engineer, surveying engineer, surveyor (see Chapter 11), transportation engineer, structural engineer, civil engineering technician.

Where to go from here

American Society of Civil Engineers: www.asce.org; 1801 Alexander Bell Drive, Reston, VA 20191-4400; 703-295-6300; Fax: 703-295-6222, 800-548-2723.

Mechanical engineering

Mechanical engineering entails designing, manufacturing, and testing mechanical parts, machines that produce power, such as engines and turbines, or machines that use power to run, such as refrigeration and production equipment. Your ability to look at problems analytically and from different vantage points allows you to find new solutions to mechanical problems.

As you gain more and more experience, you may have greater independence in your job. Keep in mind, however, that even though you may do some project work on your own, the overall project may be a team event, making good communication skills a must for success.

Out-of-the-box angles

As the broadest engineering discipline, your specialty options are vast. Computer-aided design, manufacturing, energy development, and heating and cooling systems are a few among many. By focusing your efforts on a specialty, you build your expertise and boost your employability.

Although 60 percent of mechanical engineers work in manufacturing, a growing area of employment is business and engineering services firms that work on a contract basis.

Related jobs and specialties

Mechanical engineer, nuclear engineer, petroleum engineer, acoustics engineer, mechanical design engineer, power generation engineer, fluid mechanics engineer, heating engineer, mechanical maintenance engineer, piping engineer, thermal design engineer, tool engineer, automotive engineer, refrigeration engineer, agricultural engineer (see Chapter 14), mechanical engineering technician.

Where to go from here

American Society of Mechanical Engineering International: www.asme.org; infocentral@asme.org; Three Park Avenue, New York, NY 10016-5990; 800-843-2763; Fax: 973-882-1717.

Electrical engineering

You design, develop, troubleshoot, test, and maintain electronic and electrical equipment, ranging from computers and communication systems to electric motors and radar systems. Although you spend most of your time working out the technical aspects of your project, you can also expect to spend up to 40 percent of your time in meetings with team members, developing strategic plans and tracking project progress. As a result, communication skills are crucial to your success in this field.

Out-of-the-box angles

Specialties abound and tend to develop early in this field. Pay attention to the areas of the field that attract you during school and focus your efforts there. You may choose acoustics, quantum electronics, power generation, communications, electrical equipment, manufacturing, aviation, electronics, or robot control systems.

With rapid changes in technology, companies must stay ahead of the game by dedicating time, money, and resources to research and development endeavors. By keeping up your skills in cutting-edge areas, you enhance your chances of employment.

Hand-held devices, such as personal digital assistants (PDAs), dedicated e-book devices, palm personal computers, medical patient trackers, and wireless e-mail devices, are finally making their mark in the marketplace. If you want to participate at the cutting edge, watch this industry carefully to spot the next trend.

Related jobs and specialties

Electrical engineer, hardware engineer, electronics engineer, digital design engineer, analog engineer, power systems engineer, telecommunication engineer, control systems engineer, electrical design engineer, microwave systems engineer, electrical systems planning engineer, electrical process control engineer, radio systems engineer, roadway lighting design engineer, electronics test engineer, transmission planning engineer, avionics engineer, electrical network engineer, television systems engineer, instrumentation and control engineer, electrical distribution planning engineer, electrical engineering technician, electronics engineering technician, electromechanical engineering technician.

Where to go from here

Institute of Electrical and Electronics Engineers, Inc.: www.ieee.org; 445 Hoes Lane, P.O. Box 1331, Piscataway, NJ 08855-1331; 732-981-0060, 800-678-4333; Fax: 732-981-1721.

Industrial engineering

You help the company you work for produce a higher quality product in less time while using all human and material resources as efficiently as possible. To do this, you must combine your expertise in manufacturing, your observations of how the work is currently being done, and a keen understanding of the company's culture and business needs. After you develop your recommendations, you must find a tactful and effective way to communicate your findings to the management team and to implement the changes necessary to produce the desired results.

Out-of-the-box angles

Because your skills are transferable, you can also use them outside manufacturing by consulting with companies providing engineering, management, and business services, as well as utilities.

Employers tend to hire people with specialties in production, manufacturing, administrative paperwork practices, assembly, or raw-product processing. With one of these specialties, you can work as an internal manager or a consultant hired on a per-project basis.

Related jobs and specialties

Manufacturing engineer, industrial engineer, mechanical engineer, industrial designer, packaging engineer, consultant, industrial engineering technician.

Where to go from here

The Institute of Industrial Engineers: www.iienet.org; ca@iienet.org; 25 Technology Park, Norcross, GA 30092; 770-449-0460, 800-494-0460; Fax: 770-441-3295.

Computer engineering

Whether you help a company design a new computer system, or attempt to squeeze more resources out of an existing one, you must understand the company's goals and future needs, their budget, and their existing system in great detail. After the company approves the system, you build the system, test it, and configure it for optimal use.

In addition to having strong problem-solving skills, practical hands-on experience, and the ability to attend to details while multi-tasking, you also need to have a flexible, pleasant disposition so that you can work effectively with people who ultimately use your computer system.

Out-of-the-box angles

Rather than hire employees, more and more companies hire specialists as they need them to get the job done. This practice creates a number of alternative employment options, including temporary work, contract work, and self-employment.

A growing demand for sharing information via networking, using the Internet for e-commerce, and setting up systems to enhance online security creates great career opportunities for computer scientists.

Related jobs and specialties

Computer engineer, systems analyst, systems developer, systems architect, network systems administrator, computer systems administrator, network systems and data communications analyst, telecommunication specialist, computer hardware engineer, computer security analyst.

Where to go from here

Institute of Electrical and Electronic Engineering Computer Society: `www.computer.org`; `membership@computer.org`; 1730 Massachusetts Avenue, NW, Washington, D.C. 20036-1992; 202-371-0101; Fax: 202-728-9614.

Software engineering

Using your strong analytical skills, patience, and attention to detail, along with your ability to conceptualize and solve abstract problems, you create code that allows computers to function and perform myriad tasks.

Regardless of whether you work as an application programmer, systems programmer, database engineer, or Web programmer, you must have good communication skills to participate on development teams and considerable endurance to handle the long days required during the intense development phase.

Out-of-the-box angles

Entry into this field depends more on the computer languages you know and your portfolio of completed projects than on your degree or grades in school.

Depending on your expertise and area of interest, you can apply your skills in one of these key software markets: system software, utilities, education, personal productivity, finance, Web site, games, or reference materials. Pay close attention to the market to determine which area has the most potential for growth.

Although Silicon Valley, in the San Francisco Bay area, is known as the mecca for those with high-tech skills, a number of other regions are blossoming around the United States and the world. Look to Research Triangle in North Carolina, Dallas, Denver, Atlanta, Boston, Minneapolis, and New York City for possible employment. Outside the United States, check for opportunities in Ireland, Germany, and Asia.

Always keep an eye on the ever-changing tools and technology in your profession so that your skills do not become obsolete.

Related jobs and specialties

Software designer, software engineer, software developer, software architect, applications programmer, systems programmer, computer scientist, bioinfomatics programmer, computer security programmer, education software programmer, game developer, Web programmer, software tester, software quality assurance analyst, database administrator, database engineer (see Chapter 8), application programmer, implementation consultant.

Other intriguing options

Aeronautical engineering: Your engineering expertise allows you to be part of an extensive team that designs, produces, and installs vehicles that fly, including aircraft or missiles. For more information, contact the American Institute of Aeronautics and Astronautics: www.aiaa.org; custserv@aiaa.org; 1800 Alexander Bell Drive, Suite 500, Reston, VA 20191; 703-264-7500; Fax: 703-264-7551.

Chemical engineering: Take discoveries made by chemists and convert them into products that can be mass-produced. For more information, contact the American Institute of Chemical Engineers: www.aiche.org; xpress@ aiche.org; 3 Park Avenue, New York, NY 10016-5991; 800-242-4363.

Engineering technology: If you are interested in moving into a technical career, but don't have the four-year degree or a graduate degree required by most engineering specialties, becoming an engineering technician may be your answer. By participating in a two-year associate degree program in engineering technology, you are qualified to build research equipment and collect research data, perform quality control, or participate in product design and production. Technician positions of this kind are available within each engineering specialty. For more information, contact the National Institute for Certification in Engineering Technologies: www.nicet.org; 1420 King Street, Alexandria, VA 22314-2794; 888-476-4238.

Computer consulting: Combine your technical knowledge of computers, your ability to troubleshoot, and your interpersonal skills to work in-house or on your own helping people keep their computers in tip-top shape. For more information, contact the Independent Computer Consultants Association: www.icca.org; info@icca.org; 11131 South Towne Square, Suite F, St. Louis, MO 63123; 314-892-1675, 800-774-4222; Fax: 314-487-1345.

In total, more than 25 branches of engineering exist, and many of these branches have recognized subdivisions. If you want to explore even more options, consider careers in structural, robotics, materials, mining, petroleum, nuclear, ceramics, stationary, architectural, biomedical, environmental, or marine engineering.

Where to go from here

Institute of Electrical and Electronics Engineers, Inc.: www.ieee.org; 445 Hoes Lane, P.O. Box 1331, Piscataway, NJ 08855-1331; 732-981-0060; 800-678-4333; Fax: 732-562-5445.

Working with Money

With a good head for figures, you can excel in any number of financial careers. If you have any of the following skills or interests, one of the careers in this section may intrigue you.

Analyzing	Discerning relationships and connections among information	Reasoning
Categorizing	Estimating	Recognizing patterns
Comparing	Explaining	Seeing cause and effect
Counting	Problem solving	Straight-forward calculations
Creating spreadsheets	Processing logic questions rapidly	Strategizing
Critical thinking	Quantifying	

Keeping the books

As you audit a company's financial records, prepare taxes, or take care of bookkeeping tasks, you provide an honest picture of a company's or individual's financial picture.

To do this job well, you must keep an eye on the accuracy of the smallest detail, while remembering the big picture and large-scale implications of the company's financial decisions. The skill with which you can communicate sometimes difficult technical information to clients and peers adds to your success.

Out-of-the-box angles

As borders melt in the globalization of business dealings, the move to establish international accounting rules is heating up. This globalization may have an impact on your work.

A new career in this field entails using your knowledge to show companies how to streamline operations and services, enhancing their bottom line.

Due to the wide variety of opportunities, you can practically choose your own work environment in this field. If you want to work on your own or in a small office, set your sights on becoming a certified public accountant and preparing taxes and consulting with small businesses. If you want to work in a large company, target the Big Five or a regional public accounting firm.

Related jobs and specialties

Accountant, associate accountant, staff accountant, senior accountant, auditor, internal auditor, external auditor, cost accountant, government accountant, bookkeeper, certified public accountant (CPA), enrolled agent (EA), tax preparer, bookkeeping clerk, accounting clerk, auditing clerk, management accountant, investigative accountant (see the following section).

Where to go from here

American Institute of Certified Public Accountants: www.aicpa.org; 1211 Avenue of the Americas, New York, NY 10136; 212-938-3000; 888-777-7077.

Making loans

If you are highly motivated, can develop good working relationships with clients, and feel comfortable with computers and finances, consider becoming a loan officer for a bank or mortgage broker. In this business, you develop a customer base, work to understand your customers' financial needs, and guide your customers through the loan application process. Then you use your computer to analyze the risk associated with granting the loan.

Your hours need to be flexible enough to meet your customers' needs, which may mean working long hours, especially when interest rates are low and your business booms.

Out-of-the-box angles

Payment options vary in this field. Be sure to find out whether your compensation is in the form of a salary, commissions only, or a salary plus a commission or bonus.

The increased variety and complexity of loans and the banks' dependence on loans to succeed indicate that the demand for loan officers may remain strong.

Related jobs and specialties

Loan officer, salesperson, business loan broker, venture capitalist, commercial loan officer, credit specialist, credit manager, mortgage loan officer, business loan officer, consumer loan, loan counselor, loan collection officer.

Where to go from here

National Association of Mortgage Brokers: www.namb.org; 8201 Greensboro Drive, Suite 300, McLean, VA 22102; 703-610-9009; Fax: 703-610-9005.

Managing money

Use your understanding of finances, your analytical skills, and your sense of the operations of your company and the state of the economy to help your company reduce financial risks and maximize profits. Whether you oversee your company's financial functions and formulate plans and policies, or you invest funds and manage cash, your creative problem-solving skills, your clear communication style, and your knowledge of computers contribute to your success. Thanks to computers, you now spend less time preparing reports and more time doing analysis, developing strategies, and offering advice to management about how to increase profits.

Out-of-the-box angles

Because more and more companies contract out their accounting and financial functions, or hire finance managers for temporary stints to handle particular problems or projects, a number of alternative work options exist in this field, from part-time and contract work to self employment.

To enhance your employability, gain as much knowledge as you can about how companies can use computers to make their financial operations more efficient.

As the global economy touches more and more companies, financial managers must have a good feel for international finance and may even need to speak another language.

Related jobs and specialties

Chief financial officer (CFO), vice president of finance, controller, treasurer, financial officer, credit manager, cash manager, insurance manager business owner, entrepreneur, banker, branch manager.

Where to go from here

Financial Management Association International: www.fma.org; fma@coba.usf.edu; University of South Florida, College of Business Administration, Tampa, FL 33620-5500; 813-974-2084; Fax: 813-974-3318.

Investing

To succeed as an investment broker, you must perform under pressure at a fast pace. You must make profits for your company and clients using your mathematical aptitude to evaluate stocks based on research. You need a thorough understanding and gut sense of the market, and you must possess a high tolerance for risk. Be prepared to take the blame if your client's portfolio takes a significant dive in value as a result of market movements.

Out-of-the-box angles

The investment landscape has changed tremendously over the last decade with the advent of electronic trading, large discount brokerage operations, and changes to security exchanges. More change is on the horizon as the industry considers round-the-clock automated trading. Stay tuned to understand how these changes may impact your career.

More and more people invest as they move closer to retirement, which indicates a good future for this career.

After you build your clientele, your income bumps up as a result of increased commissions.

Related jobs and specialties

Stockbroker, financial planner, financial advisor, investment advisor, investment broker, investment manager, investment banker, retirement consultant, venture capitalist, portfolio manager, account executive, trader, options trader, day trader, brokerage clerk, transfer clerk, receive-and-deliver clerk, purchase-and-sell clerk.

Where to go from here

National Association of Security Dealers: www.nasd.com; 1735 K Street, NW, Washington, D.C. 20006-1500; 202-728-8000, 301-590-6500; Fax: 202-293-6260.

Analyzing financial research

Whether you predict the performance of specific stocks, evaluate the impact of economic policies, or screen business plans for possible venture capital funding, expect to spend the majority of your time immersing yourself in financial trends, crunching numbers at your computer, and reading annual reports and policies. To handle your intense workload and strict deadlines, you must prioritize, work well alone or as part of a team, and have an innate ability to work with and understand numbers.

Out-of-the-box angles

With the global economy, increased competition, and a greater reliance on analyzing financial data, people with analytical skills are in a fine position for employment in this career.

Because most of the jobs in this field are in banking and financial institutions, expect to enter a rather formal company culture that insists on a highly professional dress code, umpteen required social outings, and socializing with coworkers during your off hours.

Other intriguing options

Financial planning: Use your financial expertise to assess your clients' current financial situation, their life goals, and build a financial plan that suits their needs and tolerance for risk. For more information, contact the National Association of Personal Financial Advisors: www.napfa.org; info@napfa.org; 355 West Dundee Road, Suite 200, Buffalo Grove, IL 60089, 1-888-FEE-ONLY.

Appraising: Provide independent, credible, and impartial appraisals that accurately reflect the market value of tangible and intangible properties, such as businesses, gems and jewelry, machinery and equipment, personal property, and real estate. For more information, contact the American Society of Appraisers: www.appraisers.org; asainfo@appraisers.org; 555 Herndon Parkway, Suite 125, Herndon, VA 20170; 703- 478-2228; Fax: 703-742-8471.

Making the right impression means immersing yourself in this culture, whether it fits your style or not. Make sure that you are willing to participate in this culture before you embark on this career.

For a financial analyst, bonuses for great performance can equal or exceed the annual salary. Don't be deluded, however; you work very hard to put this extra cash in your pocket.

Related jobs and specialties

Financial analyst, budget analyst, budget officer, management analyst, market research analyst, insurance underwriter, risk manager, credit analyst, management consultant, management accountant, economist, financial researcher, claim adjuster, loss-control specialist, program evaluator, market researcher, mystery shopper, Web site evaluator, researcher.

Where to go from here

Association for Investment Management and Research: www.aimr.org; info@aimr.org; P.O. Box 3668; 560 Ray C. Hunt Drive; Charlottesville, VA 22903-0668; 804-951-5499, 800-247-8132; Fax: 804-951-5262.

Organizing People, Data, and Things

Even if you aren't enthralled with scientific or technical topics, your logical, organized way of thinking can position you well for several careers. If you have any of the following skills or interests, one of the careers in this section may intrigue you.

Analyzing	Event planning	Reasoning
Categorizing	Explaining	Recognizing patterns
Comparing	Investigating	Research
Counting	Organizing	Scheduling
Creating spreadsheets	Prioritizing	Straight-forward calculations
Critical thinking	Problem solving	Strategizing
Dividing up tasks	Project planning	
Estimating	Quantifying	

Event planning

You plan and produce events that fit your clients' needs, making sure that each event runs smoothly and comes in on budget. This work entails tracking myriad details associated with site selection, negotiations, travel arrangements, registration, food and entertainment, audio-visual equipment, public relations, marketing, and program evaluations.

One hitch in your work can spell disaster, so it pays to be extremely organized and efficient. Your oral and written communication skills also contribute to your success by helping you head off potential misunderstandings with clients or subcontractors and negotiating the best deals for your clients. Whether you work for a company or for yourself, you focus on building a reputation and a network of vendors; these two assets are in the end what you sell to clients.

Out-of-the-box angles

For events with budgets in the millions, corporations and large associations often look for planners with specialties in accounting, marketing, or public relations to ensure that their events run smoothly. Specializing in these fields helps improve your employability and your salary.

Although many meeting planners are self-employed, you can find job opportunities in companies, professional associations, convention venues, or visitors bureaus.

Related jobs and specialties

Event planner, meeting planner, convention planner, trade show coordinator, festival producer, professional party planner, association manager, conference hall exhibit manager, media escort, wedding planner, reunion planner, special events coordinator, caterer, travel agent, adventure trip organizer, tour guide (see Chapter 10).

Where to go from here

Meeting Professionals International: www.mpiweb.org/home.asp; 4455 LBJ Freeway, Suite 1200 Dallas, TX 75244; 972-702-3000; Fax: 972-702-3070.

Collecting

Use your ability to organize, your flair for design, and your desire to maintain documents and objects of historical value. In this field, you acquire items for a collection, preserve and restore pieces, classify and inventory items, and design and plan exhibits.

Due to the detailed and sensitive nature of your work, you must have extensive training in a particular specialty to get into this line of work. Depending on your role in the institution you work for, you may also be called upon to book tours for your exhibit or participate in public relations duties.

Out-of-the-box angles

Although specific protocols are still evolving, specialists in this field expect computers, multimedia, and the Internet to revolutionize the way collections are stored and shared with the public. Stay tuned for details as they emerge.

In addition to working for museums and libraries, consider religious organizations, professional associations, conservation organizations, private collectors, and research companies as other sources of employment.

Because this is a field of great interest to many, enhance your chances of being hired by getting as much hands-on experience as possible through volunteering, interning, or working part-time.

Related jobs and specialties

Curator, conservator, museum technician, museum director, registrar, genealogist, survey researcher, anthropologist, archeologist, artifacts conservator, ethnologist, folklorist, historian, painting restorer, horticulturist, botanist, zoologist (see Chapter 14), document controller, database administrator, archivist, archive technician, librarian (see Chapter 8).

Where to go from here

Society of American Archivists: www.archivists.org; 600 South Federal Street, Suite 504, Chicago, IL 60605.

Buying

If you are a strong negotiator, hard worker, good planner, and quick decision maker who can act effectively on fast-changing data, you may have a future as a buyer. Whether you buy products for a retail store or purchase parts for a manufacturer, your goal is to get the highest quality merchandise at the best possible price.

To succeed in the long run, you must continually track inventories, review sales figures, and stay attuned to factors that impact the supply and demand of the products and materials you buy. Another key to success is building a reliable network of suppliers whom you trust and feel comfortable dealing with.

Out-of-the-box angles

Computers have revolutionized many of the routine tasks of sales and inventory control, allowing buyers to spend more time selecting the right items and building relationships with suppliers. A good working knowledge of computers and the appropriate software is definitely a plus to employers.

To be competitive in this field, you must continue to hone your skills. Many companies prefer to hire those who have a certification.

Related jobs and specialties

Buyer, merchandise manager, purchasing agent, purchasing manager, commodity manager, commodity buyer, supply manager, contract specialist, contract manager, government purchasing agent, government purchasing manager, merchandising executive, wholesale buyer, retail buyer, planner, scheduler, inventory specialist.

Where to go from here

American Purchasing Society: www.american-purchasing.com; propurch@aol.com; North Island Center, 8 East Galena Boulevard, Aurora, IL 60506; Fax: 630-859-0270.

Investigating

As long as you don't mind a bit of confrontation on the job, your ability to follow leads, interview, interrogate, and think on your feet make you a prime candidate for doing detective or investigative work. You use surveillance, computer research, searches, and interviews to verify facts, gather information, or solve crimes. You can expect to work irregular hours, some of which you spend out in the field doing surveillance and conducting interviews.

Out-of-the-box angles

One out of every four investigators and detectives is self-employed, and many work part-time. You may think of including this as part of your composite career. (See Chapter 7 for more information on composite careers.)

Although you may think of detectives as working for police stations or private investigators, your options are actually a bit broader than that. Consider being a detective for a store or hotel or an investigator in a corporate, legal, or financial setting.

If you are intrigued by detective work, you can build a viable specialty based on a previous career in finance, accounting, investigative reporting, law, or insurance.

Your ability to use the Internet and other electronic databases to gather investigative data and help solve cases may prove to be a good selling point when you look for a job.

Related jobs and specialties

Private investigator, police investigator, criminalist, police detective, polygraph operator, private detective, investigative accountant, investigative reporter, criminal investigator, corporate investigator, internal investigator, external investigator, legal investigator, intellectual property investigator, store detective, plainclothes investigator, inspector, accident reconstructor, bounty hunter, fingerprint expert, firearms expert, polygrapher, freelance undercover agent, medical examiner, forensics.

Where to go from here

International Crime Scene Investigators Association: PMB 385, 15774 South LaGrange Road, Orland Park, IL 60462; 708-460-8082; Fax: 708-460-8843.

Other intriguing options

Project managing: You ensure that the projects you head up come in on time and within budget with as few snags as possible. To do this, you must tap your technical expertise, negotiation skills, time management tactics, and people management skills. For more information, contact the Project Management Institute: www. pmi.org; pmihq@pmi.org; Four Campus Boulevard, Newtown Square, Pennsylvania 19073-3299; 610-356-4600; Fax: 610-356-4647.

Virtual assisting: With the appropriate equipment, you can partner with clients all over the country or the world to assist them in running their businesses. You can do your work without leaving your office. If you want to start your own home-based business, this may be the answer you are looking for. For more information, contact AssistU.com: www.assistu.com; help@assistu.com; 76 Cranbrook Road, Suite 192; Cockeysville, MD 21030; 866-829-6757.

Professional organizing: Use your natural ability to organize and create useable systems to help others manage the chaos in their homes and offices. For more information, contact the National Association of Professional Organizers: www.napo.net; P.O. Box 140647, Austin, TX 78714; Fax: 512-454-3036.

Relocation work: Make a huge difference in people's lives by coordinating their national or international moves and helping them get settled in their new homes and communities. For more information, contact the Employee Relocation Council: www.erc.org; 1720 N Street NW, Washington, D.C. 20036; 202-857-0857.

Chapter 10

If You Connect Well with Others

In This Chapter

▶ Using your skills to help people heal physically and emotionally

▶ Exploring ways to help others enjoy life more

▶ Assisting others in the work place

▶ Keeping people safe as your line of work

All of the careers that I describe in this chapter require you to enjoy working closely with patients, clients, coworkers, guests, customers, or the general public. To do this work well, you must have strong interpersonal skills that allow you to sense what others need, to encourage them, and to guide them.

The people who excel in these interpersonal careers tend to have the following skills.

Ability to discern perspectives of others	Empathizing	Putting people at ease
Building relationships	Extracting information from others	Recognizing cultural values and norms
Collaborating	Getting advice	Sensitive to others' moods
Comforting others	Getting along well with others	Trusted confidant
Cooperating	Nonverbal communication	Verbal communication

As you read through the career descriptions in the chapter, notice which careers feel most comfortable and are most consistent with who you are. If the careers in a certain section don't appeal to you, just skip right over them to check out another section.

Helping Others Heal Physically

Some people with interpersonal skills enjoy helping people who are ill or facing health challenges.

If you have any of the following skills or interests, one of the careers in this section may intrigue you.

Acknowledging others	Helping others brainstorm	Providing customer service
Clarifying vision	Helping others see possibility	Setting goals
Giving advice	Interviewing	Trusted confidant
Giving feedback	Motivating others	

Nursing care

As you work directly with patients, helping them through their diagnosis, treatment, and rehabilitation, your sympathy and compassion are essential. Inherent parts of your job include following instructions to provide patients with proper care and making quick, sound decisions about when to call in others for consultation and assistance. The records you keep, your discussions with patients, and the hands-on care you give must be done meticulously to prevent errors and accidents.

Out-of-the-box angles

One in four nurses works part-time. One in ten works more than one job. Due to the round-the-clock nature of this work, alternative schedules are the norm and on-call status may be required at times.

Although a large demand for nurses is expected to continue, recent shifts in the health care industry mean that nurses must look beyond traditional hospital settings for work and must be flexible in rotating among various settings if necessary.

Due to the aging population, technological advances that allow procedures to be performed outside hospitals, and people's desire to heal at home, the areas of growth in this field are expected to be in home health, long-term care, ambulatory care, outpatient hospital centers, rehabilitation, chemo-therapy, and surgicenters.

Trends toward increased specialization mean nurses focus their efforts on particular populations, such as children, elder care, rehabilitation, and cardiac patients. Doing so may increase your employability.

Related jobs and specialties

Registered nurse, hospital nurse, office nurse, nursing home nurse, licensed vocational nurse, certified nursing assistant, home health nurse, school nurse, hospice nurse, paramedic, emergency medical technician (EMT), physician assistant, physician, doctor, EMT instructor, nurse practitioner, public health nurse.

Where to go from here

American Nurses Association: www.nursingworld.org; 600 Maryland Avenue, SW, Suite 100 West, Washington, D.C. 20024, 800-274-4ANA.

Rehabilitation

Within any of the rehabilitation specialties, you help patients improve how they function in their work, home, school, and social environments. You bring out their creativity, confidence, and problem-solving abilities while teaching them new social and life skills.

You evaluate what patients can and can't do, review their medical histories, and create treatment plans to bring about the desired outcome, whether it's a greater range of motion, the ability to use a computer, techniques to alleviate pain, or ways to compensate for the permanent loss of a particular motor function. Over time, you assess your patient's progress and modify the treatment plan as necessary.

To succeed, you must have compassion, a desire to help, and the ability to communicate with your patient and his family. In some cases, you must be fit enough to handle the physically demanding tasks of moving equipment and helping patients with limited capabilities.

Out-of-the-box angles

Within this field, you have some flexibility in arranging your work life. Part-time work, private practice, or a combination of self-employment and employment with a company are possible.

Rehabilitation specialists of all varieties may be in demand as the population ages and becomes more vulnerable to heart attacks and chronic debilitating conditions that require rehabilitation.

Combine your expertise in a creative media, such as art, recreation, dance, drama, or music, with training in rehabilitation methods to create a viable specialty in the field of rehabilitation.

Related jobs and specialties

Physical therapist, rehabilitation specialist, speech therapist, occupational therapist, respiratory therapist, ergonomic specialist, speech pathologist, audiologist, rehabilitation counselor, recreation therapist, recreation therapy paraprofessional, music therapist (see Chapter 13), dance therapist (see Chapter 12), art therapist, orientation therapist, prothetist, orthotist, special education counselor, industrial therapist, physical therapist aid.

Where to go from here

National Rehabilitation Association: `www.nationalrehab.org`; `info@nationalrehab.org`; 633 South Washington Street, Alexandria, VA 22314; 703-836-0850; Fax: 703-836-0848.

Holistic medicine

As a chiropractor, acupuncturist, herbalist, or other alternative medicine practitioner, you combine your extensive knowledge of the systems that make up the human body, your compassion, and your ability to listen to find ways to ease your patients' pain.

Using the diagnostic system and devices preferred in your specialty, you evaluate your patient to determine what is out of alignment based on the symptoms the patient shares with you. Then you use treatments, such as chiropractic manipulations, acupuncture, herbs, biofeedback, or massage, to strengthen the body's weaknesses.

With every patient comes the requisite paperwork, so know up front that you may divide your day between patient care and billing.

Out-of-the-box angles

The demand for alternative medicine has almost doubled since 1990. If you decide to begin a practice, your clientele may be well-educated Baby Boomers who can afford to finance alternative care out of their own pockets.

Other intriguing options

Midwifery: Combine your medical background and your passion for life to help women with family planning, pre-natal care, giving birth, and caring for their newborns. For more information, contact The American College of Nurse-Midwives: www.acnm.org; info@acnm.org; 818 Connecticut Avenue, Suite 900, Washington, D.C. 20006; 202-728-9860; Fax: 202-728-9897.

Nutrition: Use your scientific knowledge of food and your ability to work with people to help clients increase their state of health and well being by eating better. For more information, contact the American Association of Nutritional Consultants: www.aanc.net; registrar@aanc.net; 302 East Winona Avenue, Warsaw, IN 46580; 888-828-2262; 219-267-2614.

Some alternative healing methods, such as chiropracty, acupuncture, and massage, are becoming more and more mainstream; some insurance companies now include these treatments in their standard coverage, which could encourage additional interest and growth in this field.

Equipment costs may drive more chiropractors to pool their resources in larger practices, but for now, sole proprietorships and small practices are the norm.

Related jobs and specialties

Chiropractor, chiropractic assistant, acupuncturist, reflexologist, naturopath physician, osteopath, massage therapist (see Chapter 12), medical intuitive, aromatherapist, day spa worker, homeopathist, homeopathic physician, herbalist, Chinese medicine practitioner, light therapist, biofeedback specialist, sound healer (see Chapter 13), vitamin therapist, nutritionist (see the following sidebar).

Where to go from here

Complementary Alternative Medical Association: www.camaweb.org; cama@mindspring.com; P.O. Box 373478, Decatur, GA 30037.

Helping Others Make the Most of Life

Sometimes a little extra boost of support can go a long way. As a member of one of the following professions, you are in a fine position to help children and adults live full lives.

If you have any of the following skills or interests, one of the careers in this section may intrigue you.

Acknowledging others	Finding common ground	Networking
Building consensus	Giving advice	Receiving feedback
Building others' self-esteem	Giving feedback	Role playing
Clarifying vision	Helping others brainstorm	Sensing others' motives
Coaching	Helping others see possibility	Setting goals
Creating and maintaining synergy	Interviewing	Understanding group process
Facilitating group discussion	Motivating others	

Counseling

If you like listening to people and helping them resolve personal, family, relationship, educational, and mental health situations, consider a career in the field of counseling. Regardless of the setting, you begin your relationship with each client by getting a full grasp of their situation and what isn't working. From what they say, how they say it, and what they don't say, you discern their needs and help them gain the perspective, the skills, and possibly the medication they need to resolve their difficulties.

Confidentiality, trust, and objectivity are essential elements of your work. Although much of your work takes place in one-on-one meetings with your clients, you may also confer with other specialists to coordinate support. Due to the emotionally intense nature of this work, you must pay attention to your own needs so that you don't suffer from burnout.

Out-of-the-box angles

Besides establishing a private practice, consider working in hospitals, long-term care facilities, home health agencies, private social services agencies, schools, employee assistance programs, rehabilitation settings, and employment centers.

Most health insurance covers brief stints of therapy, as long as counselors on their preferred provider lists provide the care. When first starting out, counselors may have a difficult time getting on these lists, which means that they can only work with clients who pay for their own care. Many counselors use a sliding fee scale to allow those who aren't covered to have access to the care they need. If you choose to enter this profession, stay abreast of developments in health insurance so that you won't be taken by surprise when you complete your degree. The climate could be completely different than it is now.

Specializing in an area that serves the aging Baby Boomers and the increasingly diverse population is a good strategy to increase your employability. Stress management, gerontological counseling, and multicultural counseling are all potential areas of specialization.

Related jobs and specialties

Therapist, counselor, social worker, grief counselor, employee assistance planner, clinical psychologist, psychiatrist, psychiatric nurse, drug and alcohol counselor, school counselor, school psychologist, sports psychologist, music therapist (see Chapter 13), dance therapist (see Chapter 12), art therapist (see Chapter 11), hypnotherapist, residential counselor, human service worker, community outreach worker, mental health aide, case management aide, clinical psychologist, health psychologist, neuropsychologist, development psychologist, employee assistant plan manager, employee welfare manager, clergy, child protective services social worker.

Where to go from here

American Counseling Association: 5999 Stevenson Avenue, Alexandria, VA 22304-3300; 703-823-9800; 800-347-6647; Fax: 703-823-0252.

Childcare

You help children develop and grow physically, emotionally, socially, and intellectually through play, cooperative activities, and instruction. To accomplish this goal, you plan a series of events for the day, knowing, of course, that those plans may change as the day unfolds. Tracking your charges' progress, creating a plan to work with their special needs, and sharing your ideas with parents are integral aspects of your job.

To succeed in this work, you must have the physical stamina and energy to keep up with an active group of young children throughout long days, have the imagination, wonder, and patience to participate in their activities, and the common sense and knowledge to respond appropriately in times of crisis.

Out-of-the-box angles

Self-employment and part-time work arrangements are usually available in this field.

Other intriguing options

Personal and professional coaching: Help people clarify their life dreams, create a workable action plan, and stick with it to reach their goals. You can apply your talents in a corporate setting as well as the private sector. For more information, contact the International Coach Federation: www.coachfederation.org; icfoffice@coachfederation.org; 1444 "I" Street NW, Suite 700, Washington, D.C. 20005; 202-712-9039; 888-ICF-3131.

Undertaking: Help grieving families lay their loved ones to rest by handling the logistics of the funeral service while taking into account the families' requests. For more information, contact the National Funeral Directors Association: 13625 Bishop's Drive, Brookfield, WI 53005.

More government subsidization and tax deductions for child care mean that your services are in more demand. This is especially true if parents see that a preprimary education is beneficial to their children.

Related jobs and specialties

Daycare provider, child care worker, family child care provider, nanny, preschool teacher, teacher assistant, tutor, early childhood program director, child psychologist, school counselor, guidance counselor, development psychologist.

Where to go from here

National Association for Education of Young Children: www.naeyc.org; naeyc@naeyc.org; 1509 16th Street, NW, Washington, D.C. 20036-1426; 202-232-8777; 800-424-2460; Fax: 202-328-1846.

Helping Others Enjoy Their Leisure Time

If you like giving people the times of their lives, you may enjoy the following careers in the travel and recreation industries.

If you have any of the following skills or interests, one of the careers in this section may intrigue you.

Acknowledging others	Finding common ground	Networking
Building consensus	Giving advice	Providing customer service
Building others' self-esteem	Helping others brainstorm	Putting people at ease
Clarifying vision	Helping others see possibility	Setting goals
Creating and maintaining synergy	Interviewing	Understanding group process
Facilitating group discussion	Motivating others	

Recreation

If you are creative and outgoing, and you enjoy organizing events, consider working in recreation. As a recreation leader, you plan events, teach necessary skills, facilitate activities, and encourage participants to engage in activities. Your motivational skills and your ability to sense who needs an extra boost of confidence can go a long way toward making you a success. In addition to the activity-centered tasks you do, you may take care of the administrative aspects of running the facility where you work.

Out-of-the-box angles

Look beyond your local parks and recreation department for employment possibilities; try cruise ships, urban community centers, summer camps, nursing centers, residential care facilities, amusement parks, health clubs, apartment complexes, corporate wellness programs, and clubs.

If you work outside, your work may be seasonal, so think about including this profession in a broader composite career (see Chapter 7 for more information on composite careers).

The increased interest in health and fitness and the need for recreation activities for older adults increases the demand for people in this profession.

Related jobs and specialties

Recreation leader, activity specialist, recreation supervisor, director of recreation and parks, camp counselor, recreation therapist, certified leisure technician, lifeguard, craft specialist.

Where to go from here

National Recreation and Park Association: www.activeparks.org; 22377 Belmont Ridge Road; Ashburn, VA 20148; 703-858-0784; Fax: 703-858-0794.

Travel

Your clients depend on your patience, research abilities, organizational skills, and knowledge of the travel industry to book them on the best, most economical tours or trips available. You assess their travel needs by asking a series of questions, come up with the options that best fit their desired parameters, and book the arrangements they choose. The more you know about the destinations, the transportation carriers, the accommodations, and the local culture and customs, the more likely your clients are to come to you for your suggestions.

Out-of-the-box angles

The Internet gives travelers unprecedented opportunity to make their own travel arrangements. However, several factors indicate that the travel industry is going strong: more business travel as managerial and sales positions increase, more global business travel, more tours for foreign tourists, and increased tourism as Baby Boomers retire with money and the desire to travel.

Travel agents can telecommute thanks to networks and advanced computer systems.

Creating specialized tours for a targeted market is one way to niche yourself in this field. Adventure travel, art buying trips, and singles tours are examples of specialty tours. Think of a population you want to target and create a trip that appeals to them.

Related jobs and specialties

Travel agent, travel counselor, location tour guide, adventure travel organizer, reservation agent, ticket agent, travel clerk, gate agent, station agent, member services counselor, passenger rate clerk, rental car agent, entertainment director, resort social director, camp counselor, cruise director, camp director, relocation specialist (see Chapter 9).

Where to go from here

American Society of Travel Agents: www.astanet.com; 1101 King Street, Suite 200, Alexandria, VA 22314; 703-739-2782; Fax: 703-684-8319.

Hospitality

As an employee or manager within a hotel, you put in long days completing the myriad tasks that keep the establishment in tiptop shape. You may secure fresh flowers for the lobby, choose furnishings for the next upgrade, plan the restaurant menus, orchestrate onsite meetings and conventions, or verify that repairs have been completed.

Your ability to interact easily with people of all backgrounds, work as part of a team, manage your time and multiple projects, and solve problems in a timely manner contribute to your success in this industry.

Out-of-the-box angles

Many hotel managers are self-employed, owning the establishment they manage. Many people in this field act as property managers, looking after a property for long distance owners.

The hotel industry shows two trends. One is a move toward economy hotels with clean rooms, but few other amenities. The other is suite hotels that cater to business travelers who are in the area for extended stays.

If you work for someone else, investigate your compensation package, which may include significant bonuses and perks, such as free laundry and parking.

Related jobs and specialties

Hotel manager, bed & breakfast owner, front desk clerk, concierge, general manager, resident manager, executive housekeeper, front office manager, food and beverage manager, convention services manager, assistant manager, restaurant manager, food service manager, restaurateur, sommelier, apartment building manager, retail manager, property manager, spa manager, catering manager (see Chapter 9).

Where to go from here

American Hotel & Motel Association: www.ahma.com; infoctr@ahma.com; 1201 New York Avenue, NW, #600, Washington, D.C. 20005-3931; 202-289-3100; Fax: 202-289-3199.

Helping Others in a Business or Public Setting

The careers in this section allow you to exercise your interpersonal skills while helping people live and work better.

If you have any of the following skills or interests, one of the careers in this section may intrigue you.

Acknowledging others	Facilitating group discussion	Managing
Building consensus	Finding common ground	Networking
Building others' self-esteem	Giving advice	Providing customer service
Clarifying vision	Giving feedback	Receiving feedback
Coaching	Helping others brainstorm	Sensing others' motives
Creating and maintaining synergy	Helping others see possibility	Setting goals
Determining who is best to do the job	Interviewing	Trusted confidant
Extracting information from others	Leading	Understanding group process

Staffing

Use your ability to put people at ease, your knack for getting them to talk freely about themselves, and your aptitude to discern what is needed in a situation to become a successful recruiter. Your skills allow you to get a good sense of what the employer wants and a clear idea of what skills and experience each applicant brings to the party. You find and hire the best candidate for each job. To do your job well, you must judge people impartially and communicate your assessments effectively with executives and hiring managers as well as applicants at all levels.

Out-of-the-box angles

As more and more companies rely on temporary workers and contract employees to get the work done, they turn to recruiting specialists to fill open positions. The forecast is good for this field.

Recruitment and staffing functions are outsourced more and more often, which means that opportunities to work independently or in small agencies exist.

Check into your compensation package carefully. Those who place temporary workers may receive a salary, and those placing highly-skilled individuals may have some commission-based pay.

Related jobs and specialties

Headhunter, personnel recruiter, staffing specialist, personnel development specialist, employment interviewer, personnel consultant, human resources coordinator, employment manager, placement manager, temporary agency owner, casting director.

Where to go from here

Recruiters Network: www.recruitersnetwork.com; info@recruitersnetwork.com; 5464 North Port Washington Road, Suite #196, Milwaukee, WI 53217; 414-357-8350; Fax: 414-357-8333.

Supporting employees

If you have strong interpersonal and communication skills, the desire to help employees make the most of their work experience, and the ability to juggle multiple tasks, consider a career in human resources.

Depending on your interests, you may work with compensation issues, labor issues, benefits, or the allocation of resources. You help the company utilize the skills of the personnel in a cost-effective and quality way. To do this, you must be well informed about the company's strategy, goals, and constraints. In some circumstances, you may do the dirty work of letting poor performers go, laying off part of the work force, or explaining reductions in benefits to employees.

Out-of-the-box angles

Two specialties are emerging in this field: international human resource managers, who grasp how to handle the needs of a global and culturally diverse work force; and information systems people, who are well-versed in the programs used in human resources.

Legislation in areas such as safety, equal employment opportunity, wages, family leaves, and health insurance mean human resource specialists may be in demand to implement and monitor more programs.

Related jobs and specialties

Human resource specialist, labor relations specialist, management consultant, organizational development consultant, group facilitator, succession planning consultant, trainer, labor relations specialist, international human resource manager, human resource information systems specialist, safety specialist, training materials development specialist, compensation specialist, employee relations manager, human resource clerk, benefits specialist, corporate coach, professional coach (see the previous section).

Where to go from here

Society for Human Resource Management: www.shrm.org; shrm@shrm.org; 1800 Duke Street, Alexandria, VA 22314; 703-548-3440; Fax: 703-836-0367.

Managing businesses

Managers and executives create strategies, policies, and procedures to achieve a company's long-term and short-term goals. To do the job well, you must have the ability to scan an infinite amount of information from sources inside and outside the company and synthesize this information in ways that help you make sound decisions. After seeing what needs to be done, you must clearly articulate what you want and delegate tasks to appropriate members of your staff.

If you work in a large company, you may be held accountable for a narrow aspect of the operations, such as marketing, purchasing, finance, or property management, but if you are a manager of a smaller organization, you may be responsible for several of these areas or all of them. You can expect traveling, attending meetings, and giving presentations to be integral parts of your work life.

Out-of-the-box angles

The growth of the global marketplace brings new challenges and opportunities for managers. Experience in international economics, global marketing, information systems, and other languages puts you in a strong employment position.

Although most companies in the past promoted their management team from within, you can, with sufficient experience and background, make your way into a management position from outside the company. An expertise in finance, a well-rounded background in the business side of your industry, or experience as an entrepreneur help position you to become a manager. If this is your goal, start building the experience you need by taking on more management tasks within your current job. Consider volunteering to chair a committee, taking on a team leader position, or volunteering as a member of a non-profit's Board of Directors.

As you move into management, position yourself in an industry that is growing steadily to insure that you have as many options as possible.

Related jobs and specialties

Chief executive officer, manager, general manager, operations manager, office manager, leader, education administrator, financial manager (see Chapter 9), mayor, governor, health club manager, business manager, team manager, executive director, staff director, volunteer coordinator, management consultant, entrepreneur.

Where to go from here

American Management Association: www.amanet.org; mworld@amanet.org; P.O. Box 169, Saranac Lake, NY 12983; 800-313-8650; Fax: 518-891-0368.

Keeping the public safe

Your communication skills, your ability to handle sensitive, perhaps even explosive, situations with a calm demeanor, and your talent for thinking well on your feet make you a good candidate for a career in public safety. Because a fair amount of the work in this field is physical, you must be in exquisite shape, both strong and agile, fast and enduring. Whether you direct traffic during an emergency, respond to a call, or investigate a crime, you protect the safety of those in the community. In each situation, you use as little force as necessary to turn a difficult situation into a peaceful resolution.

Out-of-the-box angles

Opportunities in federal law enforcement exist, including the Federal Bureau of Investigation (FBI), Drug Enforcement Administration (DEA), Immigration and Naturalization Services (INS), Bureau of Alcohol, Tobacco, and Firearms (ATF), Customs, United States Secret Service, and Bureau of Diplomatic Security.

If you are a psychologist, photographer, chemist, biologist, or accountant, you can find work in police departments helping police officers solve crimes.

Other intriguing options

Corrections work: Use your interpersonal skills and inner strength to oversee people who have had trouble with the law. The environment requires that you play the role of police officer, social worker, counselor, teacher, and security guard. For more information, contact the International Association of Correctional Officers: P.O. Box 81826, Lincoln, NE 68501.

Related jobs and specialties

Police officer, law enforcement officer, sheriff, deputy sheriff, marshal, deputy marshal, state police officer, college police officer, highway patrol officer, correctional officer, probation officer, security guards, house or store detective, private investigator, (see Chapter 9), fire marshal (see Chapter 12).

Where to go from here

American Federation of Police: www.aphf.org; 3801 Biscayne Boulevard, Miami, FL 33137; 305-573-0070.

Chapter 11

If You Have a Good Eye

● ●

In This Chapter

▶ Investigating careers with an artistic flair

▶ Exploring careers with spatial implications

● ●

*T*he careers in this chapter may intrigue you if you think in pictures, translate visual images into physical form, manipulate three-dimensional structures in your head, or have a good sense of direction.

This chapter consists of four sections, each devoted to a different career category. To determine whether you are interested in the careers in a particular category, read the introductory paragraph and check out the skills highlighted in the box. (See Chapter 6 for more information on the skills listed in these boxes.)

Keep your journal nearby as you read this chapter. Record any ideas that you find intriguing so that you can look at them after you put the book down.

Working on a Two-Dimensional "Canvas"

Although visual images have always had a place in society, the explosion of new technological media has caused a surge in the use of visual imagery. You see photographs, video clips, and animation just about anywhere and everywhere you look. These visual images, which you see in entertainment, education, and advertisements, were designed by a person with artistic capabilities.

If you have any of the following skills or interests, one of the careers in this section may intrigue you.

Cartooning	Drawing	Pictures and photography
Color schemes	Forming mental images	Sense of aesthetics, beauty and balance
Creating patterns and designs	Imaginative	Sense of perspective
Designing graphic representations	Manipulating images	Visualizing

Graphic design

You use images, type, color, and various two-dimensional media to create distinctive and descriptive logos and images. Your work conveys information or establishes a recognizable brand for your clients' products or companies.

You translate your clients' ideas into results that fit within their purpose, budget, time frame, and design limitations. In addition to producing images, often with computer manipulation, you spend a considerable amount of time talking with your clients at key points in the development process. After each discussion, you take their thoughts into account as you brainstorm solutions to create finalized images.

To excel in this field, you must have a command of various computer software programs that are widely used, and you need to stay up on the latest technology.

Out-of-the-box angles

One third of all graphic designers are independent contractors. Due to the lively market for visual images, this number may grow in future years.

Telecommuting is a distinct possibility with this career, as long as you have access to the high-end equipment needed to communicate with clients and perform the tasks involved.

Web design is the newest application for graphic design skills and may be an area of tremendous growth for years to come. On the Web, graphic designers use their skills to create the look, feel, and navigational system for Web sites with the goal of attracting visitors and keeping them coming back for more. Because the Web changes constantly, anyone entering this field must spend a considerable amount of time keeping up with the technological advancements inherent in this market segment.

Those trying to break into Web design may find that an excellent portfolio brings them more visibility and results than academic achievements.

Related jobs and specialties

Graphic designer, digital graphic artist, desktop publisher, computer artist, Web designer, Web programmer (see Chapter 9), biomedical visualization specialist, medical illustrator, demonstrative evidence specialist, electronic typesetter, layout designer, production artist, animator, illustrator, marketing communications specialist (see Chapter 8).

Where to go from here

Graphic Artist Guild: www.gag.org; 90 John Street, Suite 403, New York, NY 10038; 800-500-2672.

Photography

You blend artistic sense with technical knowledge to capture photographic images that evoke a certain mood or feeling about a person, place, or event.

In some niches of this field, such as photojournalism, you must get results within a couple of frames to record the essence of the moment or event. In other niches, you take up to 1,000 pictures before you find one that catches what you need. No matter what your subject, being in the right place at the right time is the name of the game.

Out-of-the-box angles

More than half of all photographers are self-employed. They work in their own studios, sign contracts with advertising agencies or magazines, or supply photographs to stock photo agencies for a fee.

The explosion of new media outlets in entertainment, education, communication, and marketing creates a growing and constant demand for more visual images and the photographers who make them.

Digital cameras and scanners allow photographs to be processed, manipulated, edited, and enhanced more readily than ever before. This change not only impacts the work process, but also extends the creative parameters within which photographers work. This technological revolution influences all aspects of photography. By staying on top of the changes as they develop in this field, you have a much better chance of catching the next wave.

Photography has many niches. Choose a niche that appeals to you and fits your lifestyle, and then build your expertise! Your choices include commercial, landscape, product, editorial, industrial, forensic, portrait, aerial, scientific, archeological, event, live performance, news, medical, and entertainment photography.

Other intriguing options

Painting: Wield a paint brush to create murals, design fabrics, paint signs, decorate furniture, produce portraits, or render pictures. Persistence, natural talent, and technical training are the keys to your artistic and financial success. For more information, contact the National Watercolor Society: www.nws-online.org; 915 South Pacific Avenue, San Pedro, CA 90731.

Art directing: Create a design concept and then direct artists and writers who transform the design into form. Your role as an art director resembles that of an editor — coming up with the original parameters of a piece and then giving guidance and suggestions to strengthen the final product. For more information, contact the Art Directors Club: www.adcny.org; 106 West 29th Street, New York, NY 10001; 212-643-1440.

Related jobs and specialties

Staff photographer, still photographer, freelance photographer, photojournalist, foreign correspondent, studio camera operator, motion picture photographer, camera operator, cinematographer, videographer, steadicam operator, photographer assistant, camera assistant, photographic retoucher and restorer, photo editor, file editor.

Where to go from here

Professional Photographers of America, Inc.: www.ppa.com; csc@ppa.com; 229 Peachtree Street, NE, Suite 2200, Atlanta, GA 30303; 800-786-6277.

Working on a Three-Dimensional "Canvas"

Not all creative design happens on a two-dimensional surface. Some people with artistic talents visualize and work in three dimensions. For example, artists and people in the fashion industries are masters at thinking in and working in 3-D. If this form of creativity is in your blood, you can't ignore it!

If you have any of the following skills or interests, one of the careers in this section may intrigue you.

Active imagination	Drawing	Recreating experience in mind
Arranging objects (such as furniture or accessories)	Forming mental images	Sculpture
Color schemes	Imaginative	Sense of aesthetics, beauty, and balance
Creating patterns and designs	Painting	Visualizing

Self-expressive art

Create unique pieces that express a feeling, vision, thought, or notion using one or more media. Finding ways to get your pieces into galleries and museums or noticed by collectors helps you build your career and a name for yourself.

Unfortunately, a career focusing on self-expressive art rarely pays the bills, especially during the early years. If you can forgo some of the time you spend creating self-expressive art, you can translate your talents into a financially rewarding career (see the preceding section for ideas on how to do this).

No matter which path you decide to pursue with your art, your natural talent, enhanced by formal art training and experience, and persistence are your best bets for success.

Out-of-the-box angles

Think about incorporating several of your talents into a composite career that allows you to have the time and mental space to be creative in a self-expressive manner. Some of the most lucrative avenues to pursue as an artist include graphic design, commercial photography, advertising, product design, art direction, and computer art.

 To create a profitable art career, you need to know about the business side of art. Knowing how to price, promote, and sell your art allows you to run your business with confidence. If you aren't skilled in these areas or have no desire to master them, then partner with a good manager, or join a co-op to propel the business side of your art.

Related jobs and specialties

Sculptor, neon sign maker, craftsperson, glass blower, woodworker (see Chapter 12), floral designer, needlework, weaver, textiles, mosaic designer, etcher, lithographer, installation artist, stained glass artist, quilter, ceramic artist, carver, metal arts worker, weaver, balloon artist.

Where to go from here

National Artists Equity Association: `http://artists-equity.org`; `info@artists-equity.org`.

Fashion design

You translate the pulse of the culture, the times, and the trends into clothing and accessories the public wants to buy. You have strong technical training, a good eye for color, line, and style, excellent pattern-making skills, and a sense of what is practical and functional for your customers.

For the majority of designers, the road to success starts with learning the ropes and paying dues in low-paying assistant positions. Some designers find their niche in such assistant positions, while others strike out on their own.

Out-of-the-box angles

If you are serious about making a place for yourself in this industry, take whatever opportunities present themselves as long as the jobs give you chances to learn the ways of the industry and to make the connections you need to launch your career. You just never know how, when, or where your break may happen.

Although formal training helps, this is another career where outstanding portfolios can open doors.

With the right niche, self-employed fashion designers can make their mark by designing for individual clients or high-end boutiques.

If you aren't interested in the high-stakes game of fashion design, but love the industry, look into some of the more stable careers within the industry, including trim buyer, fabric buyer, textile designer, merchandiser, sample maker, quality control specialist, and image consultant.

Related jobs and specialties

Head designer, assistant designer, specialty designer, pattern maker, sample maker, costumer, wearable artist, tailor (see Chapter 12), seamstress, clothing buyer, wardrobe specialist, textile designer, jewelry designer, shoe designer.

Other intriguing options

Image consulting: Use your sense of fashion to help others enhance their visual appearance by recommending appropriate colors and styles for any given event or setting. For more information, contact the Association of Image Consultants International: www.aici.org; info@aici.org ; 910 Charles Street, Fredericksburg, VA 22401; 800-383-8831.

Cosmetology: Help your clients build self-confidence with the hairstyles, hair colors, nail colors, and makeup that bring out their natural beauty. For more information, contact the National Cosmetology Association: 401 North Michigan Avenue, Chicago, IL 60611; 312-527-6765.

Where to go from here

Council of Fashion Designers of America; 1412 Broadway, Suite 2006, New York, NY 10018.

Creating Environments

One form of 3-D creativity takes a sense of design and mixes it with spatial reasoning and building. Most people with this combination of talents work with buildings and structures in some way, such as through design, construction, or decorating.

If you have any of the following skills or interests, one of the careers in this section may intrigue you.

3D thinking	Creating charts and diagrams	Spatial implications
Abstract spatial imagery	Forming mental images	Spatial reasoning
Accurate perception from different angles	Making models	Taking things apart and putting back together
Assembling	Recognizing spatial depth and dimension	Visualizing
Building	Sense of direction	Working with charts and diagrams

Architecture

To design a building, you must use your sense of design and spatial relationships to balance a number of factors, including aesthetics, functionality, safety, economic limitations, and the desires of those who are to occupy the space. From the initial conversation with your client until the building is completed, you play an active role. During the initial phases, design and engineering are your key functions. After building begins, you supervise the construction and verify that the plans are built to your specification.

Much of the work you do takes place under deadline with a distinct likelihood of revisions at every turn. Your ability to communicate your ideas to clients using words and visual representations is crucial to your success.

Out-of-the-box angles

The majority of architects work in small companies with fewer than five employees. About 30 percent of architects are self-employed.

Technological advances, including the creation of the computer-aided design drafting program known as CADD, have changed this industry and made it easier to make revisions and communicate changes. Take the courses and training you need to stay proficient in these technologies.

If you want to specialize, look beyond the typical residential home and business office to designing dream homes, multifamily dwellings, health care institutions, schools, and ecologically friendly buildings.

Related jobs and specialties

Architect technologist, drafter, entertainment architect, intern-architect, industrial designer (see Chapter 9), landscape architect (see Chapter 14).

Where to go from here

American Institute of Architects: www.aiaonline.org; 1735 New York Avenue, NW, Washington, D.C. 20006; 202-626-7300; 800-AIA-3837; Fax: 202-626-7547.

Construction

Although you must have stamina, ability, and balance to build structures, you must also read blueprints accurately, have good spatial perception, and have the ability to visualize how something needs to be put together. Your knowledge of the tools and methods required to transform a pile of materials into a building in accordance with the architect's plans minimizes errors, costs, and delays.

Out-of-the-box angles

Employment in this profession depends on the local economy and tends to be seasonal, cyclical, and limited to short-term projects. The variable work schedule makes this profession worth investigating if you want to build a composite career. One third of all carpenters are self-employed.

To encourage steady work, develop a set of well-rounded skills so that you can take work in a variety of areas depending on what's available.

Related jobs and specialties

Structural carpenter, detail carpenter, construction worker, installer, plumber, electrician, finisher, cabinetmaker, steel structure worker (see Chapter 12), home remodeler, home inspector, expediter.

Where to go from here

National Association of Home Builders: www.nahb.com; info@nahb.com; 1201 15th Street, NW, Washington, D.C. 20005-2800; 800-368-5242, ext. 0.

Interior design

You take empty rooms or buildings and design the spaces to be both functional and aesthetically pleasing to the owners, while coming in under budget within the stated time frame. You rely on your artistic abilities as well as your technical knowledge about materials, construction methods, and safety regulations.

Because creating a space is often a joint effort, communication and coordination are keys to your success. As with any design field, you must stay up-to-date with trends and be open to incorporating new influences into your designs.

Out-of-the-box angles

Don't limit your thinking to residential design. With technological and management style changes in the workplace, offices originally designed to control employees are likely to need makeovers to foster better communication and workflow. Also, don't forget that many people work at home now, and you may find a niche by specializing in designing home offices.

Your portfolio is your ticket to success, especially if you are a freelance designer who depends on a steady stream of clients. Begin each job with a "before" picture and then follow up with vivid "after" pictures to demonstrate your design sense. They say a picture is worth a thousand words, so two pictures must say even more!

Related jobs and specialties

Interior designer, interior decorator, feng shui specialist, office space planner, set designer, lighting designer, furniture designer (see Chapter 12), kitchen designer, stager, window display, merchandise display designer, retail space designer, exhibit designer.

Where to go from here

American Society of Interior Designers: www.asid.org; 608 Massachusetts Avenue, NE, Washington, D.C. 20002-6006; 202-546-3480.

Mapping and Navigating the World

The careers that I list in this section tap a different aspect of visual intelligence, one that relies less on a sense of design and more on spatial reasoning abilities, mapping expertise, and navigational skills.

If you have any of the following skills or interests, one of the careers in this section may intrigue you.

3D thinking	Forming mental images	Sense of direction
Abstract spatial imagery	Mapmaking	Spatial implications
Accurate perception from different angles	Map reading	Spatial reasoning
Creating charts and diagrams	Navigating	Visualizing
Finding the best route	Recognizing spatial depth and dimension	Working with charts and diagrams

Surveying

Use your ability to visualize distances and shapes and to measure, calculate, and plot the terrain to provide civil engineers, architects, and local authorities with the surveying measurements that they need to build projects and establish legal boundaries.

Because your work is the first step in long-term projects, precision and accuracy are crucial; any mistakes you make prove costly and time-consuming for those using your measurements as a starting point. Although more and more technology helps you with your work, fieldwork is still the name of the game. Therefore you must have the physical stamina, coordination, and strength to do the job. Surveying is by definition a team event, so your ability to cooperate and communicate — verbally and with hand signals — is vital to your success and that of your team.

Out-of-the-box angles

New technologies, such as Geographic Information System (GIS) and Global Positioning System (GPS), have made surveyors more accurate and more productive than ever before. To take advantage of this edge, today's surveyors must be more technically savvy than in previous decades.

Eight out of ten surveyors are employed by the government and engineering and architectural companies. If you want to search beyond these traditional employment options, look into urban planning (see the following section), mapping, and searching for natural resources.

Related jobs and specialties

Land surveyor, licensed surveyor, surveying engineer (see Chapter 9), surveying technician, surveying assistant, surveying party chief, geophysical prospecting surveyor, geodetic surveyor, marine surveyor, geographic information specialist, cartographer, cartographic technician, topographer, photogrammetrist, geologist (see Chapter 14).

Where to go from here

American Congress on Surveying & Mapping: www.acsm.net; 6 Montgomery Village Avenue, Suite 403, Gaithersburg, MD 20879; 240-632-9716.

Urban planning

You help communities determine long-term and short-term plans for land usage, especially in times of growth and community revitalization.

To do this work, you must take the needs and ideas of various groups and visualize and develop spatially-sound and inviting plans for the area. At key points in the planning process, you must effectively communicate the newest version of the picture to the city's citizens and officials to work through any potential conflicts and to enhance the plans. Clearly political diplomacy and the ability to build consensus among various groups are crucial skills in this profession.

Out-of-the-box angles

Although six out of ten planners are employed by local governments, more and more opportunities are opening up in the private sector as companies search for ways to plan for the future in areas such as tourism, environmental protection, transportation, economic development, and historic preservation. Urban planners can also be called upon to handle public relations issues and conduct research and testing.

Affluent areas experiencing rapid population growth provide the best employment possibilities for planners.

Related jobs and specialties

City planner, community planner, regional planner, public sector planner, community planning director, land developer, civic leader.

Where to go from here

American Planning Association: www.planning.org; APAInfo@planning.org; P. O. Box 97774, Chicago, IL 60678-97774; 312-431-9100.

Piloting

Whether you fly planes, helicopters, or balloons, you deposit your passengers or cargo in their final and desired destination. Your extensive training and experience in the air provides you with the knowledge you need to do your job well. Your understanding of the equipment, controls, weather patterns, and emergency procedures is crucial to your success, as are flawless eyesight and good spatial reasoning skills.

Out-of-the-box angles

Aside from flying as a commercial airline pilot, consider one of the following flying niches: charter, sight-seeing, cargo delivery, air-taxi service, flight instructor, rescue service, agricultural, mail delivery, fire fighting, aerial inspections, test pilot, or traffic monitoring.

Irregular hours are an inherent part of this job. And to add to the potential stress, many of these hours are spent away from home on overnight layovers. To maintain your sense of self, discover a hobby that you can take with you or find in any city you visit.

This job is the ultimate flex-place position. Your flying assignments dictate whether you find yourself in a series of humdrum destinations in the middle of nowhere or in exotic vacation destinations.

Related jobs and specialties

Captain, co-pilot, navigator, flight engineer, air traffic controller, flight dispatcher, check pilot, examiners, balloonist, tour guide (see Chapter 9), driver, ship captain.

Where to go from here

Air Line Pilots Association International: www.alpa.org; P.O. Box 1169, Herndon, VA 20172; 703-443-2110.

Chapter 12

If You Want Your Work to Be Physical

In This Chapter
▶ Finding ways to do precision work
▶ Exploring careers where you can use your hands to create
▶ Discovering work that is physical
▶ Using your body to be creative

For some people, the thought of sitting at a desk all day can send them into the doldrums. They prefer to be in motion throughout the day, using their bodies to perform their work.

As you read the four sections in this chapter, notice any jobs that appeal to you. Make note of what interests you, even if it's just one aspect of a job. Each clue you discover helps you build a picture of the career you want.

Use the out-of-the-box angles and the related jobs and specialties to help you see other possibilities in similar fields. If you spot a job title that looks interesting, add it to your list of intriguing career ideas to explore later.

Chapters 11 and 13 describe careers that rely on using your physical senses.

Doing Precision Work

Your eye for detail and your ability to produce precision results make you a candidate for any of the following careers. Decide on your medium of choice and specialize.

If you have any of the following skills or interests, one of the careers in this section may intrigue you.

Eye-hand coordination	Handling objects skillfully
Finger dexterity	Precision work with hands

Metal working

If you have fine vision, a passion for doing precision work with your hands, and excellent eye-hand coordination, you may be cut out to be a machinist. After reading the blueprints, you plan the steps necessary to produce the specified pieces and measure and mark your materials accordingly. Then you use an extensive collection of devices to shape the metal and sophisticated lasers or optical measuring devices to verify the precision of your work to the one-ten-thousandth of an inch. In the final phase of each project, you assemble the pieces that you make and polish the surfaces as required.

Out-of-the-box angles

Although the predicted number of job openings in this field is expected to decrease due to a rise in computerized manufacturing techniques, if you have the appropriate training and skills, you may be in great demand because employers are having a difficult time finding qualified workers.

As more and more manufacturers bring in new equipment and change their production techniques, they rely on machinists to retool the operations.

Related jobs and specialties

Machinist, toolmaker, die maker, mold maker, instrument maker, metal worker, machine tool programmer, welder, locksmith, metal pattern maker, gunsmith, blacksmith, automotive machinist, agricultural machinist, grinder, polisher, roller, forger, heat treater.

Where to go from here

National Institute for Metalworking Skills, Inc.: www.nims-skills.org; NIMS@nims-skills.org; 3251 Old Lee Highway, Suite 205, Fairfax, VA 22030; 703-352-4971; Fax: 703-352-4991.

Jewelry work

Combine your eye for detail and design with fine dexterity, good eye-hand coordination, and concentration to become a jeweler. Whether you specialize in design, repair, or cutting, setting, and polishing stones, you can include appraisals as one of your services if you can identify stones and assess their value.

When designing jewelry or making repairs, your goal is to satisfy your customers' needs. You may work under deadline with extremely high quality requirements. Physical stress is a daily part of this career because you do very fine, precise handwork for hours at a time.

Out-of-the-box angles

Nearly one-third of all jewelers are self-employed as retailers, repair people, or designers.

 Technology has made its mark in this field as more and more jewelers use lasers to cut stones or engrave jewelry, and use computer-aided design (CAD) to design and manufacture jewelry. Familiarizing yourself with these tools significantly improves your chances for success.

Related jobs and specialties

Jeweler, jeweler designer, jewelry maker, watchmaker, locksmith, engraver, clock repairer, polisher.

Where to go from here

Jewelers of America: www.jewelers.org; 52 Vanderbilt Avenue, 19th Floor, New York, NY 10017; 646-658-0246; Fax: 646-658-0256.

Dentistry

Use your fine dexterity to help others care for their teeth and gums. Whether you are a hygienist, who cleans teeth, takes and develops x-rays, applies fluoride and sealant, and educates patients; a dental assistant, who prepares patients and works alongside the dentist; or the dentist, who fills cavities, prepares crowns, and evaluates overall dental health, you must work with a variety of tools and interact with patients who may be more than a little bit nervous. For certain tasks, you work as part of a team, so communication and cooperative work patterns are essential.

Out-of-the-box angles

Great opportunities for flexible work schedules exist in this occupation, as part-time and alternative shifts are available. If you prefer to be self-employed, consider becoming a dental laboratory technician.

Other intriguing options

Woodworking: Convert your love of working with your hands, your sense of design, and your precise nature into a woodworking career, such as cabinet making, furniture making, milling, boat building, finishing, musical instrument building, carving, or framing. For more information, contact The Cabinet Makers Association: www.cabinetmakers.org; 6551 City West Parkway; Eden Prairie, MN 55344; 952-947-9705.

Tailoring: Whether you make suits, evening gowns, or hats, your ability to fashion fabric into beautifully finished pieces is your gift. For more information, contact the National Association of Milliners, Dressmakers, and Tailors: 157 West 126th Street, New York, NY 10027; 212-666-1320.

The demand for hygienists is expected to grow, making it one of the fastest-growing occupations around. The expected growth is due to more and more people retaining their original teeth and younger dentists delegating more tasks to hygienists and dental assistants.

Related jobs and specialties

Dental hygienist, dental assistant, dentist, oral surgeon, dental technician, dental laboratory technician, dental ceramist, orthotics technician, prosthetics technician, optician, ophthalmic laboratory technician.

Where to go from here

American Dental Hygienists' Association: www.adha.org; mail@adha.net; 444 North Michigan Avenue, Suite 3400, Chicago, IL 60611; 312-440-8900.

Working with Your Hands

For some people who like to work with their hands, precision work is too meticulous and intricate. They prefer working on a larger scale, repairing, building, or creating objects of various forms.

If you have any of the following skills or interests, one of the careers in this section may intrigue you.

Creating with hands – large scale	Good sense of timing	Using body in complicated ways to accomplish goals
Creating with hands – medium scale	Quick response time	
Eye-hand coordination	Sign language	

Equipment repair

Combine your ability to work with your hands, your knowledge of electronics, and your passion for troubleshooting to repair electronic and mechanical equipment. When a machine goes down, you arrive in a timely manner, assess what is wrong, and make repairs on the spot or in the shop by replacing the defective parts, resetting the machine, or reinstalling new parts or software. To perform your work, you use a variety of diagnostic and repair tools.

Out-of-the-box angles

As more and more businesses and individuals depend on computers and computerized equipment for productivity and entertainment, they increasingly need immediate, high-quality repair service. With the right skills and experience, you can set up your own shop or travel to your customer's site to meet their needs.

Alternative schedules are available, as your services are needed 24 hours, 7 days a week. Be prepared. If you work for a computer-repair service, shifts may be assigned according to your tenure in the job.

Related jobs and specialties

Computer repairer (see Chapter 9), bench technician, automated teller machine repairer, office machine repairer, electronic home entertainment equipment repairer, telecommunications equipment mechanic, installer, commercial and industrial repairer, automotive repairer, engine repairer, home appliance repairer, mechanic, aircraft mechanic, aircraft service technician, line installer, line repairer.

Where to go from here

Electronics Technician Association: www.eta-sda.com; eta@tds.net; 502 North Jackson, Greencastle, IN 46135; 765-653-4301; 765-653-4287.

Other intriguing options

Musical instrument repair: Combine your knowledge of music and musical instruments and your ability to work with your hands to repair musical instruments. Choose a specialty in percussion, strings, winds, brass, pianos, or pipe organs. A fine home-based business idea. For more information, contact the Piano Technicians Guild: www.ptg.org; ptg@ptg.org; 3930 Washington Street, Kansas City, MO 64111-2963; 816-753-7747; Fax: 816-531-0070.

Massage therapy: Eliminate your clients' aches and pains with a soothing, restorative massage using your hands. For more information, contact the American Massage Therapy Association: www.amtamassage.org; 820 Davis Street, Suite 100, Evanston, IL 60201-4444; 847-864-0123; Fax: 847-864-1178.

Culinary work

Chefs train hard and work long, unusual hours under considerable pressure to do what they love best, which is to create aesthetically-pleasing dishes that provide their patrons with unique eating experiences. Having endurance, an eye for detail and design, a keen sense of taste and smell, and the dexterity to work effectively with kitchen tools and food are essential to success in your trade. While you learn to cook, spend time honing your ability to create as a member of a team; anywhere you work, your success depends on others, and their success depends on you.

Out-of-the-box angles

Specialization is a key to success in this field, whether you are known for pastries, regional cuisine, or a style of entrée.

Before you think of launching your own restaurant, get experience, build a name for yourself, and create a concisely-worded description of your vision that you can present to financiers.

In the early years, consider augmenting this career with another source of income; many chefs work unusual and part-time hours to start.

The restaurant industry is expected to grow more than 20 percent over the next ten years as Baby Boomers retire and the number of busy, dual-career families grows.

Related jobs and specialties

Chef, baker, pastry creator, pastry chef, specialty food producer, preparation chef, assistant chef, short-order cook, baker, industrial baker, institutional chef, caterer.

Where to go from here
American Culinary Federation: www.acfchefs.org; acf@acfchefs.net;
10 San Bartola Avenue, St. Augustine, FL 32085; 800-624-9458, 904-824-4468;
Fax: 904-825-4758.

Working with Your Body

Some careers require you to throw your entire body into the job. Although
the work tends to be strenuous, the personal satisfaction of seeing what
you've created is great.

If you have any of the following skills or interests, one of the careers in this
section may intrigue you.

Agility	Eye-hand coordination	Natural sense of how your body moves
Aware of body sensations when active in other ways	Flexibility	Physical exercise
Balance	Good sense of timing	Quick response time
Endurance	Internal body map	Sports games
Eye-foot coordination	Martial arts	Using body in complicated way to accomplish goals

Construction

Whether you are framing a house, installing the electrical or plumbing system
in an office, or roofing a commercial building, you must be fit enough in mind
and body to handle the strenuous work and perform precision tasks accurately. Your ability to read blueprints, use your knowledge of construction to
come up with sound, workable solutions on the fly, and work safely contribute to your success. Because any construction project is a team effort,
taking directions well and working cooperatively are essential.

Out-of-the-box angles

Depending on the specific trade you choose, intermittent, seasonal work is a possibility. Use your creativity to find several niches that help even out the dips in employment during the year.

Demand for your specialty may depend on any number of factors. Do research to discover ways that you can capitalize on trends within the trades. For example, more and more electricians now step beyond residential construction to install robots and automated manufacturing systems, or specialize in pre-wiring residential homes for computers and entertainment systems.

Due to a decrease in the number of people training to work as plumbers and pipefitters, experts expect a shortage of skilled workers in these fields. If you gain the skills, you may be highly employable.

Related jobs and specialties

Plumber, electrician, mechanic, carpenter (see Chapter 11), steeplejack, bricklayer, sheet metal worker, elevator installer, millwright, boilermaker, carpenter, stonemason, carpet installer, floor finisher, cement mason, drywall installer, drywall finisher, glazier, insulation worker, painter, framer, structural carpenter, paperhanger, plasterer, stucco mason, roofer, structural and reinforcing metal worker, detail carpenter, security system installer.

Where to go from here

National Electrical Contractors Association: www.necanet.org; 3 Bethesda Metro Center, Suite 1100, Bethesda, MD 20814; 301-657-3110; Fax: 301-215-4500.

Training and coaching

Use your fitness experience and knowledge of your sport, your understanding of how the body functions, and your enthusiastic nature to help your clients and class participants become more fit. Depending on your interests, you may specialize in some combination of weight training, assessing fitness, or consulting on weight management and general lifestyle issues. You must be able to explain in very specific terms how your clients can improve their form. Helping them articulate their goals and keeping them motivated are also key skills in this work.

Out-of-the-box angles

In this field you can specialize in supporting a specific population, such as children, seniors, pre- and post-natal women, or rehab patients, or focus on training people in a particular kind of exercise, such as yoga, water aerobics, step, kickboxing, cycling, or strength training. Training in several related specialties allows you to reach more clients and increases your chances for success.

Various employment arrangements are available, from working in-house at a fitness or rehabilitation center to working solo in people's homes. Choose the format that works with your life and goals.

Related jobs and specialties

Personal trainer, yoga instructor, aerobics instructor, physical education teacher, group fitness instructor, clinical exercise specialist, fitness aide, exercise physiologist, athletic trainer, outdoor exercise leader, physical therapist (see Chapter 10), lifestyle and weight management consultant, coach.

Where to go from here

American Fitness Professionals & Associates; www.afpafitness.com; afpa@ afpafitness.com; P.O. Box 214; Ship Bottom, NJ 08008; 609-978-7583.

Firefighting

If you can keep your mental and physical edge while vacillating between the extreme adrenaline rush of an emergency and the ultimate boredom of a day with no alarms, you may succeed as a firefighter. You must perform physically strenuous tasks during long shifts under potentially dangerous working conditions, all the while thinking decisively enough to protect people and their property from risk. You must be a team player; your life and the lives of those around you depend on it.

Out-of-the-box angles

If you want to break into the field, move to a fast-growing area; an increasing population is the best indicator of future fire department expansions.

Technological advances and new techniques are always on the horizon. Keep your skills up-to-date by attending seminars and conferences.

Related jobs and specialties

Firefighter, fire marshal, fire investigator, fire captain, fire safety consultant, firefighter academy instructor, paramedic, EMT (see Chapter 10), police officer, guard (see Chapter 10).

Where to go from here

International Association of Firefighters: www.iaff.org; 1750 New York Avenue, NW, Washington, D.C. 20006; 202-737-8484; Fax: 202-737-8418.

Creating with Your Body

If your body is your instrument of creativity, consider exploring the careers I describe in this section.

If you have any of the following skills or interests, one of the careers in this section may intrigue you.

Agility	Expressive or creative dance	Mimicking
Aware of body sensations when active in other ways	Eye-foot coordination	Mind/body connection
Balance	Eye-hand coordination	Movement to music
Body language	Flexibility	Natural sense of how your body moves
Choreography	Folk/creative dance	Quick response time
Drama	Good sense of timing	Role playing
Endurance	Internal body map	Using body in complicated way to accomplish goals
Expressive gestures	Mime	Using body to express yourself

Acting

Use your body and your ability to express emotions, verbally and non-verbally, to entertain and inform your audience. Starting out, you must do what you can to get experience and build a set of favorable reviews. Your hours are long and irregular, and you may need to travel to film locations or to perform on the road, which requires a great deal of stamina. Through it all, you need talent, creativity, the ability to transform yourself into a character, and a degree of stage presence.

Out-of-the-box angles

Although training and formal education may help your chances of success, auditioning for paid and unpaid parts in local, low-budget productions and commercials are probably your best bet to get you started. Commercials accounted for over half the revenue for actors this year.

A number of factors indicate a growing demand for actors, including a rising demand for films in foreign markets, the growth in cable, satellite, syndicated television, and music videos, and the desire of the public to see more live performances.

As your career advances, consider hiring agents and managers to help you find work and negotiate your contracts.

Related jobs and specialties

Actor, mime, impersonator, look-a-like, clown, comedian, juggler, stunt double, narrator (see Chapter 13), director, acting coach, acting teacher.

Where to go from here

Screen Actors Guild: www.sag.org; 5757 Wilshire Boulevard, Los Angeles, CA 90036.

Dancing

You rely on your body's grace, flexibility, and stamina to allow you to express yourself with movement to music. The practice required to perform is time consuming, physically taxing, and takes discipline and dedication. Whether you perform in theaters, concert halls, amusement parks, music videos, or commercials, you work with a choreographer and other performers to achieve the desired effect. Due to the nature of the field, rejection and periods of unemployment are part of daily life in dancing.

Out-of-the-box angles

Consider creating a composite career that allows you to bring in money in the down times, while giving you the flexibility you need to practice and perform.

Dance is becoming more popular with the general public, so explore teaching opportunities.

Related jobs and specialties

Dancer, choreographer, dance instructor, artistic director, dance coach, expressive dancer, dance therapist, movement therapist (see Chapter 10), dance critic (see Chapter 8), ice skater.

Where to go from here

National Dance Association: www.aahperd.org/nda/nda-main.html; nda@ aahperd.org; 1900 Association Drive, Reston, VA 20191; 703-476-3400; 800-213-7193.

Chapter 13

If You Have an Ear for the Sound of Music

● ●

In This Chapter

▶ Making music for a living

▶ Working with sound

▶ Using your voice to launch your career

● ●

*T*his chapter consists of three sections, each one devoted to a different musical career category. To find out if you are interested in the careers in a particular category, read the introductory paragraph and check out the skills highlighted in the accompanying box (see Chapter 6 for more information on identifying the skills that are important to you). If you aren't intrigued by what you see, skip to another section.

As you read each section, use the out-of-the-box angles and the related jobs and specialties to spark new ideas about how you can implement your own career ideas.

When you see an idea that may work for you, circle it, star it, or record it in your journal for later review.

Making Music

If you can compose or perform music, or help others do so, bring music into your career and the lives of others by exploring the career ideas in this section.

If you have any of the following skills or interests, one of the careers in this section may intrigue you.

Actively listening to music	Improvising	Pick up beat easily
Arranging	Intervals	Sensing tonal qualities
Composing	Keeping time	Tonal patterns

Playing an instrument

Although your musical abilities may not guarantee fame, they are an essential component of your success in the music industry. Although some musicians make a living using their music as a form of self-expression, most musicians perform to the specifications set out by a conductor, director, or producer. Practicing, sight-reading music, and taking musical direction are essential to your success.

In many careers, establishing a defined niche or specialty ensures success, but for musicians, versatility is the key. The more musical styles and instruments you can play, the better your chances of getting work.

Out-of-the-box angles

A good way to pull in a reliable salary as a musician is to align yourself with a religious organization. Two out of three musicians work for such organizations.

To soften the financial ups and downs of intermittent employment, round out your income base by creating a composite career using other aspects of your musical talent, such as teaching or copying music.

New, affordable, high-quality electronic instruments and audio visual equipment make it possible for up-and-coming musicians to make their mark with exceptional sound. Do what you can to gain access to electronic equipment so that you can build the experience you need to succeed.

A number of new distribution channels also make it easier for you to succeed in the music business. Watch for new independent labels and cable music stations — they are multiplying constantly.

Related jobs and specialties

Instrumentalist, background musician, studio musician, freelance musician, back-up musician, orchestra member, instrumental soloist, session musician, general business musician, floor show band member, rehearsal pianist, accompanist, theater musician, church organist, section member, classical musician, piano tuner, instrument repair (see Chapter 12).

Where to go from here

American Federation of Musicians: www.afm.org; join@afm.org; 1501 Broadway, Suite 600, New York, NY 10036; 212-869-1330; 212-764-6134.

Teaching music

You help students create music of their own. You may focus on music theory and history, arranging, or performance. The specifics of what you teach depend on the age and skill level of your students as well as the education guidelines specified by the institution that pays your salary.

In addition to teaching students, you may be responsible for planning concerts, parades, music festivals, or recitals. Creativity and innovative teaching methods bring results and an air of excitement to each session.

Out-of-the-box angles

If you are a musician by trade, teaching music can be a good addition to your composite career (see the preceding section for more information on being a musician).

If you want to be a self-employed music instructor, build a relationship with a music store by sponsoring an event, posting your card, and teaching classes. Doing so adds to your credibility and increases your visibility in the community.

Related jobs and specialties

Private music instructor, elementary school music teacher, secondary school music teacher, college or university music professor, conservatory professor, choir director, music supervisor, music department head.

Where to go from here

Music Teachers National Association: www.mtna.org; mtnanet@mtna.org; The Carew Tower, 441 Vine Street, Suite 505, Cincinnati, OH 45202-2814; 513-421-1420.

Music therapy

Combine your love of music with counseling skills to help people of all ages navigate a variety of life situations, including rehabilitation, age-related disorders, and physical, mental, and emotional disabilities. By encouraging clients to write, create, and listen to music, you assist them in enhancing their self-esteem and developing key motor skills, life skills, and socialization skills.

Other intriguing options

Composing: Use your musical training and talent to write original music for any purpose, from jingles and songs to symphonies and movie scores. You may create with an instrument or computer keyboard in hand. For more information, contact The American Society of Composers, Authors, and Publishers: `www.ascap.com`; `info@ascap.com`; One Lincoln Plaza, New York, NY 10023; 212-621-6000.

Conducting: Channel your musical talents to help a choir, band, or orchestra produce their finest performance. Your tasks include auditioning and selecting musicians, choosing the music to be performed, planning the performance details, and directing the musicians during the performance. For more information,

contact The American Choral Directors Association: `www.acdaonline.org`; `acda@acdaonline.org`; 502 SW 38th Street, Lawton, OK 73505; 580-355-8161; Fax: 580-248-1465.

Copying: Use your knowledge of music and music theory and your extreme attention to detail to transcribe a full musical score into sheet music for individual parts. Being a copyist is a great addition to a musically-focused composite career. For more information, contact the American Society of Music Copyists: `http://members.aol.com/asmc802/home.htm`; `asmc802@aol.com`; P.O. Box 2557, Times Square Station, New York, NY 10108; 212-246-0488.

To support clients, most music therapists work as part of an interdisciplinary team, which includes medical professionals, teachers, therapists, and the patient's family.

Out-of-the-box angles

A vast number of niches exist within this profession, including the following:

- ✔ **Setting:** Focus on working in schools, hospitals, correctional facilities, rehabilitation units, mental health agencies, or geriatric environments.

- ✔ **Population:** Concentrate on working with the elderly, adults, adolescents, or children.

- ✔ **Condition:** Specialize in a variety of conditions, including psychiatric disorders, pain management, stress reduction, mental and physical disabilities, labor and delivery, grief, post traumatic stress disorder, or substance abuse.

Good self-employment possibilities exist that allow for flex-time and flex-place work.

Related jobs and specialties

Music therapist, music therapy consultant, music therapy supervisor, art therapist, drama therapist, creative arts therapist, dance therapist, occupational therapist, audiologist, speech pathologist (see Chapter 10).

Where to go from here

American Music Therapy Association: www.musictheraphy.org; info@musictherapy.org; 8455 Colesville Road, Suite 1000, Silver Springs, MD 20910; 301-589-3300; Fax: 301-589-5175.

Enhancing and Appreciating Sound and Music

If you enjoy music and have a good ear for it, but are not cut out to be a musician yourself, consider using your talents to enhance the music others create. In the following careers, you play an important role in getting high-quality music to those who enjoy it.

If you have any of the following skills or interests, one of the careers in this section may intrigue you.

Arranging	Keeping time	Tonal patterns
Improvising	Pick up beat easily	
Intervals	Sensing qualities of a tone	

Live performance

As a sound technician for live performances or broadcasts, you make the musicians and performers sound great by blending the voices and music to create a pleasing, balanced sound. Your ear for sound, your knowledge of acoustics and the venue, and your ability to identify solutions to eliminate problems on the spot lead to your success.

For a successful career, you must understand the traditional tools of the trade as well as the latest analog and digital technologies. Clearly, an aptitude for working with electronic equipment is a plus!

Out-of-the-box angles

As a sound technician for a traveling show, you have the ultimate flex-place position with very short stints in all sorts of locations. Think carefully about your ability to live with this lifestyle.

Alternative schedules are the norm in this career, because most radio and television stations are on the air 24 hours, 7 days a week, and most theater and film work takes place on tight, project-dependent deadlines.

Growth in the cable industry and enhancements to Internet access mean an increased demand for audio programming.

Related jobs and specialties

Audio technician, broadcast engineer, live sound reinforcement engineer, location recording engineer, sound technician, sound designer, assistant engineer, audio control engineer, touring technician, resident sound technician.

Where to go from here

Audio Engineering Society (AES): www.aes.org; HQ@aes.org; 60 East 42nd Street, Room 2520, New York, NY 10165-2520; 212-661-8528; Fax: 212-682-0477.

Recording

You record tracks for CDs, films, television shows, and other media according to specifications set by the producers and artists. For films or television, you re-record numerous tracks of dialogue, music, sound effects, foley, and narration, adjusting the volume and balance while also producing fade-ins and fade-outs. Clear communication and accurate artistic translation of the client's vision are the name of the game. Your hours in the studio may vary, possibly for long stretches at a time. Endurance and the ability to work under pressure are key attributes in this career.

Out-of-the-box angles

Technological advances in equipment and recording and distribution media mean that you must stay on your toes to keep up with the ever-changing technical side of your work. Read trade journals, attend conferences, and keep track of enhancements to equipment. When you get the chance, practice using cutting-edge equipment.

After you have a good reputation and considerable experience, going freelance is a distinct possibility in this field. Word of mouth spread through your network helps produce a flow of clients.

Related jobs and specialties

Audio engineer, audio specialist, sound mixer, music mixer, re-recording mixer, re-recording engineer, digital audio editor, post-production engineer, digital remastering engineer, audio engineer for video, sound FX editor, dialogue editor, foley artist (see the following sidebar).

Other intriguing options

Foleying: You use your acute sense of hearing and your creativity to create or enhance incidental sounds in movies. Your work provides the audience with a rich, realistic experience at the movies. For more information, contact The Cinema Audio Society: CinAudSo@aol.com; 12414 Huston Street, Valley Village, CA 91607; Fax: 818-752-8624.

Music journalism: If you are a writer and are knowledgeable about the music industry, combine your talents as a music journalist. In addition to writing reviews of live performances, you may interview bands or write a regular column about the music scene. For more information, contact the Music Critics Association: www.musiccritics.org; info@musiccritics.org; 818-766-0443.

Music sales: You love music, but don't have the talent to perform. Don't give up — consider a career in music sales, instead! Sell music, records, or instruments to bring music into people's lives. For more information, contact the National Association of Recording Merchandisers: www.narm.com; 9 Eves Drive, Suite 120, Marlton, NJ 08053; 609-596-2221; Fax: 609-596-3268.

Management: Whether you are a business manager, booking agent, club manager, artist and repertoire (A&R) coordinator, or studio manager, your knowledge of music, combined with your ability to organize and manage, can mean success in the business side of the music industry. For more information, contact the National Conference of Personal Managers: www.ncopm.com; 46-19 220 Place, Bayside, NY 11361.

Where to go from here

Society of Professional Audio Recording Services: www.spars.com; spars'ars.com; 364 Clove Drive, Memphis, TN 38117-4009; 901-821-9111, 800-771-7727; Fax: 901-682-9177.

Producing

If you know a hit song when you hear one, you may have a future as a record producer. As a producer, you take raw talent and make the necessary decisions and choices to produce a well-arranged, well-recorded hit. If you don't have the technical skills to create the recording yourself, you must communicate with the engineer to articulate the feeling and sound you desire. Aside from the creative side of producing, you also manage the business side of the equation. That means bringing the project in on time, within budget, and with as few personal disputes and technological problems as possible.

Out-of-the-box angles

Although some producers are employed by record companies, others work as freelancers, hired by either the artist or the record label. As a producer, you can expect to earn a salary and negotiated royalties on the projects you produce.

Related jobs and specialties

Record producer, radio producer, film producer, television producer, synthesist, music executive, independent producer, staff producer, production coordinator, MIDI pre-producer, talent scout.

Where to go from here

National Academy of Recording Arts and Sciences: 3402 Pico Boulevard, Santa Monica, CA 90405; 310-392-3777; Fax: 310-399-3090.

Using Your Voice

If you have a wonderful singing or speaking voice, you can use your voice as the cornerstone of your career. Consider the careers that I describe in this section.

If you have any of the following skills or interests, one of the careers in this section may intrigue you.

Blending	Perfect pitch	Remembering melody
Good singing voice	Relative pitch	Singing melody
Harmonizing	Remembering lyrics	Vocal sounds/tones

Singing

By mixing your vocal talent with determination and perseverance, you can create a viable singing career. To do so, you must have a versatile voice, be able to sing any style of music, have the ability to sight read, and exude confidence while performing. The key to success is building a reputation for excellence and dependability. As with most music careers, the hours are irregular, and travel is frequent.

Out-of-the-box angles

Even if you were born with a great singing voice, invest in a voice coach who can instill good habits that enable you to have a life-long singing career.

Although a lucky few have full-time jobs, most vocalists are freelancers who work through agents to audition for jobs. Many vocalists make singing part of a composite career, which lets them stabilize their income while still allowing them to utilize their greatest asset.

Related jobs and specialties

Performing artist, recording artist, singer, vocal soloist, rock star, opera singer, background vocalist, back up singer, jingle singer, studio singer, studio vocalist, choir member, cantor, church soloist.

Where to go from here

American Guild of Musical Artists: 1727 Broadway, New York, NY 10019; 212-265-3687; Fax: 212-262-9088.

Voiceover

Combine your voice, sense of timing, and acting ability to do voiceovers for television, radio, cartoons, and non-broadcast, industrial narration. To excel in this profession, you must modify the tone, pacing, and quality of your voice on command.

Out-of-the-box angles

The money you spend to have your own voice coach is a worthwhile investment. Just as actors and singers continue their training throughout their careers, with a coach you can continue to enhance your skills, which helps you land bigger and better assignments.

Your demo tape is your entry pass into this field. You must make the best impression possible when potential employers hear your tape. Invest as much as you can to have your tape professionally produced.

Although you can build a career by connecting with an agent and paying her 10 to 15 percent of your paycheck for each job, you can also build your own business by sending out demo tapes, following up by phone, negotiating your own deals, and building repeat business.

Doing voiceovers can be a good element of a composite career as long as your other work allows you the flexibility to attend auditions and taping sessions.

Other intriguing options

Voice coaching: Use your finely-tuned ear to help actors, singers, speakers, and other professionals strengthen and develop their voices for artistic and professional uses. For more information, contact the Voice and Speech Trainers Association: www.vasta.org.

Related jobs and specialties

Voiceover talent, actor, cartoon voice, radio announcer, narrator, master of ceremonies.

Where to go from here

Great Voice: www.greatvoice.com; info@greatvoice.com; 616 East Palisade Avenue, Englewood Cliffs, NJ 07632; 800-333-8108; Fax: 201-541-8608.

Chapter 14

If You Love Nature and Its Creatures

In This Chapter

▶ Discovering work that taps your green thumb

▶ Connecting with careers that connect you with animals

▶ Finding careers to aid the earth itself

*I*f you enjoy being outdoors, studying nature, and preserving the environment, you may be intrigued by the career ideas that I include in this chapter.

For the most part, all of the career ideas listed in this chapter rely on several common skills:

- ✔ Picking up nuances between large numbers of similar objects
- ✔ Discriminating among living things, such as plants and animals
- ✔ Discerning patterns of life
- ✔ Examining things in nature
- ✔ Using scientific equipment to observe nature
- ✔ Being sensitive to formations in nature
- ✔ Keeping detailed records of observations
- ✔ Creating hierarchies that make sense
- ✔ Classifying things into hierarchies

What differs in the careers in this chapter is whether you apply your skills to plants, animals, or the earth as a whole.

Use the description of each career idea as a launch pad for exploration and creative thinking. Pay close attention to the out-of-the-box angles and the related jobs and specialties; ideas in these sections may help you expand how you think about your career ideas.

Working with Plants

If you have a green thumb, you no doubt know it. Plants grow and flourish in your care. The career ideas in this section help you use your talent and knowledge in a variety of ways.

If you have any of the following skills or interests, one of the careers in this section may intrigue you.

Collecting	Organizing collections	Plant identification
Labeling collections	Plant Care	

Botany

As someone who understands and is fascinated by plants and their functions, you have a wide variety of careers to choose from. Perhaps you are interested in discovering new plants, classifying plants, keeping plants healthy, or understanding how plants work.

Depending on your specialty, you may work outside or in a laboratory conducting research for universities or institutes. Your ability to observe, classify, and ask good questions makes you a valuable researcher in your field.

Out-of-the-box angles

Biotechnical advancements are the cutting edge in this field. Although still somewhat controversial, genetically altering crops may produce a demand for scientists for some time.

Your knowledge puts you in a good position to address issues related to the global food-supply by improving crop yields and minimizing the effects of stresses such as drought and pests on crops.

As the push to preserve the environment takes hold, botanists are needed to evaluate lands and create plans to preserve and restore existing plant life.

Related jobs and specialties

Botanist, agricultural scientist, agricultural engineer, agricultural chemist, food chemist, plant breeding technician, seed technologist, agriculture technologist, botanical technician, food bacteriological technician, food product technologist, crop scientist, agronomist, genetic engineer, plant taxonomist, plant explorer, plant collector, research ethnobotanist, international sourcing specialist, plant pathologist, biochemist.

Where to go from here

Botanical Society of America: www.botany.org; hiser.3@osu.edu; 1735 Neil Avenue, Columbus, OH 43210-1293; 614-292-3519; Fax: 614-247-6444.

Growing plants

If you want to live close to the land and have a hands-on business, growing plants may serve you well. Do your research to find a crop that flourishes in your climate and then identify the growing methods that can maximize your production. Your knowledge of plants, your ability to track your business, and your hard work contribute to your success.

Out-of-the-box angles

The majority of people in this career are self-employed. The work tends to be seasonal, so combine this work with other jobs to create a viable composite career. (Chapter 7 tells you more about composite careers.)

If you are looking for a viable small business, consider using your green thumb to grow herbs, orchids, or organic produce to meet the needs of specialty markets.

As the number of parks and recreation areas increase, you may find work as a horticulture technician working to enhance and beautify private or public lands. To boost your employability in this area, focus on a specialty such as floriculture, nursery operations, arboriculture, or turf care.

Related jobs and specialties

Farmer, farm manager, horticulturist, horticulture technician, hydroponics farmer, organic farmer, nursery owner, nursery worker, greenhouse worker, nursery manager, farm labor contractor, farm crew leader, farm manager, hydroponics technician, holiday tree farm operator, flower grower, garden center owner, vineyard manager, viticulturist, forest seedling grower, hothouse worker, herb grower, orchid grower, bonsai grower, landscaper (see the following sidebar).

Where to go from here

American Society for Horticulture Science: www.ashs.org; webmaster@ ashs.org; 113 South West Street, Suite 200, Alexandria, VA 22314-2851; 703-836-4606; Fax: 703-836-2024.

Designing landscapes

By becoming a landscape architect, you have a unique opportunity to combine your love of nature, your creative sense, your communication skills, and your ability to work with your hands. Each project, which follows the same basic process, begins by assessing the soil, sunlight, water, drainage, and slope of the property, while gaining a clear understanding of the purpose and needs for the site. After analyzing the information, you create a preliminary design and present it to your clients for review.

As with architecture, your ability to accurately articulate your vision is crucial to your success. While you rework and refine your design, you keep close contact with other professionals working on the project, which may include surveyors, architects, and contractors, to ensure that your design fits the overall plan. As a landscape designer, you may or may not participate in the actual construction of your design.

Out-of-the-box angles

Although most landscape designers created their plans by hand in the past, the technological revolution has provided a new set of useful tools for the job: computer-aided design, geographic information systems, computer mapping, and video simulation of plans. Skilled use of these tools gives you more employment opportunities.

A growing concern for the environment and the increased need for developers to meet environmental regulations means an increased demand for environmentally-sound designs. You can help meet this need by taking on projects such as preserving historic sites, conserving natural resources, reclaiming land, planning wildlife parks, refuges, and recreation parks, and refurbishing sites that already exist.

If you don't want to do pure design work, explore opportunities in regional and urban planning, environmental impact and feasibility research, cost studies, or site construction.

Forty percent of landscape architects are self-employed, and most others work for fairly small design firms.

Related jobs and specialties

Landscape architect, landscape designer, interiorscaper, landscape consultant, landscape architectural technician, environmental planner, urban planner, intern landscape architect, architect (see Chapter 11).

Where to go from here

American Society of Landscape Architects: www.asla.org; 636 Eye Street, NW, Washington, D.C. 20001; 202-898-2444; Fax: 202-898-1185.

Other intriguing options

Landscaping: Use your knowledge of plants to maintain parks and recreation facilities or to help others enhance and maintain the beauty and value of their surroundings. Because landscaping is seasonal and dependent on weather conditions, consider this job as part of a composite career or as a viable part-time job. For more information, contact the Associated Landscape Contractors of America: www.alca.org; webmaster@alca.org; 150 Elden Street, Suite 270, Herndon, VA 20170; 703-736-9666; 800-395-2522; Fax: 703-736-9668.

Horticultural therapy: Combine your love and knowledge of plants and gardening with your psychological background to help people who are disabled or disadvantaged gain confidence, motor skills, and social-interaction skills by working as a team to grow a garden. For more information, contact the American Horticultural Therapy Association: www.ahta.org; ahta@ahta.org; 362A Christopher Avenue,

Gaithersburg, MD 20879; 301-948-3010; 800-634-1603; Fax: 301-869-2397.

Food science: Find ways to improve how food is processed, preserved, stored, and delivered using your understanding of the chemical and microbiological nature of food. For more information, contact the Institute of Food Technologist: www.ift.org; info@ift.org; 221 North LaSalle Street, Suite 300, Chicago, IL 60601-1291; 312-782-8424; Fax: 312-782-8348.

Soil science: Use your knowledge of the chemical, biological, and mineralogical composition of soils to map and classify soils, minimize erosion, or recommend ways to enhance plant growth. For more information, contact the Soil Science Society of America: www.soils.org; 677 South Segoe Road, Madison, WI 53711; 608-273-8095.

Managing forests

You use your knowledge of trees to manage the lands and the resources within the forest by balancing the ecology of the area with the harvest of the trees. Your tasks include maintaining an inventory of the size and variety of trees in the forest, reforesting, directing the harvest, preventing fires, controlling insects and invasive plants, and managing environmental and conservation programs.

To excel at forest management, you must have a solid scientific background, exceptional health and a strong constitution, and good planning and problem-solving skills. Although you may work on your own a fair amount of the time, you also work with a wide variety of people, including landowners, farmers, loggers, government officials, special interest groups, and the general public.

Out-of-the-box angles

Although currently a tight market, the public's interest in environmentally-responsible wood products, environmental issues, and sound land management may increase the demand for this profession.

To do your work, you may be expected to travel frequently to isolated, remote locations.

Related jobs and specialties

Forester, forestry technician, forest worker, forestry professional, range manager, range conservationist, range ecologist, range scientist, appraisal forester, consulting forester, district forester, forest engineer, forestry inventory officer, forest economist, forest operations manager, forestry technologist, forestry technician, forestry worker, forest survey technician, silviculture technician, silviculture worker, cruising technician, fire suppression officer, forest fire fighter, range manager.

Where to go from here

Society of American Foresters: www.safnet.org; 5400 Grosvenor Lane, Bethesda, MD 20814; 301-897-8720; Fax: 301-897-3690.

Working with Animals

Whether you work with pets, farm animals, wild animals in captivity, or animals in their native habitats, you want to strengthen your connection with the animal kingdom. The careers in this section give you the opportunity to do so.

If you have any of the following skills or interests, one of the careers in this section may intrigue you.

Aware of animal needs	Interacting with living creatures	Pattern recognition
Characteristics of animals	Labeling collections	Understanding animal behavior
Collecting	Organizing collections	

Zoology

You observe animals in their natural setting, conduct experiments in a controlled setting, or dissect animal specimens to gain a thorough understanding of how animals function, why they behave as they do, where they came from, and what sort of habitat they need to thrive.

Library Resource Center
Renton Technical College
3000 N.E. 4th St.
Renton, WA 98056

For this career, basic research skills in observation, experimentation, and analysis create a strong foundation for future career growth.

Out-of-the-box angles

Launch your career with a broad education in zoology and then specialize on a specific species or topic area that intrigues you. By creating a depth of knowledge in a certain topic, you improve your employability.

Your greatest employment opportunities are with educational institutions, museums, zoos, and governmental agencies. Working as a volunteer, intern, or apprentice can help you get your foot in the door. To work independently on projects in these organizations, you must have a doctorate.

Related jobs and specialties

Zoologist, animal biologist, marine biologist, aquatic biologist, limnologist, wildlife biologist, fishery biologist, endangered species biologist, herpetologist, mammalogist, carcinologist, morphologist, ichthyologist, ornithologist, physiologist, developmental scientist, biology technician.

Where to go from here

Society for Integrative and Comparative Biology: www.sicb.org; SICB@BurkInc.com; 1313 Dolly Madison Boulevard, Suite 402, McLean, VA 22101; 703-790-1745.

Training animals

Combine your love of animals with your patient nature to help animals learn new behaviors. To succeed in this work, you must enjoy working with and being around animals as you spend much of your time repeatedly training, rewarding, and caring for your charges. Your specific working conditions depend on the animals you train.

Out-of-the-box angles

Numerous niches exist in this profession, including training animals for entertainment purposes, protection, service, show, law enforcement, or rescue operations.

With the appropriate on-the-job training, or a stint as an apprentice, this career can provide good self-employment opportunities.

Related jobs and specialties

Animal trainer, animal keeper, animal behaviorist, canine handler, pet therapist, professional handler, obedience instructor, show judge, canine police

Library Resource Center
Renton Technical College
3000 N.E. 4th St.
Renton, WA. 98056

officer, termite dog trainer, drug dog trainer, exotic animal handler, search and rescue dog trainer, horse trainer, companion pet trainer, race horse trainer, marine mammal trainer, snake handler, jockey, circus trainer.

Where to go from here

The Professional Handlers' Association: `www.infodog.com/misc/pha/phainfo.htm`; 17017 Norbrook Drive, Onley, MD 20832; 301-924-0089.

Caring for animals

If you want to spend your days surrounded by animals, you may find caretaking of interest. Although you can expect strenuous, long days, you may be rewarded with lots of love and affection from your animal clients. Patience, physical strength, and an even temper are essential for success. By the way, don't forget that communicating with human owners is an inherent part of the package.

Out-of-the-box angles

Look to animal shelters, vet hospitals, vet clinics, stables, labs, zoos, pet stores, aquariums, wildlife management facilities, kennels, and rehabilitation centers as possible places for employment or volunteer experience.

In areas where pet owners are busy working and traveling, pet-walking or pet-sitting companies can produce profits with very little start-up cost.

If you want to build your own business, get your creative juices flowing. Because many people treat their pets as members of the family, they pay for some interesting services. Ideas others have converted into businesses include pet transport, creating pet jackets, rent-a-pet services, doggie camps, doggie day care, and pet cemeteries.

Related jobs and specialties

Groomer, animal caretaker, zookeeper, ranch hand, kennel owner, curator, animal care attendant, pet sitter, dog walker, boarding kennel operator, kennel aide, pet day care owner, zoo manager, animal welfare advocate, animal control officer, pet store owner, animal shelter foreman, stable manager, animal protector.

Where to go from here

National Dog Grooming Association of America: `www.nauticom.net/www/ndga`; `ndga@nauticom.net`; P.O. Box 101, Clark, PA 16113; 724-962-2711; Fax: 724-962-1919.

Healing animals

You combine your love for animals and your ability to sense what they are experiencing with your scientific knowledge to treat the animals in your care. To prepare for your profession, you must undertake extensive training and then devote time to keeping up with constant medical and technological advances. In addition to attending to the health of animals, you also provide support to the people who own the animals, so your bedside manner must calm both the pets and their owners.

Out-of-the-box angles

The vast majority of vets are self-employed. Those who succeed focus some of their attention on mastering the business side of the profession.

If you want to live in a rural area, farm animal vets are in great demand.

Interested in veterinary medicine, but want something besides a private practice? Look at other options, including space medicine, wildlife management, circuses, aquatic animal medicine, zoos, military service, food hygiene and safety, private research firms, and colleges.

Related jobs and specialties

Veterinarian, small animal veterinarian, large animal veterinarian, zoo veterinarian, veterinary dermatologist, veterinarian dentist, veterinary pathologist, veterinary physiologist, veterinary surgeon, exotics veterinary, avian veterinary, vet tech, veterinary assistant, veterinary inspector, animal nutritionist, equine musculoskeletal therapist, movement therapist, perinatologist.

Where to go from here

American Veterinary Medical Association: 1931 North Meacham Road, Suite 100, Schaumburg, IL 60173; 847-925-8070; Fax: 847-925-1329.

Managing wildlife

You tend to the needs of wildlife, both game animals that are harvested for sport or for food and non-game species. Through research and careful data collection, you discover and solve problems for species in your area while striving to maintain the habitat that the species needs to survive.

For the long-term survival of wildlife, you spend a considerable amount of time educating the public about animals and what they need. Understanding scientific details and translating them into entertaining, everyday language that the public can understand is a key talent in your line of work. Depending on your job, you may also spend a considerable amount of time lobbying, testifying, advocating, and creating legislation on the behalf of wildlife.

Out-of-the-box angles

In addition to working for the government, look to conservation agencies, city or county governments, private industry, and teaching institutes for work.

Eighty percent of wildlife lives on private lands, so much of your attention must focus on coordinating efforts with private landowners to insure healthy habitats for wildlife. Your interests may lead you to protect wetlands, assist farmers in finding ways to continue farming their lands, help groups that want to establish a wildlife habitat on their lands, or conduct an ongoing inventory of soil and water quality throughout the country.

Related jobs and specialties

Wildlife expert/manager, wildlife management specialist, game warden, park ranger, game officer, fishery officer, conservation officer, fish and wildlife officer, forest ranger (see the previous section), trail guide, interpretive center docent, wildlife educator, naturalist, wildlife conservationist, fish and wildlife technician, fish hatchery worker, refuge manager, park manager.

Where to go from here

International Association of Fish and Wildlife Agencies: `www.teaming.com/iafwa.htm`; 444 North Capitol Street, NW, Suite 534, Washington, D.C. 20001.

Other intriguing options

Breeding: Use your understanding of animal genetics to breed animals to improve their performance, productivity, or appearance. For more information, contact the National Pet Dealers and Breeders Association: Route 2, Box 40, Humboldt, NE 63876.

Entomology: Control or eliminate insect pests in ways that do not harm the environment. For more information, contact the Entomological Society of America: `www.entsoc.org`; `esa@entsoc.org`; 9301 Annapolis Road, Lanhan, MD 20706; 301-731-4535; 301-731-4538.

Beekeeping: Raise bees to produce honey and pollinate crops that must be fertilized by honey bees to produce a harvest. For more information, contact The American Beekeeping Federation: `www.abfnet.org`; `info@abfnet.org`; P.O. Box 1038, Jesup, GA 31598-1038; 912-427-4233; Fax: 912-427-8447.

Nurturing Nature and the Earth

The earth's systems and resources need management and care, and if you have any of the following skills or interests, one of the careers in this section may intrigue you.

Collecting	Observing natural phenomenon	Sensitive to formations in nature
Keeping detailed records of observations	Organizing collections	
Labeling collections	Pattern recognition	

Working with land and water

Use your scientific expertise and extensive knowledge of geological formations to explore the earth's surface for natural resources (such as water, oil, gas, and minerals), clean up the environment, guide appropriate land use and construction, and predict future earth-changing events.

To do this work well, you must visualize the earth's structure and movements in three dimensions. Although some of your work takes place in an office or laboratory, you also do extensive fieldwork, on land or at sea, anywhere on the surface of the globe. The intense nature of your fieldwork assignments requires stamina, physical strength, and a flexible lifestyle. The upside is that you may be rewarded with longer-than-usual vacations. Because you work as part of a team on nearly all of your projects, you must have the ability to communicate clearly, sometimes in more than one language.

Out-of-the-box angles

Work in this field depends on an intense use of new technology, including global-positioning systems, remote sensing, computer modeling, and digital mapping. To be employable, you must stay current with these advances.

Increased environmental laws mean that companies must hire geologists to comply with the regulations.

To be successful, self-employed consultants to industry or governmental agencies must stay alert to the changing needs of their clients and reposition themselves accordingly.

Related jobs and specialties

Geologist, geophysicist, petroleum geologist, engineering geologist, mineralogist, paleontologist, stratigrapher, glaciologist, volcanologist, geodesist, geomagnetist, seismologist, geochemist, paleomagnetist, environmental geologist, exploration geologist, development geologist, prospecting geologist, sedimentologist, oceanographer, ground water geologist, hydrologist, physical oceanographer, chemical oceanographer, geological oceanographer, geophysical oceanographer, biological oceanographer, groundwater technologist, oceanographic chemist, reservoir engineering technician, water quality engineer.

Where to go from here

Geological Society of America: www.geosociety.org; P.O. Box 9140, Boulder, CO 80301-9140; 303-447-2020; Fax: 303-447-1133.

American Society of Limnology and Oceanography: www.aslo.org; business@aslo.org; 5400 Bosque Boulevard, Suite 680, Waco, TX 76710-4446; 254-399-9635; 800-929-2756; Fax: 254-776-3767.

Ecology

Use your natural science background to understand the interactions between organisms and their environment. Not only do you gain a better understanding of how nature works, you can teach others, help communities solve environmental problems, manage resources, and restore ecosystems in an effective manner.

Your work may include field observation as well as laboratory research. Strong writing and presentation skills, well thought out research methods, and accurate statistical analysis are required in your field. A working knowledge of social sciences, such as geography and economics, can enhance your work.

Out-of-the-box angles

As you search for jobs in this field, you may not find the term "ecologist" in the job titles. Look at the intent and focus of the job to see if it fits your skills and interests.

Your best bet for employment is in private companies, pre-college schools, and non-governmental agencies.

You may be required to write grants to fund your own projects, so honing your grant-writing skills now may well lead to greater employability and job security later.

Related jobs and specialties

Ecologist, environmental consultant, research scientist, environmental planner, field researcher, park naturalist, wildlife specialist, wildlife biologist, forester, natural resource manager, environmental analyst, field ecologist, science specialist, outdoor educator, education coordinator, lobbyist, program manager.

Where to go from here

Ecological Society of America: http://esa.sdsc.edu; esahq@esa.org; 1707 H Street, NW, Suite 400, Washington, D.C. 20006; 202-833-8773; Fax: 202-833-8775.

Working with the weather and air

Your observation, measurement, and computer skills put you in a good position to be a meteorologist, whose primary goals are to observe, understand, analyze, and forecast the weather. Your work guides key decisions, such as when to plant and bring in the harvest, when to start a prescribed burn, when to activate preparations to protect against major weather events, and whether or not to travel by air, sea, or ground transportation.

To excel in this field, you must have strong analytical and mathematical skills, good map-reading skills, and the ability to visualize in three dimensions. As you deepen your understanding of this topic, you may gravitate toward a specialty, such as severe weather, climatology, numeric weather prediction, tropics, or satellite weather.

Out-of-the-box angles

Television and radio weather forecasters account for only an eighth of the positions in the field. Your other options include the following:

✔ Working for the National Weather Service as an operational forecaster gathering and interpreting data to create forecasts on an ongoing basis.

✔ Conducting basic research using observation and computer models to better understand weather and climate phenomenon such as tornadoes, hurricanes, and lightning, which can ultimately lead to better prediction.

✔ Doing applied research to help design aircraft, buildings, and transportation systems that weather storms with less damage.

✔ Applying your understanding of how weather systems disperse pollutants throughout the atmosphere to help determine how to prevent and solve air pollution problems.

This field has good potential for building an interdisciplinary career by combining atmospheric science with other specialties such as astronomy, civil engineering, environmental engineering, electrical engineering, computer science, mathematics, physics, biology, or agriculture.

Specialties include radar, polar, severe weather, tropics, satellite, climatology, atmospheric optics, electricity, and numeric weather prediction.

Related jobs and specialties

Meteorologist, atmospheric scientist, weatherman, atmospheric physicist, climatologist, air quality meteorologist, hydrometeorologist, meteorological technician, climate service technician, aerological technician, climate date processor, climate service specialist, meteorological inspector, weather station officer-in-charge, port meteorological inspector, surface weather observer, avalanche controller, ice service specialist, weather service specialist, climatologic geographer, air quality engineer, noise control specialist, consulting meteorologist.

Where to go from here

American Meteorological Society: `www.ametsoc.org/AMS/amshomepage.cfm`; 45 Beacon Street, Boston, MA 02108-3693; 617-227-2425.

Waste management

Managing waste of all varieties — from household garbage to toxic industrial waste — requires a strong background in the sciences, including geology, chemistry, physics, ecology, or some combination. Whether you work in the field finding and implementing a solution to an ongoing waste problem, cleaning up a recent spill, or working in a governmental agency devoted to waste management, you prepare written statements and give presentations to pitch project proposals and provide status updates. To excel in this field, you must adhere to safety regulations and find your way through government guidelines to make the impact you strive to make.

Out-of-the-box angles

A number of opportunities exist in this profession. Depending on your interests, you may get into reducing waste at the source by redesigning packaging, developing recycling programs and inventing products made from recycled materials, finding safe ways to incinerate waste to create energy, or managing landfills.

Negligence, lack of enforcement of hazardous waste regulations, heightened health concerns, and dwindling disposal sites increase the need for waste management professionals.

If you are willing to take on the risks of working with hazardous materials, job opportunities abound for those with the required training.

Related jobs and specialties

Waste management engineer, asbestos abatement worker, lead abatement worker, decontamination technician, decommissioning and decontamination (D&D) worker, treatment, storage, and disposal (TSD) worker, water and wastewater treatment plant operator, water pollution biologist, environmental engineer, sanitary landfill operator, recycling plant operator, incinerator operator, hazardous material transporter, hazardous waste site worker, emergency responder, environmental toxicologist, industrial hygienist, radioactive waste engineer.

Where to go from here

Air and Waste Management Association: www.awma.org; info@awma.org; One Gateway Center, Third Floor, Pittsburgh, PA 15222; 412-232-3444; Fax: 412-232-3450.

Part IV
Weaving It All Together

The 5th Wave By Rich Tennant

STAND UP COMEDIAN MAKING TRANSITION TO TAX ATTORNEY

"Hey – what's the deal with all these statutes?
Hey – what's the deal with all these books?
Hey – what's the deal with the Bar Exam?
Hey – and what if I don't pass it... ?"

In this part . . .

With a good career idea or two in hand, this part tells you how to investigate your options, blend your ideal vision with the realities of how you live, and identify the training you need. When you are ready to take action, the last two chapters in this part provide guidance on starting your job search and preparing your business.

Chapter 15

Preparing Your Game Plan

- -

In This Chapter

▶ Clarifying your immediate goals

▶ Becoming familiar with your target careers

▶ Building your list of questions about a career

▶ Talking with people about your target career

- -

After you have a good career idea or two (see Parts I through III of this book to help you formulate some ideas), it's time to deepen your understanding of each of them. Having accurate, up-to-date perspectives on your target careers is essential to verifying that the careers match your needs.

Throughout this chapter, you find strategies and resources that you can use to transform your career ideas into a workable plan.

Although you may feel like you have hit pay dirt with one of your career ideas, take the time to verify that your career ideas do in fact fit you and your lifestyle before you launch your job search, accept a job offer, or start a business.

Staying Focused and Up-to-Date on Your Goals

The world is far too complex and changing far too fast to rely solely on written material or one person's opinion about a career. To get an up-to-date picture of a potential career, you need to gather information from a variety of sources and situations.

No matter how you explore your career ideas, keep yourself focused on your goals:

- ✔ **Verify what you think you know.** Sometimes it's tempting to act on your own beliefs about a career or what you've heard without confirming that you have your story straight. Stay conscious and check out the facts before you act. For example, if you assume that you can't make any money doing what you love, you may turn away from an idea that's actually viable. Or if you have heard that working from home is a great option for parents who want to spend more time with their kids, take the time to verify that this set-up actually works for you and your family.

- ✔ **Find out what you know you don't know.** Researching what you don't know is an obvious strategy. The key is to admit what you don't yet know. Dig deep to get the full scoop. As you gather information about the field, pay extra attention to any new information you discover that shows you angles you have not thought of before.

- ✔ **Track down valuable resources.** Always keep your eyes open and your ears tuned to pick up clues about new resources — new books, people, Web sites, businesses, and conferences that could help you in your search. The resource you just happen to hear about in passing may be the one that opens the door to your future.

Familiarizing Yourself with a Career

Before you speak to other people to get their ideas and insights about your target careers, you must spend some time becoming familiar with the field on your own. As you spend time exploring your career ideas, you can:

- ✔ Confirm that each career is what you think it is.

- ✔ Verify that you are interested in pursuing a career after all.

- ✔ Acquaint yourself with pertinent profession-specific terminology, which enhances your credibility as you talk with people about their careers.

- ✔ Determine what information you need to target during your informational interviews with contacts.

Using online career and industry profiles

In the past, you had to go to a library or a career center to find thorough career profiles. With the advent of the Internet, you are just a click away from a number of extremely valuable resources.

The following Web sites provide the best online career and industry profiles. Read the description of each site to discover what information they have in their profiles. You may want to check out several sites to compare and contrast what the various sources say about your target careers:

- ✔ **Occupational Outlook Handbook** (`http://stats.bls.gov/ocohome.htm`): On this site, each career profile includes a description of the nature of the work, working conditions, training and education requirements, job outlook, earnings, related occupations, and sources of additional information. You can access career profiles on this site using an alphabetical index, an occupations index, or the site's search engine.

- ✔ **Wetfeet.com** (`www.wetfeet.com`): Click on the Careers and Industries link to reach the career profiles. Each profile consists of five separate pages: career overview, requirements, job outlook, career tracks, and compensation. Next to each profile is a list of additional resources, including profiles of related jobs, industry profiles, associations, and discussion boards.

- ✔ **Princeton Review** (`www.review.com`): Although primarily a resource for students making decisions about their education, this site has 180 detailed profiles that consist of an unusual mix of information, such as a look at a day in the life of a career, paying your dues, associated careers, past and future of the field, quality of life, statistics about who is in the profession, salary information, what professionals read, movies and books that feature the career, major employers, who you are likely to associate with, and key professional associations. To reach the profiles, click on the Career tab, then click on Find a Career. Enter the name of the career you want to access. The results provide any direct hits and other related possibilities. You must sign up as a member of the site to access these profiles.

- ✔ **Cornell University's Career Zone** (`www.explore.cornell.edu/newcareerzone`): Click on the career cluster that matches your interests to find a list of jobs. Although there may be anywhere from 100 to 600 jobs listed per cluster, you can make the review process more manageable by sorting the jobs by required education or expected wages. Each job profile includes a job description, interests, work activities, tasks, skills, abilities, knowledge, education, school programs, wages, job outlook, and similar jobs. Videos accompany some of the profiles.

Check out the following sites to find discussions, articles, chat rooms, and lists of relevant links associated with certain careers and industries:

- ✔ **About.com** (`http://home.about.com/careers`): If you want to know more about what it is like to be in a particular profession, visit this site. After clicking on your desired career, you find a wide variety of articles, links, discussions, and related sites that the About.com guide has pulled together to give an up-to-date, relevant look at the career area. Take your time surfing this content-rich site to discover the lingo used by members of the occupation.

✔ **Votech Education** (http://votech.about.com/education/votech/): If you want to get a feeling for what it takes to enter a profession, check out this page. Scan the left-hand column for a career category that matches your interests and then click away until you find what you are looking for. Although part of the previous site, About.com, the career discussions on this page tend to focus on what you need to know to get into a career.

Plugging keywords, such as job titles, commonly-used equipment and supplies, or professional awards, into your favorite Internet search engine can lead to additional information about a career, such as the Web site of someone who currently does the work, additional professional groups, informative articles about the profession, resources for the tools and equipment these professionals use in their work, and job boards for future reference.

If your first set of keywords doesn't give you what you want, try another keyword. Sometimes just a slight variation in the words you use in your search can pull up a different set of links.

Using offline resources

The career section of your local bookstore or the reference section in your local library may also have some useful resources to help you gain a more thorough perspective on your career ideas. Look for the following:

✔ *The Occupational Outlook Handbook:* Published by the U.S. Department of Labor, Bureau of Labor Statistics. Provides the same information as their Web site (see the preceding section) but in a book format.

✔ *The Dictionary of Occupational Titles:* Provided by the U.S. Department of Labor, Employment Training Administration. Includes short descriptions of 12,741 occupations, which are organized by occupational categories. Each occupation is also coded according to the work functions performed in each job. If you know from your exploration that you like to work primarily with people, data, or things, paying attention to these codes may expand your horizons.

✔ *The Encyclopedia of Careers and Vocational Guidance:* Compiled by JG Ferguson Publishing Company. Consists of three volumes, each with detailed descriptions of various careers. Each entry includes a definition of the job, its history, the nature of the work, alternative titles and specialties, special requirements and suggestions for entering the field, ways to explore and experience the work, advancement opportunities, the employment outlook, and sources for additional information.

Cool Careers For Dummies, 2nd Edition, by Marty Nemko, published by Hungry Minds, Inc., also offers lots of information about great careers.

Contacting professional associations

Professional associations provide another great source of career information. Whether you visit an association's Web site or send for more information, you gain valuable information about training and education requirements, salary standards, education sources, conferences, and local chapters by connecting with relevant associations.

Check out the associations listed in any of the career profiles you read (see the preceding section) and the associations listed in the descriptions of the career areas included in Chapters 8 through 14.

If you want to search out associations that are more closely related to your target careers, visit the following Web sites:

- ✔ **American Society of Association Executives (http://info.asaenet. org/gateway/OnlineAssocSlist.html):** This search engine allows you to access over 6,000 professional associations. Just type in a word you know is in the name of the association, or select one of the keywords the site provides. From the resulting list of links, click on the most relevant association to go directly to its Web site.

- ✔ **Directory of Associations (www.marketingsource.com/associations):** Access 2,500 business-related associations around the world through this site's search engine or by browsing under particular categories. Web site addresses are listed when available.

If you don't have access to the Internet, or you want to do additional offline research, ask the reference librarian in your local library to direct you to the following resources:

- ✔ *Encyclopedia of Associations:* Published by The Gale Group. Lists 23,000 national and international associations. Each entry provides contact information, a description of the purpose of the organization, its publications and affiliations, and convention information. If you are interested in regional, state, or local organizations, look for the volume dedicated to these groups.

- ✔ *National Trade & Professional Associations Directory:* Compiled by Columbia Books Inc. each year, this index provides information about 7,600 trade associations, professional societies, labor unions, and technical organizations. You can use this book to find contact information and a description of an association even if you only know the acronym, subject area, or location of the organization.

Gathering salary information

Estimating the salary associated with a particular job title is a very complex operation. Generally, your salary depends on a number of factors including your job responsibilities, performance, tenure, training, experience, the company's size, company pay scales, the industry, and your geographic location.

Rather than piecing together a salary estimate on your own or depending on the industry grapevine, use one of the following two Web sites to obtain accurate, reliable salary estimates based on the compilation of salary surveys from various research organizations and government sources:

- **Salary.com** (www.salary.com): In addition to wonderful articles about compensation and benefits, this site's greatest tool is a salary calculator:

  - Choose a job category and enter your zip code, or choose from a list of states and cities.

  - Identify your target job title. If you need more information to make your choice, check out the job descriptions provided for each title.

  - Click on Create Salary Report to see a graph showing the base salary for your area.

  - With one additional click you can see how that salary compares to the national average, to the salary for the same job in a different location, or to a related job in the same location.

- **America's Career InfoNet** (www.acinet.org/acinet/): Click on Wages and Trends and choose a job family or enter a keyword for a specific search. In the next screen, select a specific occupation from the list and highlight your state. The results include a brief description of the job, the wages for the United States and the state you selected, and the employment trends. With just one click you can also see how the salary for a job in your state compares with the salary for the same job in all 50 United States on the basis of median wage or employment-growth trends.

Your best offline resource for researching compensation trends is the *American Salaries and Wages Survey,* published by The Gale Group. This book pulls data from over 300 sources to create geographic-specific salary data for 2,660 occupation classifications and 4,800 individual jobs.

Asking the Right Questions about a Career

After you create a solid overview of your careers of interest (see the previous section), you should have a better idea of what you don't know about each one. At this point in your research, you need to talk with people in the profession to fill in the blanks.

Before you talk with someone about a career, create a list of questions so that you can make the most of your question-and-answer time. As you build your list, hone in on the questions you absolutely must have answers to before you continue your investigation of a career.

If you talk with more than one contact about a career, ask similar questions so that you can compare and contrast what you hear.

As your conversations with your contacts clarify and answer your first set of questions, another layer of unknowns may surface, and then another. For example, your first line of questions may provide more details about a particular flex-time or flex-place arrangement. Later, you may need to know more about the education and training requirements. Finally, you may want to confirm your impression of the industry outlook before you move forward with your search.

At each step in your questioning, you have another opportunity to confirm that the career is a good fit, or to decide that you need to go back to the drawing board, or to come up with a better slant, or to drop the idea entirely.

The following questions provide a starting point as you build your list of questions for an informational interview:

✔ **The profession in general**

- What is the outlook for this profession?

- What training or education is required?

- What sort of advancement possibilities exist?

✔ **A specific job**

- What is your day like?

- What are your key job responsibilities?

- What are your favorite and least favorite parts of your job?

✔ **The industry in general**

- What is the long-term outlook for this industry?

- What is at the cutting edge of this industry?

- What are the pros and cons of working in this industry right now?

✔ **A company and its culture**

- What is the future outlook for this company?

- What are the pluses and minuses of working for this company?

- What is an example of an unwritten policy in this company?

✔ **The business format**

- What is it like working for this kind of company?

- What are the pros and cons of working for a company this size?

- What is it like getting paid this way?

✔ **The form of work**

- What are the pros and cons of your schedule?

- How did you negotiate your flexible work arrangement?

- Did you experience any unexpected surprises when you started this schedule?

✔ **The lifestyle**

- How does this job impact your life?

- How much flexibility do you really have?

- How much travel should I expect?

✔ **The contact's career path**

- How did you get into this field?

- What jobs have you held?

- Do you know anyone who entered this field with my background?

Although you should plan to spend 15 to 20 minutes interviewing any one contact, create a thorough list of questions so that you are prepared if you have the opportunity to talk longer than you expected or you find the person's expertise is slightly different than you expected.

Making Contacts

With a list of questions in hand, you can begin talking with the people who work in the career that you are investigating.

The thought of asking people to talk with you about their professions may be a bit daunting, but in my experience, people are generally happy to talk with you as long as you are genuinely interested in hearing about their work.

Priming the pump

To minimize your own sense of being overwhelmed, start by talking with people you know. Make a list of your:

- ✔ Family and friends
- ✔ Former colleagues
- ✔ Neighbors
- ✔ School friends

Write down as many names as you can. At this early stage, don't worry about whether they know anything about your target field. Instead, focus on whom you know to be well connected.

Choose five people you feel comfortable just calling or e-mailing out of the blue. Set up a time to talk by phone, have coffee, or go for a walk.

Begin by asking them if they know anything about the career you are interested in. If they do, ask the questions you've prepared. In addition to paying attention to their answers, notice how effectively you communicate what you are looking for. These interactions are as much to gain information as they are to practice and polish your spiel. At the end of your interview, ask if they know anyone else you should talk to and how you can contact them.

 Never end an informational interview without asking about additional contacts. This one question allows the size of your network to snowball. You can even be more direct and ask if your contact knows anyone who works in a particular company or is a member of a specific association. You may be surprised whom your friends know!

If your personal network doesn't produce the kinds of contacts you need, consider contacting people through an alumni group, sorority or fraternity, or career center. These groups often offer career networks as part of their services.

Setting up additional informational interviews

When you begin your second round of informational interviews, you may need to talk with people you don't know well or at all. Use the following steps to set up your informational interviews:

1. **Think about the information you still need to know to verify that a career is a good fit.**

   Be clear about your key focus.

2. **Make your initial contact with a letter, an e-mail, or a phone call.**

   Ask your original contacts for permission to use their names in your initial communication with each new contact. If you do need to contact someone cold, be polite, yet persistent. Even if you run into what seems like an endless series of no's, just keep calling on a regular basis. Your perseverance may pay off in the long run.

3. **Follow up with a phone call or e-mail to set up a 15- to 20-minute appointment.**

4. **Conduct your interview either in person or by phone depending on what is most convenient for your contact.**

   When possible, stick to your list of questions and your prearranged time slot.

5. **Thank those who talk to you, even if your conversation only lasts five minutes.**

6. **Keep your contacts informed of your progress as you fine-tune your ideas.**

   Even if you refocus your direction even slightly, make contact. Sharing your new angle may bring to mind a new set of contacts.

   Later, when you are clear about your direction, your informational interview contacts may be some of your best sources for job leads.

Staying objective in your quest

During your interviews, remember that you are there to gather information to help you better understand a potential career. Be sure to:

- **Ask the tough questions:** Especially those you aren't sure you really want to know the answer to.

- **Confront your worst fears:** Remove your rose-colored glasses to get as accurate a picture as possible about a career, company, or work format.

- **Remember your purpose:** Don't change an informational interview into a job interview even if the contact mentions a job opening. Because you are meeting with your contact to gather information to see if the field is a good fit for you, you are not in a good position to jump into a job interview scenario. Stay true to your original intention. If you are genuinely interested in hearing more about the position, set that appointment up as soon as you can after your informational interview.

When possible, conduct two or three informational interviews before you make pivotal decisions about your career. Compare what you hear from different sources and send a follow-up e-mail to your contacts to clarify anything that doesn't quite add up.

If you are still doing informational interviews, it is too early to make any binding career decisions. Focus you attention on verifying that each career is a good fit and on gaining experience in the new arena, as I describe in Chapter 16. If a fantastic job offer does come your way, evaluate it very carefully before you make a final decision. Refer to Chapters 17 and 19 for help in thinking through the various issues.

Chapter 16

Testing the Waters of a Potential Career

In This Chapter

▶ Trying your career ideas on for size

▶ Finding out what the work is really like

▶ Experiencing the lifestyle of a potential career

A career idea has captured your attention. You know something about this potential career from visiting Web sites, doing informational interviews, and the reading you have done, but you still don't know if it is the right career for you.

Now is the time to test the waters by using the following methods to find out all you can about the work that you want to do. Depending on how familiar you are with your idea, your exploration may take a couple of weeks to several months.

Use what you don't know as the starting point to guide your investigation, and then implement the following exploration methods that feel relevant to your situation. You need to find out as much as you can to make a good decision about how well each career idea fits your needs and your life. This doesn't mean you need to know everything; you just need enough information to feel comfortable pursuing your choice. After you reach that point, move to Chapter 17 to iron out the details.

Keep track of your discoveries. After every conversation, meeting, or volunteer activity, take a moment to:

✔ Notice your first impressions

✔ Pay attention to how you feel participating in the activity

✔ Note any questions the experience brings to mind

✔ Keep track of any new contacts you make

Because your exploration may take awhile, write down your observations as you go along so that you won't have to reconstruct it all when the time comes to make your decision.

In your exploration, if you run across information that surprises or startles you, take a moment to calm yourself down and then ask questions and do more reading until you have a full, informed picture of the situation. With this information in hand, consider your options and get creative to find a way to make the career work for you. If you need help, check out Chapter 17.

Immersing Yourself

Before you talk to people, look at ads, take a class, or go on an interview, surround yourself with information about the potential career. Find out as much as you can about the idiosyncrasies surrounding the career.

As you prepare to experience your career ideas first-hand, keep up with reading newspapers, Web sites, association newsletters, and other materials related to the field so that you are up-to-date. See Chapter 15 for more information on familiarizing yourself with a career.

Taking a class

Pick up class schedules for the schools in your area to find a course that you can take to get a taste of your potential career. Remember to check out the following:

- Classes sponsored by your city
- Community colleges
- Universities with local satellite campuses
- Personal-growth centers
- Bookstores

Your goal at this point is not to get fully trained in the field, but to explore whether the field is a good fit for you. Take a one-day or an evening class that introduces you to your field or an aspect of it.

If you discover a degree or certification program during your search, make note of it for future reference. In Chapter 18, you find information about how to select your best training options.

Do not commit to a full degree or certification program at this point, even if it looks like a perfect match. If you decide to start a program now, you prematurely limit your career investigation and your future career direction. At this stage of the game, you need to wait until you have a clearer sense of your ultimate direction before committing yourself to a particular education program.

Imagining being on the job

As soon as you get a sense of your target career, begin to imagine yourself on the job at that career. Pay attention to any aspect of the work, or its impact on your personal life, that feels uncomfortable.

If you experience this discomfort, use it as a research guide. Make a concerted effort to gather pieces of information that help you ease your concerns or confirm your impression.

Trying on the lifestyle

In some cases, your career choice means a change in your lifestyle as well. Your hours may change, you may need to move, or you may take on new and different responsibilities that have a direct impact on your family life. Take some time to verify that you are also comfortable with this type of change. One way to tell is to try on the new lifestyle.

Invent ways to mimic your desired lifestyle for a few days in your current situation. Even if your efforts aren't completely accurate, you can at least get an idea of what it might be like to live this way over time.

During the days you've set aside for your experiment, think about yourself and your life from this new point of view from the moment you wake up in the morning until the time you go to bed. As you proceed with your experiment, ask yourself the following questions:

- ✔ What do you like?
- ✔ What makes you feel uneasy?
- ✔ What do you find out?

Use the following ideas to start planning your experiment:

- ✔ **If you want your new career to be part-time:** If you are currently working, set up a week when you are in the office three out of five days or when you leave early for three days in a row. Notice how the time off impacts your life. Project how the decrease in salary might affect you.

- ✔ **If your new career is entrepreneurial:** Think about what your workday would look like as an entrepreneur. Would you work at home? Out on the road? In a small office? At client sites? Take a couple of days or a week off, if you are currently in a job, and use the time to explore this lifestyle. Even if you use the week to get your business plan in order, you can discover what it feels like to plan your own day and find the self-discipline to get done what needs to get done. If you have children, arrange for day care as you would if you were running your own business.

- ✔ **If your new career involves relocating:** If part of your plan is to move, take a couple of trips to scope out the new area. If the move means a longer commute, drive the commute several days in a row to get a feel for the traffic, travel time, and alternate routes.

Connecting with Others in the Career

After you feel you have a good overall sense of the career and know enough about it to want to take your exploration even deeper, begin connecting with others who can help you get a real-life taste of your prospective career.

Observing someone at work in the career

By watching someone interacting with clients, coworkers, suppliers, and management and doing the tasks you might perform, you have a great opportunity to evaluate how well a potential career fits you and your needs. (See Chapter 15 for information on building list of contacts that you can use for this purpose.)

Before you ask your contacts if you can shadow them for a couple hours or a day, think through what you hope to gain from the experience. Make a list of what you want to look for during the observation. Build in time at the beginning of the appointment to set up the following ground rules:

- ✔ The length of your observation time

- ✔ The appropriate time to ask questions — for example, on the spot or during a break

- ✔ Whether or not you can take notes on what you see. Some places have confidentiality issues that may disallow you making written notes about what you observe.

As you observe, you may have a visceral reaction to what you see. Whether it's love or loathing at first sight, seeing the job first hand gives you invaluable information. Pay close attention to whatever you feel; these feelings may become even more intense if you actually decide to work in the field.

Hanging out in the environment

If you can't gain access to a person you can observe, try creating a way to spend time in the environment you want to work in.

If you want to work in a setting that is fairly public, you can probably spend time in the environment without official permission. Even if you can't gain access to the entire area, you can begin to get a feel for what it might be like to work in a public place, such as a bank, restaurant, airport, school, hotel, retail store, or recreation park, simply by visiting the place as any customer would.

If you want to work in a corporate setting or in an environment that is not open to the public, you may need to find a contact who can take you on a tour of the environment you are interested in. Or you can locate a company that is similar in terms of size, industry, or product line to the one you are interested in, but is more accessible.

No matter how you gain access, as you spend time in the surroundings, remember to do the following:

- ✔ Observe the comings and goings.
- ✔ Watch to see who does what.
- ✔ Notice the interactions between coworkers.
- ✔ Pay attention to whether you feel out of place or at ease.
- ✔ Think about what it might be like to work in an environment like this on a regular basis.

If you have an opportunity to visit a company you are targeting, you can gain valuable information by observing both the environment and the people in it. During your visit, ask yourself the following questions:

- ✔ Can you see yourself working with these people?
- ✔ How satisfied do the employees appear to be?
- ✔ Can you see yourself in this particular environment?
- ✔ How do you feel as you watch the manager interact with the employees?

You can also visit a place where people in the profession congregate — a conference, a trade show, or a show, for example. This option can be an extremely relevant source of information if attending these events is likely to be an important part of the job you want.

A conference is a fabulous place to immerse yourself in a new career area. Throughout the event, you eat, breathe, and sleep the profession. Within a couple of days, you may even find yourself laughing at the in-jokes of the profession, which is a good sign that you are getting a handle on the culture. While at the conference, take note of how you feel:

✔ Are you energized?

✔ Are you drained?

✔ Are you bored?

Talking to people outside the field

To make sure that you get the full picture of your target careers, don't limit yourself to talking with only those who do the job you want. Think of others you may interact with who might provide you with a unique perspective of your target career, including:

✔ Vendors

✔ Customers

✔ Professional colleagues who work at a similar level but hold different jobs

Use your current contacts to gain access to people in these various roles. (See Chapter 15 for information on building a pool of contacts.) While you are at it, see if you can talk with someone who you might manage or report to. No matter whom you end up talking to, each person can help you reach your goal of broadening your understanding of the job.

Observing the lifestyle

A truly fulfilling career gives you professional satisfaction and also allows you to live life the way you want to. Whether you are interested in rural living, telecommuting, working part-time while parenting, or being an entrepreneur, you can gain insight about your new life by spending time with people who are living the life you want. Rather than talking with them about their work, see if you can visit them at home to get a sense of how their profession impacts their lives.

To make full use of your visit, do the following:

✔ Prepare a list of questions to ask.

✔ Observe the environment and what happens in the home.

✔ Notice the interruptions.

✔ Get a feel for the flow of activity.

Make your appointment at a time when you can witness the aspects of the lifestyle that concern you the most, which could be the morning shuffle of getting the kids off to school before work or the commute.

If you don't know someone to visit, talk about your desired lifestyle with people you know or meet. Often people pipe up and say, "Oh, Janet's sister is doing the very same thing!" Follow up to see if you can connect in person. If the potential contact lives too far away, set up a conversation by phone or via e-mail.

Finding a Community of Like-Minded People

After you connect with individuals in your desired career, and you are seriously considering becoming an active member of the profession, you should become part of the community. Doing so allows you to enrich your understanding of the career, while giving you ongoing contact with people within the profession.

Attending a meeting of professionals

Many of the professional associations that I list in Part III have local chapters so that their members can get to know and support each other. Attending local chapter meetings on a regular basis is a great way to do the following:

✔ Build a thriving network.

✔ Find a mentor.

✔ Identify local job leads.

✔ Enhance your visibility within the profession.

To find local chapter meetings in your area, try the following:

✔ Read the calendar section of your local newspaper for several months.

✔ Access your professional association's Web site to see if it lists local chapters. (I list many of the these organizations and their Web addresses in Part III of this book.)

✔ Ask your contacts which professional meetings they like most.

Some chapters allow you to attend their local meetings as a guest several times before you become a full-fledged member of the organization. To make the most of the meetings, follow these guidelines:

- **Attend several meetings before you decide whether to stop going.** This advice holds true even if you feel somewhat uncomfortable at the meetings at first. The only reason to cut this plan short is if the group's mission or purpose is clearly not a good match for you.

- **Announce yourself.** Tell the person at the door that you are attending for the first time so that he or she can introduce you to people right off the bat.

- **Think about how to introduce yourself before you walk into the meeting.** Write your introduction down if it helps to have something in front of you.

- **Introduce yourself to the people sitting around you.** Asking questions about the organization is a good way to start a conversation.

- **Notice who plays key roles during the meeting.** Keep their names and faces in mind for future reference.

The more frequently you attend chapter meetings, the more people you recognize, and the more comfortable you become. Another way to feel at ease is to reconnect with people outside the meeting. Useful strategies to follow up with people you've met include:

- **Taking your business cards with you to every meeting:** Your card gives people a way to find you again if they have a lead for you. If you aren't currently employed, you can create your own cards at an office supply store or on your own computer. As you design your new cards, include, at the very least, your name, prospective profession, phone, and e-mail address. Also remember to get the cards of those people you want to keep in touch with.

- **Sending an e-mail or making a quick call:** Several days after you meet someone, e-mail or call to share a book title, a recent article, or the phone number of a contact you discussed.

- **Inviting someone to join you for lunch or a walk:** This strategy works well if you both sense that you had a lot in common during your initial conversations. Don't expect each and every one of these attempts to result in a long-term connection. Just see what develops in the course of your interactions. Who knows — this person may lead you to just the right contact.

- **Responding when someone follows up with you:** Don't let a hot or warm connection drop away out of ambivalence or apathy on your part. Even if you aren't sure there's a match, take a chance and check it out. Later in your career you may need to be choosier, but for now, while you make your way into your profession, follow up on any lead that comes your way.

Subscribing to a newsletter

As you search the Internet for informative Web sites, keep your eyes open for free online newsletters or e-zines. Likely sources for these publications include professional associations, schools, and professionals already in the field.

Subscribe to several. They are free and take just a moment of your time to read. In return, you keep yourself up to date on the following:

✔ Hot topics within the field

✔ Key events for professionals like yourself

✔ Crucial issues that may impact how you work

✔ New techniques and perspectives you can incorporate into your work

✔ Key players in the field

Don't just subscribe. Take the time to read each newsletter and save any items that are relevant to you. As you refine the direction of your career change, review these articles to see if you can spot angles, contacts, and companies you may not have picked up on the first time around.

If you are not online, contact your professional association to see if they have a printed newsletter that they distribute to members.

Participating in an online community

You can also connect with people in your field by becoming part of an online community. You can talk with people locally or all over the world via e-mail, discussion boards, or chat rooms. The beauty of these communities is that you can do the following:

✔ Participate any time of day or night that is convenient to you.

✔ Get a feel for the community by reading others' conversations.

✔ Ask questions and get up-to-date answers.

✔ Respond to questions from your own knowledge and experience.

✔ Look at archived messages to catch up on what has happened within the community over time.

✔ Make great connections for off-line conversations.

If you have already found references to these groups during your research, check them out. If not, do a search on some of the following sites to see what communities you discover:

- **Yahoo! Groups** (`http://groups.yahoo.com`): Access a group using the search function or by scanning the groups under the categories that interest you.

- **Topica** (`www.topica.com`): On this site you can find discussion groups, e-mail newsletters, and tips on various topics. Use the list of topics to find what you are looking for.

- **Monster.com** (`http://community.monster.com/chats`): This site gives you a schedule of online chats and bulletin boards for finding a job in various industries.

- **Wetfeet** (`www.wetfeet.com/research/careers.asp`): After finding your target career or industry profiles on this site, check out the Wet Feet Resources for current discussion topics. You must become a member of the site to read or participate in these discussions.

Some of these online communities are open to anyone. Feel free to join on the spot. Before jumping into the conversation, however, you may want to just visit for a couple of days, reading the current posts and archived messages to get a sense of the community and its communication norms.

Other groups are for members only. E-mail the host to find out how you can become a member. You may need to be part of an organization or have a particular kind of training to participate. Either way, it's worth the effort to check it out.

Getting Your Feet Wet

You have the background information to know that your career idea fits you in theory. Now it's time to verify that you like doing the work as much as you enjoy thinking about doing it. To know one way or the other, you must dive in and try it out.

Although you may not have all the training you need to get started in your potential career, you may be able to do something that's similar to give you an idea of what the field is really like. For example:

- If you want to teach, try tutoring.

- If you want to be an editor, volunteer to work on a non-profit's newsletter.

- If you want to be a counselor, try participating on a hotline.

- ✔ If you want to be a sound technician, find a band that needs someone to set up equipment for performances.

- ✔ If you want to be a contractor, spend some time at a work site doing whatever is needed.

- ✔ If you want to be a computer consultant, volunteer to set up computers for a school, non-profit, or business owner.

- ✔ If you want to be a vet, try working with animals in some capacity — perhaps at the local Humane Society.

- ✔ If you want to be an artist, try working in a gallery.

Your goal is to get a sense of what this career may be like by taking a peek at the work, the environment, and the client or customers. To gain this experience, consider taking a short-term or part-time job, or doing a temporary assignment. You can also volunteer for your professional association, a project at work, a non-profit, or a friend who owns a business.

Drawing Conclusions from Your Research

After exploring and thinking about your career ideas and your lifestyle options using the ideas in this chapter, you can reach an informed decision about whether you really want to delve into the career.

As you make your conclusions, take everything you have discovered into account. Don't sweep something under the rug just because it's unappealing. Face it. Whether or not an uncomfortable issue ends your investigation, it is better to deal with it now than after you get into the profession or you change your life completely.

Take some time to consolidate your thoughts. While reviewing Worksheet 7-5, update what you love about each of your career ideas and your pros and cons for doing the work. By getting your conclusions down on paper, you can take your time assessing your options, looking at tradeoffs, and noticing if any holes exist in your logic.

Chapter 17

Getting All the Pieces to Fit

In This Chapter

▶ Making sense of inconsistencies in your picture

▶ Handling tough choices

▶ Finding the best way to describe what you want

. . . .

Throughout this book, I encourage you to focus on your ideal career and lifestyle, putting aside thoughts of whether any particular idea is feasible or not. In your exploration of potential careers, you have no doubt found aspects of your needs and desires that clash to some degree. This chapter helps you find workable solutions to resolve these conflicts.

Before you delve into how to move your ideal career into reality, take a moment to think about what you need for yourself and your family when it comes to your work. Note any specific elements you feel you must incorporate into decisions about your future career. (Chapter 3 can help you form a picture of these needs.) With those ideas in mind, let yourself sink into the picture you have created of your desired career.

Finding a way to synchronize your ideal and your reality is like doing a jigsaw puzzle. You may need to move several pieces around to get all the pieces to fit. Stay as open as you can to seeing solutions that may not be obvious at first.

Overlaying Your Must-Haves with Your Vision

As you look at ways to coordinate the must-haves in your life with your ideal vision of your future work, what do you see? Before you make any conclusions, write down the answers to the following questions to look at the pieces of your puzzle from different points of view:

✔ **In your heart of hearts, what do you need?** For you to succeed and feel fulfilled, what work configuration works best for you? What does your body, mind, and spirit need to flourish?

> ✔ **What's best for your family and home life?** Putting your needs on the back burner for a moment, what work set-up allows your family and home life to thrive?

When the Pieces Fit Together

Sometimes all the pieces of the puzzle slide together as if by magic. If that is the case for you, keep reading this section. If you see any clashes as you try to piece it all together, move on to the next section for help in taming the inconsistencies you see.

As your picture comes together, don't act on it immediately. Take a couple of days to look at your idea from several different angles and do the following:

> ✔ When you wake up in the morning, run the career scenario over in your mind.

> ✔ As you daydream during your work day, compare and contrast what you do now with what you think you may do in the future.

> ✔ Write in your journal about your career idea and its impact on your life.

> ✔ Look at the changes that may happen in your life as a result of making this change in your career.

> ✔ Make improvements to your career idea as insights strike you.

> ✔ Talk about your idea with someone you trust.

As you work through the picture of your new career, notice how you feel when you think about your new plan. Are you excited, motivated, surprised, nervous, or scared?

If you are excited about your new direction and don't feel there's anything you need to refine, jump to the section at the end of this chapter titled "Formulating One Sentence That Says It All."

If you feel uneasy, is it because you can finally see your future unfolding before you, or do you find a few little details that don't quite feel right?

If you notice something that doesn't feel quite right, make some notes in your journal so that you can brainstorm solutions to make your career idea truly work. Use the ideas in the following section to help iron out the subtle wrinkles in your picture.

When the Pieces Appear to Clash

As you look at all the pieces of your puzzle, you may discover that a couple of elements you want in your work and need in your life appear to be diametrically opposed.

At first you may feel stumped. The ideas you come up with initially may not feel feasible or practical. Although you may feel tempted to give up at this point, keep in mind that between any two options exist a host of creative solutions. You just need to know how to find them.

In your journal, describe the clash you feel. Be as specific as you can be about what doesn't work for you about the picture.

Finding the essence of what you want

To find new solutions, step away from the specifics of your picture and focus on the overriding truth of what you want in the situation. Regardless of the particulars of your clash, how do you want to feel when all is said and done? When you discover the essence of what you want, you may well feel a sense of relief as you realize that you've been focusing so much on the details that you lost track of the big picture.

For example, you may identify the following clash between your ideal career and your family life:

> To work in the industry of my choice, my commute may be a stress-filled, three-hour round trip, which means I'm going to arrive home exhausted and unable to enjoy my kids.

After thinking about the clash, you may discover that the essence of your desires is more like the following:

> I want to be calm when I walk in the door after work.

As you look at the bigger picture, don't worry about how to make it all happen, just think about the essence you want to bring about.

Having a brainstorming blitz

With your target essence in mind (see the preceding section), brainstorm as many solutions as you can. As in all brainstorming situations, all ideas are viable. Write down anything and everything you can think of. For example, if you worry that a commute from the office may leave you worn out and unable to interact well with your family at the end of the day, your brain-storming list may look like the following:

> Telecommuting, work at a satellite office, carpool, take the train, relocate closer to work, find a job closer to home, hire a driver, quit, commute during off hours, commute by plane, find a way to start a home-based business.

Boost your creative juices by eliminating any perceived or real constraints on your time, money, and resources. Be outrageous! Often elements of outra-geous ideas can become useful when looking for creative solutions. If you have had fantasies about how to handle certain clashes in the past, by all means, include them in your list.

Spotting creative solutions

Remembering what you brainstorm about any potential career-life clashes, look for any pieces that you can combine to create the essence you want. For example, following through with the example from the preceding section, you may come up with the following creative solutions:

- ✔ Telecommute two days a week and carpool the others.
- ✔ Work at a satellite office three days a week and take the train the other two days.
- ✔ Investigate career options closer to home to eliminate the commute entirely.
- ✔ Talk to friends about creating a vanpool.

Feel free to take a little of this idea and a little of that idea to come up with a solution that works with relative ease. If you feel blocked, ask a few friends to help you explore your ideas. They may see something that you don't.

Focus on the solution that gives you the essence you are searching for. If the solution still doesn't feel quite right, identify what doesn't work. Can you make a change to that one piece to make the pieces fit?

Now step away. Let your ideas sit for a couple of days. Due to the thinking you have done thus far, you may, in the course of living your life, come across a solution that resolves the clash for you.

If your clash seems insurmountable, you may be asking yourself the same series of questions again and again — a tactic that ultimately gets you nowhere. Instead, look for a new question you can ask. New questions can show you the way to new answers because they shift your perspective just enough so that you see new avenues you never ever could have seen from your old position. With the right question, perceived clashes often evaporate into thin air.

Reconciling True Differences

On occasion, you may discover clashes between two desired elements that you can't resolve. In these cases, there may be little you can do to get the pieces to fall into place exactly as you would like.

You need to discern how you can minimize the negative impact the clash has on you and your family while maximizing the aspects of it that are important to you.

Check out the following strategies to see if you can find a solution that is at least workable:

- **Use the delay tactic:** Postponing what you want until your circumstances change may cause the clash to lose its punch. Perhaps you need to wait until your kids start school, your kids get out of college, or you move.

- **Revisit your values:** Which element allows you to live closer to your values? Does this clarity help you discern which element of your clash must take priority?

- **Talk it over with your family:** Consider any way the family can adjust to allow you to meet your needs. Be honest and creative. Don't get defensive. If the words, "Yes, but" come out of your mouth, stop in your tracks to see what idea you are not allowing in.

- **Take vacation time:** Maybe you can relegate one element of the clash to your vacation or find enough satisfaction expressing this part of yourself off the job.

- **Turn the ideal into a hobby:** Perhaps you can get what you want through a hobby instead of making it part of your daily, full-time life.

As you think about your clash from these angles, notice if you can combine any of these ideas to create a workable solution. For example, you may focus your energy on a hobby basis until your children leave for college in two years. If you play your cards right, after you have the time to devote to pursuing your ideal career, you may have also gained the experience you need to break into the field.

Formulating One Sentence That Says It All

In the past, without the clarity that you have after reconciling any perceived clashes, your opening statement was probably so vague that it may have prevented your contacts from directing you to the right people.

In this section, you create one sentence that describes exactly what you are looking for. Doing so allows you to clearly articulate your mission to your informational interview contacts and to prospective employers. Your one-sentence-that-says-it-all also helps you determine whether opportunities are or are not in alignment with your mission.

To develop an accurate, detailed sentence about your career direction, look over Chapters 3, 4, and 7 to identify your most important issues.

Play with the elements you identify, personalizing them to your situation. Then string them together in various ways until you find the clearest statement to describe what you want. Start by completing the sentence, "I want to. . . ."

If you don't have a job title for the work you want to do, you can still construct a sentence that says it all. Be as specific as possible as you voice your desires. Take a look at the following examples to get started:

✔ I want to use my accounting skills in a part-time position while working from home.

✔ I want to use my creativity to teach children how to read in a way that is fun.

✔ I want to combine my interests in numeric modeling, tornadoes, and aircraft design in an internal consulting role.

After you have your sentence, write it down and try it out. Practice saying the sentence to a couple friends. Notice how they react. Do they get it? Use the questions they raise to tighten or clarify your statement.

With this sentence in your head, you can punch the internal play button whenever anyone asks what you are doing these days or what you are looking for. After a while, you may find yourself emphasizing different aspects of your sentence depending on whom you are talking with. Then you know you have fully integrated what you want. You are on a roll!

Update your sentence as your direction becomes clearer and clearer.

If you are torn between two different career directions, create a sentence for each one. As you talk about your interests with contacts, you may find more opportunities associated with one of your ideas, you may discover your skills are better suited to one option, or you may find a way to weave the two ideas together after all. Don't be concerned that you have two ideas, just proceed with both tracks at once.

Shifting Gears Midstream

If you discover at some point in your refinement process that the direction you are moving in causes you to drag your feet, stop and take a good look at what's going on.

To make a successful career change, you must feel the inner drive to go after it, so don't stay devoted to an idea just because you have been interested in it in the past.

If your career idea has lost some of its luster, see what you can do to reignite your interest. Ask yourself the following questions:

- ✔ What caused your interest to shift?
- ✔ Is there a subtle change you can make in your plan to bring life back into it?
- ✔ What catches your attention these days?

Life continues to twist and turn. Changing direction now is better than waiting until you have started a new career or quit your current position.

Admitting that you want to change your direction doesn't mean you have to start from scratch! You are way ahead of the game. By leveraging off what you already know about yourself, your needs, your interests, and your ideas, you can easily reshuffle your deck and find a direction that suits you better.

Notice where you feel uncomfortable with your puzzle and revisit Chapters 3, 4, and 6 to update your thoughts.

Setting Your Sights on Your Target Career

After you have a fairly clear picture of what you want to go after, you can make some initial decisions about how you want to transition into your new line of work.

One big question to think about is how fast do you want to make this transition. For example, ask yourself the following questions:

- ✔ Do you want to jump in and go for it?
- ✔ Do you want to ease in and test the waters before you make any big decisions?
- ✔ Do you want to get some additional training before you make any moves at all?

Making a realistic timeline

After getting a sense of how fast you want to move on this new career idea of yours, look at your life and think about a realistic time frame for pursuing your new career. Given everything else you have going on, estimate when you want to:

- ✔ Start building the skills you need
- ✔ Begin your job search or develop your business idea
- ✔ Quit your current position

If you can, plan a free week or two between jobs to give yourself a chance to complete your old position and rest up before you launch into your new work.

Trusting your gut

Any transition is a very personal process. Don't rely on other people's assessment of how fast or slow you should go. For your career change to work, your timing must be consistent with your needs.

If you push yourself too fast, you may get scared and put on the brakes prematurely, sabotaging your efforts. If you move too slowly, you may lose momentum and never get your search off the ground. Take the pace that feels right to you.

For more information about how to navigate the emotional side of your career change, check out Chapter 21.

Chapter 18

Strengthening the Skills You Need

In This Chapter

▶ Discovering what training you need

▶ Deciding how you like to learn

▶ Finding non-traditional ways to enhance your skills

▶ Evaluating your educational options

As you narrow your focus on a career, you must evaluate how much additional training you need for your new line of work and how you intend to acquire that knowledge. This chapter provides information about traditional training options, as well as some options that have entered the educational scene more recently.

Knowing What You Need to Know

Read over the career profiles and informational interview notes that you collect in the course of your research. (See Chapters 15 and 16 for tips on gathering this information.) Pay particular attention to the education requirements and the discussion of any traits and skills you need to perform in your target career. If you have any questions about what's required, check with your contacts.

After you know what training is essential, compare what you need with the education and experience you already have. Identify any hot spots you know you must address. Use the following questions to focus your thoughts:

✔ Do you need to:

- Get a degree?

- Work toward a certificate or license?

- Update your knowledge?

- Add a new key skill?

> ✔ Do you have any options in the amount of training you need, or does one standard hold for everyone in the field?
>
> ✔ Does changing your career goal slightly impact the education requirements?

Your answers to these questions can help you decide whether you need to participate in informal training options or pursue a more formal education.

Discovering How You Learn Best

If the thought of going to school makes your skin crawl or your stomach sink, don't give up just yet! In recent years, a number of new educational formats have entered the scene that expand your options far beyond the traditional classroom setting.

To find your best option, identify how you like to process new information and then build your training plan to match your preferred style.

Think back over the years. When have you learned with ease? Think about the following questions:

> ✔ In school, was there a particular kind of project or assignment that you enjoyed most?
>
> ✔ On your first few jobs, what helped you become proficient at your work?
>
> ✔ When you want to increase your knowledge about something on your own, how do you approach the topic?

Use the following questions to pin down your primary learning styles:

> ✔ **Are you a visual learner? Do you learn best by:**
>
>   • Reading about a topic?
>
>   • Looking at illustrations or pictures?
>
>   • Taking notes?
>
> ✔ **Are you a kinesthetic learner? Do you learn best by:**
>
>   • Doing a task?
>
>   • Using trial and error?
>
>   • Practicing a new skill?

✔ **Are you an auditory learner? Do you learn best by:**

- Listening to instructions?

- Attending a lecture?

- Hearing someone describe what you need to do?

As you investigate various programs and training opportunities, make sure to take your preferred learning style into account.

Finding the most workable format

Adding training to an already busy life is challenging at best. Based on what you know about your lifestyle, schedule, and work responsibilities, think about what forms of education may blend most easily with your life. They could be one or more of the following:

✔ Full-time school

✔ One course a semester with classroom time in the evenings and some weekends

✔ Evening classes

✔ Weekend classes

✔ Self-paced classes where you have to go somewhere to gain access to the materials

✔ Internet courses you do on your own schedule from your computer

✔ An ongoing internship or apprenticeship

✔ On-the-job training

✔ Mentoring from an individual, successful in your field, who helps you establish your goals, develop relevant skills, and work through difficult situations

Even if it seems impossible right now to take on the challenge of additional training, keep an open mind until you have more information about the available options. Who knows; you may discover something that works surprisingly well.

Rooting out the best location

When you think about school, you probably still think of a traditional classroom setting. Thankfully, advances in technology mean that you can find programs that afford more flexibility in time and place than ever before.

Given your preferred learning style and your lifestyle, where do you imagine you may learn best? Consider the following options:

✔ **At a school**

- Interacting with the instructor in person
- Observing the instructor via video

✔ **At home**

- By telephone
- By Internet
- Through a written correspondence course
- By video

✔ **On the job**

Another essential component of going to school is studying. You may study most effectively at home, at a public library, in a café, outside, at your office, or at school.

If you don't know where you study most effectively, observe yourself for a week or so. Find out what kind of setting you search for when you need to concentrate on a work project or think through a problem. Assess the elements of the setting to determine where you think best. Make sure that your study location incorporates as many of these characteristics as you can.

To make your study sessions as productive as possible, choose the options that feel good to you. For example, if you hate pure silence, don't think that you can suddenly force yourself to go to the library to study on a regular basis. Studying is hard enough without adding the extra burden of force to the equation. Think about your natural tendencies and leverage off those so that you can put your energy into studying rather than into getting yourself to study.

Getting Informal Training

If you just need to brush up on some skills, update your knowledge on a particular topic, or gain some experience, you may be able to get what you need without entering a degree or certification program. Depending on your education goals, consider the following options:

✔ **Taking a single class:** A class that fits your needs may be offered at a local adult school, community college, or university extension campus.

✔ **Taking an online course:** See the section "Finding potential programs" later in this chapter for more information about this option.

✔ **Taking a class on your telephone:** You can connect with others in interactive classes offered by phone. Your class may have people from all over the country and possibly the world. Check out the following Web sites for more details about the protocol and course lists:

  • www.teleclass4U.com

  • www.teleclass.com

  • www.teleclasscanada.com

Your target profession may also offer teleclasses as part of their training mandate. Do an Internet search to discover relevant teleclasses.

✔ **Volunteering your time:** Help out at an organization to gain experience and new skills that are related to your target career.

If you have access to the Internet, consider virtual volunteering, which entails using your computer to perform tasks such as editing, designing Web sites, translating, fundraising, program advising, and moderating online discussions for non-profits. For opportunities within the United States, visit www.serviceleader.org/vv/. Or if you'd prefer to address a global issue, such as hunger, you can search for appropriate volunteer assignments at www.netaid.org.

You can also contact a Volunteer Center in your area for information about local opportunities.

✔ **Apprenticing with an expert in the field:** Talk with your contacts to see if you can set up an apprenticeship or mentoring relationship with them or anyone they know.

✔ **Starting a small business related to your potential career on the side:** See Chapter 20 for ideas about how to start your own business.

Training on the Job

If you learn best by doing and you are currently employed, look around your company for experiences that can help you prepare for your career change. Although you must continue to get your work done, your personal priority is to find out as much as you can to ease your transition into your new career.

Even if your current job seems unrelated to your ultimate position, focus your efforts on strengthening key transferable skills. For example, you can participate in the budgeting process, offer to write a column for your company's newsletter, or find a way to give a series of presentations; each of these skills prove valuable in most any career you enter.

Finding a related project in your current job

Keeping what you need to know in mind, find or create a way to work on a project that gives you that experience. If you see an opportunity, try any of the following:

- ✔ Propose a new project to your boss
- ✔ Ask your boss to assign a particular project to you
- ✔ Volunteer for a committee

If someone asks why you want to do something outside your usual realm, say that you want to strengthen a skill you formerly used or build a new one. Don't feel that you must explain why in great detail.

Enjoying company-financed training

Your company may sponsor you to go back to school. That's right. Depending on how this benefit works in your company, they may pay some or all of your tuition!

Check with the human resources department at your company to determine if your company offers reimbursement for the following:

- ✔ Any course you wish to take
- ✔ Only courses related to your current job
- ✔ Only courses that are part of a degree program

Even if your company is willing to pay, don't invest your time and energy in courses that take you down the wrong road. Instead, negotiate a way to take courses that help your employer and you at the same time.

Attending conferences

A professional conference can be a great place to gain information and build your skills. As you review conference brochures that come across your desk at work, evaluate whether attending the conference could give you a better understanding of your target career. This opportunity is especially likely if your new career is in some way related to your current position.

If you see a strong link between the conference and your work and can convince your manager of its value, the company may even foot the bill for some of your expenses. If your company chooses not to fund your way to the conference, or if the conference is something you find on your own, and you feel it is an important step to your future, do what you have to do to attend. Take some vacation time, use your frequent-flier miles to get there, stay with a friend in the area, or pay for the conference yourself, if necessary.

As you set up your personal agenda for the conference, read the conference's brochure carefully for opportunities. Consider the following:

- ✔ If a session addresses a new software package that's essential for people in your target career to use, sit in on that session.

- ✔ If you see a niche or application that you've never heard of before, explore it to see if it gives you a better understanding of your new career.

- ✔ If a key expert is giving a talk on a topic that has always confused you, attend the session so that you can resolve your confusion before you enter your new field.

Check out any pre-conference workshops, as well. These workshops tend to offer more interactive, hands-on opportunities. Even if it costs more to attend these sessions, consider this an investment and evaluate the long-term return.

Taking a short-term job

A part-time job (after hours, if you currently hold a job) may be another option if you want to get a feel for the ropes of a new profession or a new skill. You don't have to keep the job forever — just long enough to gain the skill, make a good impression, and build key relationships for the future.

With some ingenuity, you may even find a way to do this within your company. After researching the organization to identify experiences that would strengthen your targeted skills, build a case for doing a rotation into that department. Be sure to lay out the benefits to the company and the details of how your proposal may work.

Have several variations worked out in your mind so that if your employer doesn't buy into your original plan, you can present her with some other attractive options. For example, your manager may flinch at the idea of assigning you to another department for several months, but see value in allowing you to do some cross-training in the same department over a period of a week or two.

Getting a Degree

In certain cases, taking a class here and doing a project there doesn't give you the training that you need to enter your new profession. To succeed in your target career, you may need to get another degree or work toward licensure.

Going to school requires you to commit your time, money, and attention for an extended period. Don't make this decision lightly. Devote the time it takes to research and think through your decision before you take action. Proceed only when you feel comfortable with your decision and your plan.

Enrolling in school because you don't know what else to do or because someone told you the degree is the ticket to more money is a bad idea. Go to school if and only if the degree enables you to do the work that you want to do.

You may find yourself shying away from your goals because you think that you are too old to go to school. News flash! You will be that much older in several years whether you go to school or not! Wouldn't it be better to have options and feel fulfilled rather than be stuck in a dead-end career going nowhere? People of all ages return to school to fulfill their dreams. Don't let your age become your excuse for passing up your dream of a satisfying career.

Clarifying your goal

A vast number of educational programs exist these days. To narrow your initial quest for appropriate programs, answer the following questions:

- ✔ **To achieve your career goal, do you need a:**
    - • Undergraduate degree?
    - • Certificate?
    - • Graduate degree?

- ✔ **What kind of program should you target?** Each school you look at may have a slightly different name for the program you are interested in. Don't limit your search to just one phrase. Explore several content areas and departments to make sure that you find all the relevant programs.

✔ **What geographic area are you willing to consider?** In addition to the schools in your area, include schools that have extension programs and distance-learning options. Think carefully about your willingness to relocate in case the right program is located out of your area.

✔ **What kinds of class formats work for you?** Take your learning style into account when you make this decision.

✔ **How much can you spend on your education?** Take a look at the section "Getting financial assistance" in this chapter for ideas about how to finance your educational goals.

Finding potential programs

If you determine that you need a degree and are interested in a traditional school setting, consider the following tips to help you locate the program that's right for you:

✔ Talk with your contacts to discover where they were trained and which programs they recommend.

✔ Visit www.collegiate.net/infob.html on the Web, a collegiate information site, to find links to numerous colleges, universities, community colleges, and specific departments.

✔ Visit the Web sites for the schools in your area and search their online course catalogs and offerings.

✔ Check your local bookstore or library for books describing schools with programs in your field.

Distance learning has also become a viable option for attaining a degree. Distance learning refers to any learning situation in which the instructor and student are not in the same place at the same time. Course work can be delivered through the mail, video, cable television, interactive television, satellite broadcasts, e-mails, message boards, Web sites, chat rooms, computer conferencing, telephone, or some combination of these methods. Distance learning can be used to take an individual class or to earn a degree.

With distance learning, you must make sure that you take courses from an accredited school with a good reputation. To check out a potential school, visit www.about.com, click on "Education," then click on "Distance Learning." Scroll down until you find the article on evaluating schools, which provides a step-by-step process for determining whether a school is reputable or not. For another opinion, check out the school of your choice on the Distance Education and Training Council Web site at www.detc.org/. *Distance Learning Online For Dummies,* by Nancy Stevenson, published by Hungry Minds, Inc., is also a valuable resource.

Converting your experience into credits

If you believe that you have the experience you need, even though you don't have the college credits to prove it, you may be able to convert your experience into credits by demonstrating that you have indeed accumulated that knowledge through self-study, volunteer activities, on-the-job training, and work experience. Depending on the school you apply to, you may need to demonstrate your expertise through:

✔ **An examination:** Some schools accept test scores as a replacement for course work. The theory is that if you can score well on the test, you must have the knowledge. If your school accepts this method, find out which of the following test's scores they accept: Advanced Placement (AP), Graduate Record Exam (GRE), Regents College Examinations, and Thomas Edison College Examination Program (TECEP).

✔ **A portfolio review:** Schools that accept this method ask you to create a portfolio that demonstrates and substantiates that your knowledge matches the objectives associated with a particular course or program. In some cases, the best way to assess your skills may be through oral questioning, responding to a case study, completing an assignment, or providing a demonstration. To be of value, your portfolio must be authentic, relevant, current, and sufficient to prove your expertise. As a result of the portfolio review, you may receive a formal grade point average or a competency rating. (For an in-depth discussion of portfolio assessment, visit www.ola.bc.ca/pla/explanation.html on the Web.)

If you earn college credits or formal recognition for your knowledge through an examination or a portfolio review, you may, as a result, be able to waive prerequisites for some classes, eliminate some required course work, and focus your attention on gaining the skills that you really need.

Two distant learning schools that are designed specifically for working adults pursuing degrees are Phoenix University (www.phoenix.edu/general/index.html) and the United States Open University (www.open.edu). Although the specific offerings depend on the school, programs in technology, nursing, administration, information technology, liberal arts, education, and more, are available.

Another resource is America's Learning Exchange (www.alx.org), which provides access to over 300,000 courses offered by over 6,000 training institutions. You can search their database by indicating the topic, your state, and the delivery method you desire.

Traditional schools often have distant learning offerings as well. Check the schools in your area to discover what distant learning opportunities they offer.

If you don't find the program you want, consider applying to a school that allows you to design a degree program that fits your interests and needs.

Check the school's Web site for links entitled individualized learning, self-designed programs, interdisciplinary studies, and joint degree programs. Although this option is not available at every school, if you find the idea intriguing, it never hurts to ask.

Choosing the right program for you

After you get information about potential programs off the Internet or from enrollment packets from each school, read over the material very carefully.

Depending on the number of schools you consider, selecting the best program may be a bit overwhelming at first. Between the amount of information you receive and the number of possibilities you are trying on, your mind may spin in all sorts of directions trying to figure out a workable plan of action. Take it one step at a time. Use the following step-by-step process to keep focused and moving forward:

1. **Get an overview of each program.**

   Pay attention to the:

   - **Program description:** Note any special features that are of particular relevance to your target careers.

   - **Faculty research interests:** Most faculty members prefer to guide students who have interests similar to their own, so if you expect to do research as part of your degree program, make sure that you find their research interesting.

   - **Degree offered:** Make sure that the training prepares you for additional certification, if necessary.

2. **Compare and contrast the various programs.**

   Each school may use a slightly different format to describe its program, so you may want to make a chart or a summary page for each program to keep the details straight. Determine what you want to know about each program and then fill in the details. Don't be surprised if there are blanks in your chart. You can fill in these answers in Step 4.

3. **Get a sense of which programs interest you most.**

   Tune in to your intuition as you study each program. Which programs feel the best to you? Your sense of excitement, or lack thereof, is a clue worth paying attention to. Make note of what about your top picks appeals to you.

4. **Check out the interesting programs.**

If you look into a traditional school, visit the school in person if at all possible. Call ahead to make an appointment to meet with a professor or an admissions counselor. Ask to talk with some current students. See if you can sit in on a class in progress. Be sure to prepare questions ahead of time based on the blanks in your detail sheet. This is a good time to ask about prerequisites and any anticipated faculty changes.

If you consider an online program, verify that the school offering the course or program is reputable and accredited by visiting distantlearning.about.com. If you haven't taken an online course before, consider taking a single course through the school to see what it's like before you commit to an entire program.

5. **Apply to your top choices.**

For any required recommendations, choose people who have some clout in your target field or a related field. The people you ask should also know you well enough to have knowledge of your talents and abilities, a sense of your ability to complete an education program, and the confidence to affirm your character.

Your references are doing you a huge favor. Do whatever you can to make their jobs as easy as possible. Start by giving your references ample time to write about you. In your packet about the recommendation, provide them with the information they need to write an accurate, detailed letter. Start by including:

- A description of what each school wants, including any forms they must fill out

- A copy of your professional resume

- A list of courses that you have taken with them

- A list of projects that you worked on with them

- A list of extracurricular activities that you have participated in, such as professional association memberships, volunteer activities, related course work, and leadership roles

- An explanation of why you are applying to the program

Be sure to thank your references and to keep them posted of your progress.

Getting financial assistance

Financial aid is not just for incoming freshman. Although you may need to be a full-time student at an accredited school to receive a full scholarship, you can find financial aid options as a non-traditional student.

To understand how to apply for scholarships or grants, visit the Free Scholarship Search Web site at `www.freschinfo.com/strategy-nontrad.phtml`. In addition to valuable how-to information, this site has a database of information about 169,000 scholarships provided by over 2,000 organizations. Or consult a printed list of scholarships, such as *Scholarships 2001,* published by Kaplan, which includes unrestricted scholarships that are worth at least $1,000 and do not have to be repaid.

While thinking about the financial side of going to school, consider the following creative ways to finance your education:

- ✔ Check with your current employer about educational reimbursement programs or scholarships.

- ✔ Talk with your accountant about tax credits for educational expenses.

- ✔ Investigate a home equity loan.

- ✔ Secure a loan using another asset, whether it's your savings account or retirement fund.

- ✔ Consider going to school part-time so that you can lower your school costs while still pulling in a paycheck.

Going to school

Becoming a student at this point in your life is bound to be a transition. Ease into the lifestyle by taking only one course your first term, especially if you plan to also work full time. That way, you get a taste of how much attending classes, doing your homework, preparing for tests, and doing projects impacts your life and your family. You may even want to do this before you enroll in a full program.

Because your time is at a premium while you are in school, you may need to rearrange some parts of your life in order to make the most of your schooling. Think about the following as you prepare to start your studies:

- ✔ **Adjusting your priorities:** With school entering the picture, your life may change form. Make a list of your three top priorities. By being clear about your new priorities, you can make decisions in alignment with your current reality.

- ✔ **Giving friends, family members, and coworkers a heads-up:** Tell the people in your life that you may not be as available as you have been and why. If you take care of this in an up-front manner, you are less likely to offend people who don't understand why you've pulled back or disappeared. Be sure to warn people when midterms and finals roll around.

✔ **Setting aside time to study:** Create a system to stay on top of your schoolwork. Keep up with reading assignments and begin thinking about projects as soon as they are assigned. You are investing too much time, money, and effort to shortchange your learning by cramming before tests and rushing to finish projects.

✔ **Finding new ways to get things done at home and at work:** Simplify wherever possible. For example, if it takes you half an hour each morning to do your hair, get it cut in a way that takes you only five. Eliminate tasks or delegate what you can by finding someone else who can accomplish the task.

You are not alone. You are part of the fastest growing segment of the student population in most colleges. To find out how others are doing it, check out these online resources:

✔ **Back to College: Resources for the Re-entry Student** (www. back2college.com): Offers oodles of articles and links to help you through your transition.

✔ **Association for Non-Traditional Students in Higher Education** (www. antshe.org/): Lets you connect with other adults returning to school and holds a conference each year.

✔ **A Room For Older College Students** (http://communities.msn.com/ Aroomforoldercollegestudents/home.htm): If you want to chat with other students over 30, visit this message board for inspiration, support, and helpful ideas.

✔ **Mom Goes Back to School** (www.suite101.com/welcome.cfm/7190): When Mom goes back to school, she may want to check out this site full of tips and articles on managing family life and school simultaneously. The site also links to Web sites that help manage stress and navigate college life.

Your time in school won't last forever. While you are there, focus as much as you can on enjoying the process of learning!

Sticking with it

If you enter a degree program, make choices that you can live with over the long haul. For example, remember the following:

✔ **Pace yourself.** Take the number of classes that you can handle reasonably, even if it takes you longer to finish the program. If you take too big a bite too soon, you may get so overwhelmed that you drop out entirely.

✔ **Choose what interests you.** When you have the opportunity to choose a topic for a paper or a project, choose one that is relevant and meaningful to you personally or professionally. That way, you can start applying what you learn today rather than waiting until you finish your degree. If you can choose electives, take courses that feed your mind and soul while you work through the required courses.

✔ **Incorporate rewards.** Whenever you see a big project or test looming before you, plan a reward for when you finish. Thinking of your day off, a weekend away, or a long soak in a hot tub can do much to keep you motivated.

✔ **Stay in balance.** Pay attention to your body, your family, and yourself while you are in school. Take some time each day to do something that's nurturing — even if you can only afford 15 minutes. The to-do lists that your work and your studies produce are always there, but without your health and your family, they don't mean much at all.

Chapter 19

Taking the Steps to Get Your Job

In This Chapter

▶ Starting your job search

▶ Handling your interview with ease

▶ Making a decision about which job to take

▶ Settling into your new job

A fter deciding what direction to take with your career, you can set your plan into motion. This chapter shows you how to search for, and get, a job in your new field. If you are interested in starting a business, turn to Chapter 20.

If you remain unclear about your direction, do not attempt to launch your job search. Setting off without a clear destination is hazardous for several reasons. You could land a "great" job only to discover that it doesn't fit your needs at all. Or you could whittle away at your self-esteem, roaming around without making any discernible progress. If you can't describe what you want in a simple sentence, don't expect your contacts to pull a job out of a hat for you. Instead, take the time you need to clarify your direction. (See Chapter 17 for tips on formulating one sentence that encompasses your career objectives.)

Notice what aspects of your future that you still feel confused about and focus your attention on those pieces of the puzzle. If you can gain more clarity in one area, the rest of the pieces may fall into place more easily. Use the following list to identify the chapter of this book that can help you make sense of your situation:

- ✔ Chapter 3 assists you in clarifying your personal needs.

- ✔ Chapter 4 lays out a variety of work environments.

- ✔ Chapter 6 helps you identify your passions and interests.

- ✔ Chapters 4 and 17 guide you to blend your needs and your desires.

You can also scan the chapters in Part III to expand on the kernel of an idea you already have. Even if you have already read a chapter, take another look if necessary. Because you may be in a different space mentally than you were when you first read the chapter, you may discover new answers. A phrase or idea that you inadvertently passed over before may be all you need to bring your picture into focus.

Launching Your Search

As soon as you can state what you want, officially begin your search by taking the steps that I describe in this section. (Chapter 17 guides you through the process of describing your career objectives clearly.)

Refocusing your resume

Of course, just about anyone you talk to about your new career direction will ask for your resume. Be prepared. Before you initiate such discussions, rework your resume so that it reflects your new direction.

If you are entertaining two similar, but different, career directions, you are embarking on two simultaneous job searches. Create a distinct resume for each one by listing your experiences in a way that highlights the skills that are particularly relevant for each career.

To be effective, your resume must catch someone's attention and hold it long enough for him to see that you are a viable candidate for the job. To increase the readability of your resume, make sure that the following crucial information is easy to spot:

- If you include an objective statement, use the title of the job you are applying for in the statement so that your resume is categorized correctly by those reading it. Avoid meaningless, showy phrases about how you want to contribute to the company.

- Use a format that gives the reader a good sense of what you did in each job you have held. Use paragraphs to describe your responsibilities and then list three or four bullets to illustrate your accomplishments in each job.

- Make your accomplishments more convincing by weaving in quantifiable results, such as creating a 50 percent increase in annual sales, managing a million dollar project budget, producing a 30 percent cost savings, or managing a team of 20 volunteers, into your resume.

✔ If you are changing careers, translate what you accomplished in your old career into the terminology of the new industry. You want the reader to get the gist of your experience without stumbling over unfamiliar terms.

✔ In the past, experts recommended limiting your resume to one page. Now, with career changes and shorter job tenures, you may need more than one page to show all your relevant experience. However, your resume should be as concise and easy to scan as possible.

✔ If you gained experience in your new area through volunteer work, part-time work, or project work in your job, incorporate the information straight into your resume. If the information doesn't fit in your resume, include a paragraph or two in your cover letter to highlight your experience.

✔ Use a carefully crafted cover letter to justify why you are the person for the job.

For additional tips on writing an effective resume, consult *Resumes For Dummies,* by Joyce Lain Kennedy, published by Hungry Minds, Inc.

Alerting your network

At this point in your career exploration, you have developed an extended network of contacts. (See Chapter 15 for more information on building your list of contacts.) Your list may consist of friends, colleagues, informational interview contacts, and people you met through professional associations. Although you may have talked to some of them fairly recently, reconnect with them to let them know exactly what you are looking for.

Be explicit in your request. Ask your contacts to forward your resume if they know of any openings that fit your description or anybody who may know of openings in your field.

If you don't already have a recruiter or two in your network, ask around to see if your friends can connect you with one. Recruiters are connected; networking is their business! If they don't place people in your area of expertise, they can refer you to someone who does. Recruiters work in several ways under several titles, including the following:

✔ **Headhunters:** Place qualified full-time applicants in a range of companies. They often serve a certain industry or profession.

✔ **Recruiters:** Work within an agency to find temporary or contract employees for a variety of client companies.

✔ **Staff or onsite recruiters:** Search for applicants to fill the staffing needs for one particular company.

Creating a multifaceted resume

Producing a polished resume printed on high-quality paper used to be the job applicant's goal, but times have changed. In today's working world, you must have a high quality resume that can be in one or more of the following formats:

✔ **E-mailed:** Send your resume in rich text format (RFT) to eliminate the need for compatible software at the other end.

✔ **Faxed:** When possible, include a specific name on the cover sheet to ensure your resume reaches the correct party.

✔ **Scanned:** Eliminate all fancy fonts and graphics if you expect the company to scan your resume into their database.

✔ **Posted on the Internet:** For details about how to do this, see the section, "Searching online and off."

✔ **Handed out in person:** Be prepared. Always bring a copy of your resume to your interview.

Before you start your search in earnest, experiment with these various media to verify that your resume comes across as intended.

Recruiters find qualified people to fill job openings. They talk with people constantly and are extremely busy professionals. Don't ask them to help you figure out what your next career should be. You can't expect them to be a walking job board. Inform them of what you want and then continue your search on your own.

The more clearly you can describe your ideal job, the better any recruiter or contact can assist you. When you call your contacts, have a carefully thought out description of what you are looking for. After your conversation, be prepared to forward your description as part of your cover letter, whether in bullet or paragraph form, to them along with your resume.

Searching online and off

In addition to tapping your network for openings, do your own footwork to find potential jobs. Start by brainstorming about the places that are likely to post jobs in your field. Consider the following resources as a place to start:

✔ Check out the jobs listed by your professional association.

✔ Visit your local career center to review their lists of openings.

✔ Attend any relevant job fairs in your geographic area.

✔ Surf Web sites related to your industry or profession for sites that provide job listings.

- Scan the want ads in your Sunday paper.
- Target key companies in your area by visiting their Web sites or their onsite job boards.

Consider posting your resume on a Web-based job board so that recruiters and hiring personnel can find you. Check out these sites if you want to pursue this option:

- Monster.com and HotJobs.com allow you to search jobs in a wide variety of locations and industries.
- Job-hunt.org, RileyGuide.com, and JobSleuth.com provide lists of job search sites for various professions, industries, and regions.
- Your professional or industry associations' job boards.

Companies pay a fee to gain access to many of these job boards, so don't refer a recruiter or contact to your posted resume unless you have verified that they have access to that particular board.

If you are currently employed, your employer may use these same job boards to find qualified applicants. Think about the ramifications of your employer finding your resume posted on one of these sites. To avoid this potential problem, you have two options:

- Some job boards provide a confidential resume option in which your name and your current company are hidden from view. Interested recruiters can send you a blind e-mail, and then you can decide whether to release your identity to them.
- You can post your resume, along with articles or examples from your portfolio, on your personal Web page. Then, when you e-mail potential employers, you can include your Web address in your e-mails. If you are sending recruiters to your site, be careful what personal information you include on your Web site. If you decide to keep this site alive even after you get a job, you can give the Web address to people who want to know more about you.

Following Up on a Lead

After you track down a qualified lead, you must be ready to act. Following the guidelines in this section gets you off on the right foot.

First you must write a cover letter to demonstrate that you can do the job. Use phrases from the want ad or online listing to strengthen your letter. If you can't get your hands on a written explanation of the job, talk with your contacts who have a working knowledge of the kind of job you are applying for to make sure that your cover letter is on the mark.

Pay close attention to all the details in the packets you send out, whether they go by mail, e-mail, or fax. Remember to do the following:

- ✔ Proofread everything. If possible, have someone else look over your resume and cover letter. Check the spellings of the company and your contacts' names.
- ✔ Verify that your own contact information is easy to locate and accurate.
- ✔ Sign your cover letter.
- ✔ Check the spacing and overall look one last time. Changing even one word can wreak havoc with formatting.

Landing the interview

When you get the call to set up an interview, you must be prepared to talk with the recruiter or the in-house interviewer about any specific expectations you have regarding your salary, benefits, vacation time, and stock options. Be up front about your needs and listen to the interviewer's comments about the likelihood of fulfilling them. Although you may not get everything you want, you are more likely to create a job that fits your needs if you speak up at this early stage.

To make the most of the call, have the following items:

- ✔ Notes in front of you so that you know with whom you are speaking.
- ✔ Calendar at hand so that you can commit to an interview on the spot.
- ✔ Pen handy so that you can take notes during the conversation for future reference.

Your first interview may last about an hour, but be prepared to interview with a series of people. If you have time constraints, make that clear when you arrange the interview. Most companies are considerate about time limitations, but sometimes interviews start later or run longer than anticipated. Take this into account when scheduling your time. As you finish your interview, inquire about the next step. The interviewer's answer gives you some idea of when you may hear word.

Preparing for the interview

Your resume is your interviewer's starting point, so you need to know your resume inside and out. Be prepared to talk about specific jobs and particular projects in detail. In your interview, you may be asked questions that require you to explain and defend your experience and how it relates to the job that you are interested in. This is especially true if you are changing careers.

If certain aspects of your resume make you feel uncomfortable, don't expect to hide them from your interviewer. Find a way to make peace with them. The more confident you feel about your explanations, the less time your interviewer may spend digging into the issue.

Come up with plausible explanations for the gaps and bumps in your employment history before the interview. Ask yourself the following questions to help you prepare:

- ✔ Were you in school, parenting, caretaking, recovering from an illness, or traveling?
- ✔ Were you laid off, fired, downsized, or right-sized?
- ✔ Did you quit? If so, why?

Give enough detail to provide an adequate explanation, but don't ever speak about your former employer or manager in a petty, blaming, or vindictive manner. If there was a problem, have a solution or an idea to share with your interviewer to show that you have a proactive attitude about the situation.

Fidgeting, breaking eye contact, or taking on an apologetic tone of voice while responding to these questions tips your hand. Recruit a friend to help you role-play your answers to a few key questions. Practice until your response rolls off your tongue without hesitation.

Asking the hard questions

Any interview is a two-way street. Just as your interviewer asks you pointed questions to verify that you are a good fit for the company's culture and the position, you must ask questions to determine if the company suits you.

To create a list of questions, do the following two kinds of research:

- ✔ **Review what you know you need in a job.** Pay particular attention to work environment issues and your personal lifestyle preferences. Ask questions to verify that the job can blend well with your life.
- ✔ **Increase your understanding of the company and the industry.** Check out the company's Web site and read about their products, technology, key players, and history. Check the local press for information about the company and the company's competition.

When you can, conduct your research several days before the interview to give yourself a chance to think about what you read. Then the night before your interview, review the information so that it is fresh in your mind.

Looking for gaps in their story

As you review your interviews, notice any gaps or inconsistencies in what you saw, heard, and sensed in each job. Don't side-step your intuition for any reason. If something doesn't add up, dig deeper to uncover the real story. Although no job is perfect, you want to go into a new career with your eyes open, as aware of the whole story as possible.

Interviewing is like dating. Each party purposely portrays themselves in the best possible light. Look and listen for clues to uncover the whole story. Does what the interviewer says match what you read in the newspaper yesterday or saw on the newsgroup discussion last night?

Getting a feel for the place

In addition to asking questions, keep your eyes and ears open during your visit. You can discover a fair amount about the company culture by observing what happens around you. Take in as much information as you can by doing the following:

- ✔ Sensing the pace
- ✔ Checking out the décor
- ✔ Noticing how work groups are laid out
- ✔ Observing interactions among coworkers

Can you imagine yourself working there?

Waiting with patience

After the interview comes the wait. This wait is not an easy one for anybody.

Depending on the job market, events at the company, the scheduling of other interviews, and what you were told at the end of your interview, you may get a call immediately, or you may not hear from the interviewer for a week or so.

If you don't hear from the interviewer or your recruiter when you think you should, place a call. Thank the person for the interview, reiterate your interest in the job, and, if they don't have any news, ask when you should follow up with them again. Listen to what they have to say. A delay does not necessarily mean bad news. They may have more people to interview, a key decision-maker may be out of town, or they may have had another job open up unexpectedly. If time passes and you still haven't heard anything, place another call.

Even as every cell in your body waits for the phone to ring, keep talking with contacts and keep track of any openings that are available in case this job offer falls through. Balance your job search activities with stress relievers such as exercising, socializing, and relaxing with a good novel.

Evaluating Your Options

By now, you may feel fairly certain about what you want and need in your work life. Just because possible jobs are falling in your lap, don't let amnesia take hold now!

Making a list of your options

Think about all you know about each job you've interviewed for so far. How well does each job fit your needs?

Create a complete list of everything you want in a job by reviewing Chapters 3, 4, 7, and 17. Then rate each job on each element of your list using the following symbols. Be as honest with yourself as possible as you complete this assessment process using the following rating system:

- ✔ "+": I am likely to have this element in this job.
- ✔ "0": I may have this element some of the time, but not all of the time.
- ✔ "-": I am unlikely to have this element in this job.
- ✔ "?": I am not sure that this element is likely to be present in this job.

A section of your list could look like this:

Short commute	+
Casual dress	0
Access to additional training	?
Able to use my writing skills in interesting ways	+
Having an office window	−

Look at the overall patterns, including the following:

   ✔ Do you see more "+'s" than "-'s"?

   ✔ Are there too many "?'s" or "0's" for your comfort? Do some research by asking your recruiter or other people who work at the company questions to gain the information you need to resolve any crucial unknowns.

   ✔ Do any of the "-'s" appear to be deal breakers? If so, see the following section, "Distinguishing deal-breakers from trade-offs."

Sometimes, at first blush, it appears that a potential job is great, but how does it really compare to the last few jobs you have held? Evaluate your previous jobs using the same elements and scoring system. Doing so helps you see whether your new options are a better fit or not. If the new position is a better fit, you are on your way. If it's not, take a moment to evaluate how taking this job improves your situation. Perhaps it gives you valuable experience in a new arena or is closer to home, which cuts your commute. Whatever your rationale, be clear about why you want to take the job.

Distinguishing deal-breakers from trade-offs

A *deal-breaker* is an element of the job that directly conflicts with your needs or those of your family. Taking a job with this kind of clash means that you sacrifice a crucial part of your desired lifestyle. Depending on your lifestyle, deal-breakers might be any of the following:

   ✔ Too much travel

   ✔ Too long a commute

   ✔ Too much required evening or weekend work

A *trade-off* is something that you can give up or take on in order to have the rest of the job which does suit you. For example, trade-offs may include the following:

   ✔ More client interaction than you would prefer

   ✔ More formal dress code than ideal

   ✔ Too far from home to walk to work

If you come face to face with a deal-breaker, share your concerns with your hiring manager or your recruiter, if you are working with one, immediately.

Do not hide your concerns from your recruiter or hiring manager. Be up front about what you have discovered. Although there is no perfect time to have this conversation, you have to share your thoughts if it is clear that both you and the company are strongly considering a deal, but before the offer is actually presented.

When you share your perspective, listen to the recruiter's or hiring manager's explanation, but hold firm if you feel the issue can't be resolved. No matter how good the job looks, if a deal-breaker lurks in the details, you face a no-win situation. Better to back off now than after you are fully embroiled in the position or lifestyle. If the job looks like a great opportunity, walking away won't be easy, but then again, trying to work and live in a situation that you know from the get-go won't work can be pure misery.

A trade-off is a different matter. In this situation, only you can determine whether you can live with the consequences of taking a position that includes this particular element.

Take some time to brainstorm ways to minimize the impact the trade-off may have on your family and your work life. Check in with your recruiter to see if anything can be done to bring the job more into alignment with your needs.

Receiving an Offer

When a hiring manager extends an offer, he expects you to say yes with great enthusiasm. If you feel confused or uneasy at the thought of receiving an offer from one of the companies you interview with, take some time to think through the situation before the offer is presented to you. Is a deal-breaker or trade-off bothering you (see the preceding section for more information on deal-breakers and trade-offs)? Are you afraid the job isn't a good fit? Talk candidly with your recruiter or hiring manager to get to the bottom of the situation.

Understanding the offer fully

Talk through the offer in detail. Ask the recruiter or hiring manager to clarify any points that seem unclear. If everyone has communicated clearly, the offer should contain no surprises.

Unfortunately, that's not always the case. If the offer comes in with a lower job title, a lower salary, or fewer benefits than you expected, ask for some time to think over your situation. Read the section "Evaluating Your Options" earlier in this chapter and rate the elements of the job with this new information in mind. Even if it is not ideal, is this job still a good opportunity to expand your experience in your target career area?

Giving your final answer

After you have a full understanding of exactly what's included in the offer, give the recruiter or hiring manager your answer:

- ✔ If the offer is not what you expected and does not give you what you need to survive or thrive, you must say no. As hard as it is to do, walk away, especially if a deal-breaker is part of the package. Although this offer didn't work out, keep in touch with the recruiter or hiring manager in case other employment opportunities arise.

- ✔ If you determine that you feel comfortable with any trade-offs present in the offer, accept the position. If you find that you need help resolving a trade-off, you may decide to make your acceptance of the job contingent on finding solutions together.

- ✔ If the offer matches what you were told during the interview process, you can take the job with some confidence in the communication channels.

Giving notice

After you accept and sign an offer, you need to give notice at your current company, if you have one.

Although it is customary to give two weeks notice, be prepared. Some companies with sensitive data may walk you out as soon as you resign, giving you only a moment to pack up your personal items. If you want to have closure with people you worked with, create a list of phone numbers and e-mail addresses and take it home with you before you give notice so that you can let these people know where you went.

If you remain for the full two weeks, continue to participate fully. Finish projects, leave instructions for whoever takes over your active projects, and create closure with those people you worked with. Feel free to daydream about your future career to help the time pass. You may also have to field questions from every corner about where you are going next. Depending on the situation, this may be fun because you get to talk about your next adventure, or it could be a bit awkward if you are going to a competitor or doing something that seems like an unusual move to your coworkers. Share as much or as little detail as feels comfortable.

Updating your network

As you leave one company to join another, share your news with everyone in your network. Thank them again for their assistance and give out your new contact information so that they can reach you if they ever need your help.

In the changing world of work, it makes good sense to keep in regular contact with your network. Although you are employed today, you may not be in the months and years to come. Having a solid, active network can make all the difference in your job search.

Feeling at Home in Your New Career

As you walk in the doors of your new career for the first time, you enter a different world with a new language, new players, and new goals. Keep these tips in mind as you settle into your new profession:

- ✔ **Stay calm in the midst of change.** Although starting something new can be exciting, you may also feel a bit unsettled or overwhelmed by the differences. Rather than fight these feelings, accept that you don't know, and can't know, all there is to know yet. Breathe and give yourself permission to ease into your new career.

- ✔ **Manage your expectations of yourself.** Before you can expect yourself to perform at the level you did in your last career, you must give yourself time to get a feel for the ropes. Expecting too much of yourself too soon can sabotage your performance. Have patience with yourself and the process of learning again.

- ✔ **Listen to the lingo.** Your first mission in a new job is to understand the language. Don't be shy. Inquire about acronyms and phrases you've never heard before. Ask if there is a glossary or translation Web page for new employees. Before criticizing yourself, remember that acronyms often crop up so rapidly that even seasoned employees have a hard time keeping track of them.

- ✔ **Get to know the players.** In your previous career, you probably knew whom to contact for what without even thinking about it. You can reach that point again — it may just take some time. Sometimes the best person to approach isn't the obvious choice. Establish a relationship with a trustworthy coworker to help you tap into the infrastructure more quickly.

✏ **Put your best foot forward, staying true to yourself.** Obviously, as you start a job in your new career, you want to make a good impression. To accomplish this, you may go out of your way to exceed your managers' expectations. Although you may win points this way, you may also significantly raise the bar of what others expect of you. Don't set up unrealistic patterns of availability or productivity if you don't want to sustain them. Be clear about your boundaries. Where you can, set limits from the start, so that your boss and coworkers know how you work.

Starting a new job is just as much of a transition as leaving your old job. See Chapter 21 for tips on navigating this time of transition.

At some point, you may find this new job isn't as fulfilling as it once was, or that a change in management or the company mission has irreparably changed your job. Take stock of your situation by reading Chapter 2. The more involved you are in the strategic side of managing your career, the fewer surprises you encounter. It pays to check in every three to six months to see how you can enliven your career.

Chapter 20

Taking the Steps to Start Your Business

In This Chapter

▶ Evaluating whether you are cut out to be an entrepreneur

▶ Pinning down the details of your idea

▶ Getting down to business with your business

▶ Setting realistic expectations for yourself and your business

*I*f you like the idea of setting your own hours and structuring your work life, or if you want to bring in some extra cash, your career path may include owning a business of your own. Before you start your business, however, take some time to look at your decision from all the angles. Only then can you know for sure that you are making the right move for you and your family.

Verifying That You Have What It Takes

Deciding to run your own business is a life decision that impacts your personal life as much as it does your professional one. Because the buck stops with you, it pays to know up front if your personality, life circumstances, and bankbooks are consistent with your dreams.

Looking at key personality traits

Although just about anyone can start a business, only those who are willing to work hard, be creative, and attend to details are successful.

As you think about converting your idea into a full-fledged business, evaluate whether you have the personality and the skills most often associated with entrepreneurial success. Ask yourself the following questions:

✔ Are you good at planning and organizing your time, multiple projects, and financial records?

✔ Do you have the initiative to step into the unknown, develop projects from scratch, and find new solutions to old problems?

✔ Are you physically and emotionally strong enough to handle the long, fast-paced hours associated with starting a business?

✔ Do you have the interpersonal skills to work with a wide variety of people, including vendors, clients, professionals, and staff people?

✔ Can you make solid decisions on your own, often under considerable time pressure?

✔ Do you have the passion and interest in what you do to carry you through the tough times?

If you have all but a couple of these characteristics, you can find ways to compensate for what you lack by increasing your training, partnering with someone else, or hiring people who have the skills you don't.

Possessing the right technical knowledge

Do you have the knowledge you need to provide your service or manufacture your product? You have to bank on these skills to make your business work, so plan to take the classes you need to update and refine your skills.

Depending on your business, you may not have to know everything yourself. You may just need to know who to consult to find out the answer. If this is the case, line up technical experts to help you on specific projects or on an on-call basis.

Having the practical business skills

Many new businesses fail because the owners don't have the skills they need to make sound business decisions.

As you make your decision to start a business, assess the skills you have and those you may need to run the business side of your venture. For example:

✔ Bookkeeping, accounting, and financial analysis

✔ Marketing and sales

✔ Inventory selection, management, and display

You don't necessarily need to be a renowned expert in these areas, but to make informed decisions, you need to know enough to oversee and converse intelligently with those handling these tasks for you. Spend the time and money required to enhance your knowledge of key topics so that your lack of knowledge doesn't sabotage your success.

Exploring potential funding options

Before you even think about launching your business, evaluate your financial situation carefully. Regardless of whether you need a couple hundred dollars to get started or more than a million, you must get a sense of your options. Think about where the money may come from to do the following:

✔ Fund the start-up phase of your venture, including the cost of developing your service or manufacturing your product, your general overhead, and your taxes and any licensing fees.

✔ Cover the business's operating expenses for the start-up period. Do some cash-flow projections to determine when your sales may begin to cover your expenses.

✔ Meet your living expenses during your start up phase.

✔ Handle personal or professional emergencies.

Although you spell out all the financial details in your business plan, to get a ball park figure for the amount of capital you need, estimate your expenses and then double or even triple that number so that you have enough funds to cover your financial responsibilities.

If you need to raise capital to start your business, consider:

✔ Your personal savings

✔ Private sources, such as family members and friends

✔ Banking institutions

✔ Entrepreneur organizations

✔ "Angel investors" who provide funding, advice, and contacts to companies in the early stages. Typically the amount of money they invest runs between $50,000 and $500,000. To read more about this concept, visit www.angelmoney.com on the Web.

✔ Venture capital firms invest in companies that need a minimum of $2 million dollars to launch.

For details about how to secure a loan, contact your local Small Business Administration office or visit the Small Business Administration's Web site at www.sba.gov/financing.

Getting emotional support

Starting a business is scary because you have to depend entirely on your own efforts to create your income. During this time, you need a support system to help you keep your feelings of fear in check.

Link up with others who are starting businesses or who are already in business. As you attend classes and networking groups, keep your eyes open for other business owners who also need support. No matter what their business, they can understand what you are going through as you deal with difficult clients, try to collect money, and figure out your pricing. Not only are you likely to feel heard and supported, you may have an opportunity to brainstorm together to find creative solutions to problems that you couldn't solve on your own.

Don't be surprised if some people in your life don't support your decision to go out on your own. Although their opinions may be hard to ignore, realize that they may feel their own fear and express it by worrying about your future. If you remain clear in your conviction, you can hold true to your goals while staying in contact with them. Or you may choose to limit your interactions with non-supporters until you have some successes under your belt.

Exploring Your Idea

Although having a business idea is a good start, you have some research to do before you can throw open your doors or Web site for business.

Defining your product or service

Begin by describing your product or service as clearly and concisely as possible. Be sure to list the key features your product or service provides as well as the benefits your customers receive.

As you write your description, don't be surprised if you notice gaps in your logic or find that you have a difficult time putting it all down on paper. Although neither of these outcomes is likely to dash your hopes of being a successful entrepreneur, you must take the time you need to sort it all out before you move forward.

As soon as you can articulate your offerings clearly with as few words as possible, you are on your way.

Defining your special niche

Many new businesses mistakenly think that if they offer anything and everything to everybody, they are more likely to be successful. Fortunately, just the opposite is often true. If your offerings are so broad that no one can clearly describe what you do, they don't become customers, and more importantly, they can't refer people to you.

You need to define your business so that it provides a particular product or service to a definable target population. Then those who hear about your business know exactly what you do and can send qualified leads your way.

For more information about establishing a viable niche, read *Nichecraft: Using Your Specialness to Focus Your Business, Corner Your Market and Make Customers Seek You Out*, by Lynda Falkenstein and published by Niche Press, or visit her Web site at www.falkenstein.com.

Talking to potential customers

With your description of your products or services in mind, approach friends and contacts who may be potential clients to see how they respond.

Listen to their questions and comments with both ears. Don't defend your idea. If they don't get it, your clients won't either, so take what you hear and revamp your product or service accordingly. Then try again.

After a few rounds of testing, you may find that people are anxious to get their hands on your product or service. After you have their attention, ask them how much they would pay for a product or service such as yours.

Checking out your competition

As you clarify your products and services, keep an eye out for others who offer something similar. As you visit their locations, read their advertisements, scan their Web sites, and review their telephone book listings, notice the key features of their offerings, how they price them, and what audience they target. Use this valuable information to help you define your niche and decide how to run your business.

If you have a hot new twist that no one else has thought of, keep it close to your chest for a while until you launch. Do your search and talk with a lawyer to determine if a trademark or patent is in order to protect your idea.

Scouting your location options

To run a successful business, you must have a location that fits your needs. Look at your business idea carefully to discern your needs. During this process, think about the following:

- ✔ How customers may interact with your business, whether in person, by phone, through other companies, or over the Internet.
- ✔ Whether you need retail, manufacturing, or office space.
- ✔ How you intend to handle shipping and receiving.
- ✔ Whether you need storage for supplies or inventory, a waiting room, or any special equipment.

If you want to work from home, check with your city to determine how it regulates home businesses.

Getting Real about Your Business

After you decide to launch your own business, a number of additional decisions rise to the surface. One of the first major decisions you must make is how you want to start your business. You have several options, including the following:

- ✔ Keep your current job and ease into your new business with a full paycheck behind you.
- ✔ Leave your current job and find a part-time job to bring in enough money to cover your basic expenses.
- ✔ Quit your job so that you can dedicate yourself full-time to your new venture.

What you decide to do is a very personal decision that depends on your finances, personality, tolerance for risk, family needs, and the kind of business you plan to start. As you read through the rest of this section, keep these scenarios in mind to see which one feels like the best fit for you and your situation.

If you don't particularly like looking at options and making decisions, you may want to rethink your decision to become an entrepreneur. As a business owner, you must make decisions, both large and small, day in and day out.

After doing your preliminary research and clarifying your business direction, begin developing your business plan. Although a requirement if you plan to borrow money, writing a business plan is a helpful exercise even if you can fund your own venture; doing so pushes you to research, plan, and estimate crucial elements of your business. The more planning you do, the fewer surprises and problems you encounter.

A typical business plan has several sections, including the following:

- **An introduction:** Describes the business, its goals, the owner, the legal structure, and its unique advantage over the competition.

- **A marketing section:** Discusses the customer demand, the market, the marketing strategy, and pricing.

- **A financial management section:** Explains your initial funding, your budget, break-even point, and methods for handling your accounting.

- **An operations section:** Outlines how you expect to run the business on a day-to-day basis.

- **A concluding statement:** Provides a summary of your goals.

For more information about what goes into a business plan, consider the following:

- Take a look at *Business Plans For Dummies* by Paul Tiffany and Steven D. Peterson, published by Hungry Minds, Inc.

- Scan the business plan outline provided by the Small Business Administration on their Web site at `www.sba.gov/starting/indexbusplans.html`.

- If you want to start a microbusiness, check out the guidelines offered by The Center for Community Futures (`www.cencomfut.com/Microbusiness.htm`).

As you develop your business plan, consider contacting the consultants in one of the following organizations:

- **Small Business Development Centers** (`www.sba.gov/SBDC`): Consultants review your plan and help you strengthen any weak spots. To locate your nearest SBDC, check your telephone book.

- **SCORE, the Service Corps of Retired Executives** (`www.score.org`): If you plan to start a larger, more traditional business, have your business plan reviewed by retired executive volunteers at SCORE. Turn to your phone book for the number of the local SCORE office.

Structuring your business

The legal structure of your business has a huge impact on its success. Do some research, consult a lawyer, and weigh the pros and cons of each option before you make your final choice about which format is best for you. Although the specifics depend on where you live, your options include the following:

✔ **Sole proprietorship:** The format for businesses run by one person

✔ **Partnership:** The structure for businesses run by two or more partners who have an oral or legal agreement to be in business together

✔ **Corporation:** A legal structure that creates a business owned by stockholders, controlled by the largest stockholder, and governed by a Board of Directors

The Small Business Administration Web site (www.sba.gov/starting/getting.html#types) is a good place to start your research. Then consider obtaining one of the Small Business Administration's Start Up Kits for corporations, partnerships, or sole proprietorships by contacting your Chamber of Commerce, visiting your local Small Business Administration Office, or downloading it from www.sba.gov/starting/indexstartup.html.

Taking Action with Your Business

After doing the proper prior planning, you can begin implementing your plan.

Creating your business identity

Developing an identity for your business typically involves creating a business name, logo, and tagline or motto that gives your potential clients a clear understanding of what your business provides. As you select your colors, font, logo, paper, and Web site design, make sure that they appeal to your target market. Whether you hire a designer or do the work yourself, create the most professional looking business identity you can afford.

Because your business focus may change as you gain more understanding of what your clients want, figure in some room for modifications and limit your first print run of printed materials until you are sure that your text is finalized.

If you plan to have a Web presence, make each page count by choosing a powerful domain name, writing compelling copy, building your site, and submitting your site to search engines. A great resource for creating a successful Web presence is Make Your Site Sell at www.sitesell.com/websolutions4.html.

Choosing a name for your business

The name of your business can't compete with the name of a similar kind of business serving the same geographic area. If you expect to have only local clients, verify that your name is available by checking with the county department that assigns fictitious names and the state government office that tracks corporations and trademarks. Use the Small Business Administration Web page at www.sba.gov/hotlist/businessnames.html to find the right state office for your research.

If you expect to have a national or international clientele, do adequate research to ensure that the name you want to use is available. Even if you aren't sure you want to establish a trademark, you need to do this research, because if someone else owns the trademark, you have no right to use the name yourself. You can conduct a free initial search, pay for a more complete research report on the availability of your name for a trademark, and apply for your trademark by visiting www.nameprotect.com or contacting a trademark lawyer.

You may also want to verify that you can obtain a domain name that works for your business. Although you may want your domain name to match your business name, consider incorporating your key benefit into your domain name. For example, I work primarily with people who are feeling stuck in their careers and their lives, so I chose www.getrollingagain.com as my domain name. Since then, I have had prospective clients recall my domain name months after I gave them my card because the benefit it describes is just want they needed. To investigate whether your preferred domain name is available, visit www.networksolutions.com/cgi-bin/whois/whois.

Establishing your work space

To be an effective entrepreneur, you must have a space dedicated to your business. If you have a store or office outside your home, carve out a place within the larger area that you can call your own. If you plan to work from home, establish a physical location for your office and set up some ground rules with your family so that they know how to interact with you while you are working.

As you design your space, pay attention to how you like to work. Don't spend big bucks on a formal desk if you prefer to sit in an easy chair or at a worktable with your laptop. Modular furniture can be a good investment because as you and your business grow, you can reform your office to fit your changing needs.

Developing sustainable marketing strategies

To get business to come to you, you must create an effective marketing strategy to get the word out to your prospective clients. For the best results, you must develop a coordinated strategy that you can sustain over time.

Marketing is an art. Begin with your best marketing piece, track its successes and failures, and then modify what doesn't work or replace it with something that has a b tter chance of working.

To be effective, you must feel comfortable enough with your marketing methods that you can make them an integral part of doing business. Having three or four strategies you employ consistently is generally more effective than a scattered approach done intermittently.

Just because your business is booming, don't think you can stop your marketing efforts. It is imperative that you market continuously, even when your business is thriving.

Feeling at Home in Your Own Business

If you've always worked in a corporate situation, becoming an entrepreneur may take some getting used to. For possibly the first time in your life, you can call your own shots, which may feel both refreshing and unnerving.

Expecting everything to take longer than you expect

In a corporate setting, a number of people are involved in making things happen. In your own business, you are responsible for everything — from keeping your supplies stocked and handling shipping to negotiating deals and delivering products or services to clients.

You may be absolutely amazed at how long it can take to get what seems like a simple letter drafted, printed, and out the door to the mail box. Just the handling of everyday correspondence, e-mails, and phone calls can consume your entire day.

At some point, you may find it worth the expense to hire someone to help out with certain tasks. Keep the following tips in mind when considering recruiting help from others:

✔ Start by making a list of all the tasks that must be done to run your business and provide your product and service to your clients.

✔ Group the tasks by functions, such as administration, development, production, marketing, sales, inventory and distribution, and customer follow-up.

✔ Identify the tasks that you enjoy doing and are good at.

✔ As you look at the remaining tasks, ask yourself if you are the best person to do a particular task. If you have the skills, but lack the desire, you can handle it, but if you lack both the skill and the desire, you are probably better off finding someone to support that aspect of your business. This is especially true if you tend to procrastinate each time you need to handle the task.

✔ Go through all the tasks and group the ones you'd rather not handle. As you look at the list, brainstorm who can help you out, which could include the following people:

- A family member who can pitch in

- A friend who may have some extra time on her hands

- An independent contractor who has the specialty that you need

- An employee you hire to take on particular tasks

If you choose to hire employees, you must look at the tax and liability implications of your decision. The Small Business Administration has a Start-Up Kit for New Employers, which outlines the basics. A conversation with your accountant is also in order.

Learning from each experience

You will make mistakes. Expect it and accept it. Whether you lack the experience, use poor judgment, or make a decision based on inadequate assumptions, you may wish you could redo any number of decisions, especially when you first start out.

Take any frustration and embarrassment you have with yourself and move it into a more proactive direction instead. First evaluate the situation. Determine if you can salvage the situation by having another conversation with the party involved, or if the next decision you make can reverse the damage. If neither scenario is possible, your only option may be to let it go.

Rather than berate yourself, think through how you would handle the situation differently if given the chance. Then the next time you face a similar situation, call upon your experience to guide you to a better decision.

Finding the balance in your new life

When you first start your business, you may find yourself eating, breathing, and sleeping your business. No matter how you look at it, a growing business takes a tremendous amount of dedication and focus.

Staying focused

Faced with your growing list of to-dos, you may feel that you must tackle everything today. The truth is that you shouldn't even try to do that.

As you begin each day or week, identify the tasks that must get done on that particular day. Then focus your attention on accomplishing those tasks and putting out any fires that crop up during the day. If you make a dent in your list, call it a good day. Over time and with experience, it becomes easier to create a focus for the day and stick with it.

Although you may have strategic decisions looming over you, discipline yourself not to obsess over them, especially if you can't or don't have all the information you need to make the decision. If you get thoughts or ideas about a decision you must make farther down the road, by all means make note of them.

Attempting to make strategic decisions while in the midst of handling your day-to-day business affairs is like mixing oil and water. Set aside a day or weekend to get away from your business environment so that you can clear your head enough to make sound, long-range decisions for your business.

And yet to succeed, you must keep yourself in tip-top shape. Find ways to eke out enough time and space for yourself, your family, and your friendships. Several strategies may help, including the following:

- ✔ **Combining activities:** If you make friends with other entrepreneurs, you can set up a regular time to problem-solve, brainstorm, or offer support while having lunch or taking a walk.

- ✔ **Creating boundaries:** Designate a certain time of day or day of the week where you step away from your business and your responsibilities. When you take this time off, you must discipline your mind to let go of work, as well.

Part V
The Part of Tens

The 5th Wave   By Rich Tennant

"The whole jungle thing got too much for me after a while."

In this part . . .

No matter how you look at it, changing careers is quite an experience. As you navigate the highs and the lows of the process, look to this part for advice on ways to stay sane when everything around you is changing. This part also features a chapter full of tips on how to stay motivated during your career change.

Chapter 21

Ten Tips for Staying Sane During Your Career Change

In This Chapter

▶ Creating space in your life to think things through

▶ Shifting your perspective from the old to the new

▶ Stepping into new options

*W*hether you are in the midst of a career change by design or by circumstances, the results of your transition can impact nearly every part of your life. As you navigate the inevitable ups and downs of this process, conflicting emotions, ranging from confusion, panic, excitement, clarity, and inner peace, can surface. The tips in this chapter can help you make sense of your journey and keep your balance during the process.

Committing One Way or the Other

If you sit on the fence about changing your career, you can tie up so much of your energy wondering whether or not to take the next step that you don't have the energy necessary to actually make your move.

Deciding to change your career does not mean you must quit tomorrow. In fact, I recommend that you stay in your current job, if you can; you can more easily make clear decisions about your future when you don't have to worry about how to make ends meet. The only exception to this is if your job is so toxic, or you are so burned out, that you can't think clearly after a day at work. If you are in either of these situations, review the options that I describe in Chapter 5.

You may also worry that if you start the ball rolling, you may lose control of the process and be forced to make decisions and choices that you aren't ready to make. A career change is a process that entails a number of decisions. At each point, you decide how and whether to move forward.

As you think about your decision to change careers, notice any other fears lurking in the back of your mind. Sometimes the fears that you believe are based in fact are actually rooted in assumption. Do you really know that you can't make the same income in another job? Do you really know that you can't negotiate the same benefits in another position? Catch these unfounded fears early on so that they won't sabotage your career change.

If you are sitting on the fence, make a choice one way or the other. Commit to focusing your attention solely on your current career for another six months or a year. Or decide to open up your exploration to include a broad range of options.

Often, the sooner you decide to launch your exploration, the more control you have over how the process takes shape.

If you work in a company that's having problems, or if you are miserable in your job, be careful not to fall into one of the following traps:

- ✔ Don't put your loyalty to the company above your loyalty to yourself.
- ✔ Don't ignore signs that you or your company are in trouble.
- ✔ Don't be lulled into thinking that your dissatisfaction may just go away one day.

Delaying your exploration leaves you with fewer options and a tighter time frame. When you have the opportunity, it pays to act sooner rather than later.

Gathering Your Resources

After you make the decision to change your career, swing into action and start gathering the resources that you need to navigate your transition.

Although you can get through this process fine all alone, you may find your journey more comfortable and productive if you get the information and support you need in the beginning rather than after you get stuck.

By picking up this book, you have, in a sense, already started gathering resources. Other career resources to consider include the following:

- ✔ A local career center or an outplacement company, if you were laid off
- ✔ The business section of your local paper
- ✔ Career-related Web sites, many of which I mention in previous chapters

You may also want to search for resources that can offer you emotional support. In particular, keep your eye out for the following:

> ✔ Friends who are also considering a career change
>
> ✔ My other book, *The Seasons of Change,* published by Conari Press, which provides a map to help you navigate and make sense of major life transitions

You also need to get a handle on your financial resources — the good, the bad, and the ugly. Doing so can actually increase your peace of mind in the long run. Although it may not be your favorite task, grit your teeth and estimate, at the very least, the following two numbers:

> ✔ **The minimum amount you could live on if you absolutely had to.** Knowing this number not only helps you budget if you are out of work for an extended period of time, it may also show you that you have more options than you thought.
>
> ✔ **The amount of money you could live on comfortably.** This number helps you get a sense of the income level you want to target.

Creating a Thinking Spot

During your career change, you may spend a fair amount of time thinking about yourself, your family situation, your interests, your dreams and passions, and your potential careers.

Although you may be used to thinking at your desk at work, in the car during your commute, or at home doing your chores, thinking while in motion doesn't allow you to think deeply enough to get the results you want.

Because you are redesigning your life, I encourage you to create a comfortable, soothing place to think things through. Ideally, this is a place where you can feel safe, think undisturbed by daily distractions, and record your thoughts easily.

Make this space as inviting as you can so that you actually want to spend time there.

Giving Yourself Time to Think

Although getting your resume together and contacting your network are important steps in building your new career, you can easily sabotage your progress by pushing yourself to act before you have a clear picture of what you want.

Before your mind is clear enough to identify and sort through the options, you may need to focus on resting and refueling, carving out time in your schedule to think, especially if you have experienced a lot of stress and strain leading up to your decision to make a career change.

Begin by identifying the time in your day or week when you have some time for yourself. Pay special attention to the times when you also have a clear enough head that you can think productively, which could be your lunch hour, a weekend morning, or the minutes before you go to sleep.

If you have a lot of work or family responsibilities, finding this time may be no small feat. Your best strategy is to experiment with different times. If your first strategy doesn't work, know you haven't failed. Keep trying different strategies until you find one that integrates well with your lifestyle.

If you have other transitions going on in addition to your career change, be gentle with yourself. If you are sick or have an incredibly heavy schedule for a couple of weeks, cut yourself some slack.

Creating Some Distance from Your Current Situation

Right now, your current career defines your identity. If you want to make a career change, you are probably not completely happy with this career and identity. It would be a shame to make a rushed decision about your future from this space.

To let go of this outdated persona, you must create a little distance between you and your world. Not 100 percent of the time, but enough of the time that you feel more comfortable and at home with yourself than you have. Only then can you make good decisions about your future that align with who you really are and what you really want.

As uncomfortable as it may be, you must slow down to do this. Stop at least once a day to reconnect with who you are as a person. Over the next couple of weeks, focus your attention on the following things:

- **Refueling your body, mind, and spirit:** Each day, attempt to put more fuel in your body than you expend living your life. By fuel, I mean healthy food, good rest, and adequate activity. Don't force yourself to do anything that feels like a struggle. Instead, nurture yourself.

- **Reflecting on your life and how you got here:** Don't try to figure anything out, just ruminate on the past. If you haven't already worked through the worksheets in Chapter 2, that is a great place to start.

During this time, do not make or act on any decisions. If you must make a quick decision, be sure it's a short-term commitment or has an escape clause of some sort. Even if you must take a job for financial sanity, continue your quest for the career that truly suits you.

After spending time reconnecting with your interests and needs, your feelings of exhaustion and panic subside, leaving room for creative insights and new ideas. You may even discover that you crave your time alone because so much healing happens during your reflection.

Letting Go of Old Strategies and Answers

As you face the unknowns inherent in finding your next career, you may be tempted to fall back on the strategies and answers that you've had in the back of your mind for the last several years.

Perhaps you have always thought of going back to school, moving into a different industry, becoming a consultant, or going into the Peace Corps. Take a moment to get these dreams you've held out on paper.

If you notice your energy sinks when you consider an option or think you should take a certain action, stop! For whatever reason, this is not the answer you are looking for.

Those plans were borne of the old you. An element or a version of the original plan may still be viable, but you won't know unless you let it go and see if it comes back in a different form.

Although you may feel some fear as you let go of the "sure thing" by releasing it from your mind, you allow a vacuum to be created by doing so. As soon as this space opens up, new ideas can come to you.

Getting out of a Rut

Up until now, you have no doubt spent a considerable amount of time going over your career situation, trying to find a solution. You may have gone down this road so many times that you are stuck in a rut. All your questions lead to the same answers, and all the answers seem to lead to dead ends.

The turning point in your career change journey occurs when you find a new way to see your situation. New perspectives point to new ideas and directions.

Start by looking at your work history and personal past. Do you see any patterns? For example, did you do any of the following:

- ✔ Report to the same nightmare of a boss in several jobs?

- ✔ Fall into jobs by taking the first offer that came along?

- ✔ Make career decisions based on your education rather than your interests?

- ✔ Get fired from several jobs?

- ✔ Have a difficult time maintaining good relationships with your coworkers?

Think about the explanations you have had for these patterns in the past. Can other reasons for the patterns exist? Experiment by brainstorming alternative explanations.

Rather than pointing your finger at someone else or the situation itself, look at your own behavior to see what you might do differently the next time around.

The following comments came from people who have experienced these patterns:

- ✔ "Looking back, I see that I had clues that the last two bosses were going to be like my first boss, but I didn't pay enough attention to my intuition during the interviews because the jobs seemed so good. In my next interview, I plan to ask specific questions to verify my prospective boss' personality and management style. No need to go down that road again!"

- ✔ "I feel so insecure about myself when I don't have a job that I just take what's there. I need to focus on building my sense of confidence so that I can hold out for the right job."

- ✔ "I never knew what I was interested in before now, so I focused on what I knew. Next time around, I know to keep my interests high on my list of priorities."

- ✔ "I didn't act very responsibly in my jobs early on, so they were right to fire me. I learned valuable lessons in each case."

- ✔ "I tend to lose ground quickly with aggressive people. I need to gain more skills in working with difficult people."

With a new understanding of why the past has been the way it has, you can see new, unexpected vistas open up before you.

Looking for breakthrough possibilities

If you have had a rocky career, you may need to look beyond your career to discover more about yourself and how you function. The following three concepts have played a tremendous role in helping some of my clients break through old patterns that were keeping them stuck. By gaining more clarity about the dynamics that have played out in their lives, sometimes since childhood, they found a better understanding of their personal style and unique way of being in the work world. With this information, they built a career and life that capitalized on their strengths. They no longer had to force themselves to live and work in ways that didn't work for them.

Each of the following Web sites offers a questionnaire that you can take to discover more

about your personal style. Even if you feel a bit skeptical, take the time to complete these questionnaires. Who knows — what you discover may provide the clue you've been searching for:

- **Adult Attention Deficit Disorder:** `http://bevkprice.com/web38.html`
- **Highly Sensitive Person:** `www.hsperson.com/pages/test.htm`
- **Success Anorexia:** `www.permissiontosucceed.com`

If you resonate with one or more of these ideas, delve into the concept to discover more about why your life and career have been the way they have been.

Finding the Open Doors

As you proceed with your career change, notice how easy or difficult it is to gain access to the information, contacts, leads, and details you need to make progress.

Do you find a pattern of "closed doors?" For example, do you do the following things:

- Lose someone's number, and then when you do reach him, he doesn't call you back as agreed?
- Miss several appointments with people in the same field for reasons completely beyond your control?
- Have trouble landing a second interview in your target industry no matter how hard you try?

Or are you finding "open doors" such as the following:

- ✔ You think about connecting with someone to ask a question, and they contact you before you have a chance to place your call.
- ✔ You start to think about moving in a new direction, and a casual conversation with a friend gives you the lead you need.
- ✔ You shift your focus slightly and land several interviews in the span of a week.

You have a choice. If you continually run into closed doors, step back to evaluate. Ask yourself the following questions:

- ✔ Are you moving in this direction because you want to or because you think you should?
- ✔ Is this the right time to take action?
- ✔ Do you need to handle something first?

Even if you have a vested interest in this direction, it may not be worth fighting against the river. Adjust your tactics a bit to see if the shift opens doors for you. Finding and walking through doors that open easily means more results in less time.

If you are running around frenetically, you may miss the signs that a door is open right in front of you. Use your reflection time to pick up on the subtle signs that something is working. Noticing these leads and acting on them comes from being calm within yourself and trusting yourself to make good decisions.

There is value in being persistent, but when your path gets blocked time and time again, listen. Take a step back to reevaluate your direction. Be brutally honest with yourself. Don't stick with something just because you said you would. If it's not working, read the writing on the wall and take a different tactic. Positive results can follow.

Creating a Plan, Then Acting on It

After you have some clarity about your direction, draw up your career plan. Put what you know down on paper. Rearrange the order until it works. Identify the gaps in your plan and then do the thinking and research to fill them in. Even if you can't assign specific dates, get a sense of what you need to accomplish first, second, and third.

By writing down your plan, you can enhance your chances of making progress and staying sane by doing the following:

✔ Setting realistic goals for yourself

✔ Focusing on one or two priorities at a time

✔ Breaking projects into bite-sized tasks so that even if you only have 20 free minutes, you can make progress

✔ Realizing that sometimes you don't have control over the timing of events. If you are waiting for information on one aspect of your plan, shift your focus to another task.

Review your plan periodically. As you receive more information, adjust your goals and priorities accordingly.

If you find yourself struggling with a task, look at it to determine what is getting in your way. Then do what you can to clear the block so that you can proceed with your plan.

Acknowledging the Transition in Your New Career

When you do land a position in your new career, realize that starting a job or a business is a transition in itself. Although this transition may not be as intense as the one you experienced getting into your new career, you are definitely in a period of adjustment. With your new career come the following things:

✔ A new identity

✔ New colleagues, company culture, and management team

✔ New patterns on the home front

✔ Loss of old friends and structures

✔ Loss of your old identity

✔ Loss of your quiet time

Rather than bolting out and jumping in to this new world, be gentle with yourself. Give yourself some time to ease into the new patterns and ways of your life.

Even though it is an exciting time, don't be surprised if you feel tired and a bit overwhelmed as you take in all the new information and meet all the new players. Depending on how much this job differs from your last one, you may take several weeks or several months to fully adjust to your new career.

Chapter 22

Ten Keys to Keeping Yourself Inspired and Motivated

• •

In This Chapter

▶ Discovering ways to keep yourself moving forward

▶ Stimulating your creativity

▶ Finding encouragement in the world around you

• •

As time goes by and you find yourself still in the midst of your career change, your spirits may take a dip. When you feel that you could use an extra boost, inspire and motivate yourself with one of the following suggestions.

Scanning the News for Fascinating Careers

Believe it or not, your local newspaper can be a great source of inspiration. Look beyond the news articles and scan for the human-interest stories, profiles of outstanding individuals, and stories about famous people that you admire.

As you read each article, see what gems you can pick up about moving from one career to the next. Ask yourself the following questions about the people and stories you read about:

✔ What is their passion?

✔ What led them into their careers?

✔ What did they do before?

✔ How did their original profession prepare or position them for their new career?

✔ Do they offer any motivating quotes or encouraging words you can take with you?

Put yourself in their shoes. Imagine what they feel as they live their lives. Think about the part of their stories that resonate with you.

Reading about the fascinating things people do expands your vision of what's possible. Sometimes the careers highlighted in these articles are inspirational in themselves because they show how, with a little creativity and ingenuity, you can create career magic. For example:

- ✔ A retired auto-repair shop owner founded a $4 million company that makes the popular Cactus Juice product from a native plant previously considered to be a bothersome weed to be burned, bulldozed, or sprayed by ranchers.

- ✔ What started out as a hobby for one man has become a successful business. He transforms corn fields into complex mazes at the request of farmers who pay him a percentage of their ticket sales, averaging about $30,000 per maze. Farmers all over the continent hire him to help them develop a secondary income source that allows them to keep their family farms.

Who knows — you may find a clue to your own future career in one of the articles you read.

Giving Yourself an Afternoon Off in a Bookstore

Sometimes the best way to reinvigorate your career search is to broaden your horizons a bit. Rather than spending the afternoon sitting in front of your computer screen or staring at your television, take the opportunity to roam your local bookstore. Even if it feels utterly counterproductive to take the afternoon off, treat yourself anyway. You may be surprised with the results.

Allow yourself to spend several hours just browsing and exploring with no time constraints, goals, or shopping lists. Let your intuition guide you. Try the following:

- ✔ Visit the sections that you are drawn to.
- ✔ Take a look in sections that you've never visited before.
- ✔ Pick up books that call to you.
- ✔ Look at any book that falls off the shelf into your lap.

When you feel bored, move on. When you feel intrigued, investigate. Pay attention to the topics and categories that interest you.

Library Resource Center
Renton Technical College
3000 N.E. 4th St.
Renton, WA 98056

If you are concerned about blowing your budget during your bookstore adventure, make a list of the interesting books that you find and promise yourself you can come back at a later time to purchase those that still call to you. If you feel you need a more fool-proof approach, leave your credit cards at home or go to the library instead.

Your bookstore journey resembles your career-change experience in more ways than one — the possibilities are endless, and sometimes overwhelming. Just immersing yourself in the unknown and getting a feel for how to navigate vast numbers of available options may help you dance more gracefully with the unknown of your own future. The more you do this activity, the more comfortable you become with making choices and trusting your sense of where to go next.

Doing a Data Dump

If your mind is filled with worries, you may not feel very inspired or motivated. Not moving forward with your plans may create even more concerns. More frustration translates into even less progress. You get the picture: a downward spiral that gets you nowhere fast.

With your mind in such a muddle, you probably can't think creatively or even logically, so don't try. Instead, focus your attention on clearing the decks by doing a data dump. Let all your worries, real and imagined, flow out of your head into your journal. Just remember, the more you get out of your head, the more room you create for new thoughts, perspectives, and solutions — exactly what you need to open the doors to progress and forward movement.

Divide a page in your journal into two columns. In the first column write down all your worries about your work or your personal life. Don't think about the order, just get them out of your head and onto the paper. Then in the second column, jot down any areas in your life where you aren't overly concerned. This column helps bring perspective to the overall picture of your life.

Now look over your lists and ask yourself the following questions:

- ✔ **How does the balance look between the two columns?** Are you surprised one way or the other? If the list of what's working is longer, you may find that you breathe a bit easier by seeing the overall picture. Or if your list of what's not working far outweighs the other list, you may feel more compassion for yourself.

- ✔ **Are most of your concerns of a strategic, large-scale nature or more nuts and bolts life stuff?** Your answer to this question can help you focus your attention on the tasks that produce the results you need to get moving again.

Library Resource Center
Renton Technical College
3000 N.E. 4th St.
Renton, WA 98056

✔ **Are some of your worries related?** Can you group any of them together? As you look at the categories, can you put some worries on the back burner for the time being so that you can focus your attention on your career change?

✔ **Could you resolve any of your worries today or this week with just a little effort?** If making a dent in this list would free up your mind to focus on your career change, set aside a week or several hours each day for a while to knock these tasks off your list. The time you spend on these items, even if they don't directly relate to your career, may prove time well spent.

Starting with What Feels Easy

Although you may think that you should tackle the hardest part of your job search first, starting with what feels easy may be far more motivating and productive in the long run! With this strategy you do the following:

✔ You make progress right off the bat.

✔ You build your sense of confidence each step of the way.

✔ You can keep moving because the next task doesn't put you off.

✔ You can apply what you discover to the tougher tasks as you go.

If you can't seem to make any progress with your career change, ask yourself the following questions:

✔ **Are you taking too big a bite?** Break down the task into smaller bite-sized bits. For example, rather than write your resume in one sitting, begin by listing and describing your positions or writing notes about your accomplishments. After you have these thoughts on paper, writing your resume isn't so overwhelming.

✔ **Is the timing wrong?** Timing is everything in a job search. As much as you want it to move quickly, you may need to wait out circumstances beyond your control in your own life or the company itself. Do you need to take care of your planned surgery or your out-of-town guests before you can focus on your career change?

✔ **Do you need more information or input before you can act?** If you are hesitant to embark on a task, sort through your thoughts to pinpoint exactly where you are getting bogged down. For example, if you don't want to talk with a key contact, think about why you are procrastinating. Would you feel more comfortable if you read up on the company, career, or lifestyle before you made contact?

> ✔ **Do you even want to do what you say you want to do?** Are you forcing yourself to pursue an out-dated career goal, a "should," or a have to? If your interests or priorities have shifted, let this career direction go and focus on what excites you with excitement today.

Rather than fighting procrastination or hesitation, use it as a signal to take a second look at the task and your motivations for doing it. Focus on doing what feels easy. Even if you accomplish only one thing each day, at least you move forward in your career change.

Letting Yourself Dream Big

Every once in a while, let your mind wander to the biggest, best expression of who you are. Let yourself dream about your next career. Don't worry about how feasible your thoughts are or how you can make them happen. Just follow your train of thought wherever it takes you.

Your enhanced vision may do the following:

> ✔ Trigger an exciting new line of thinking
>
> ✔ Remind you of something you knew at one time but had forgotten
>
> ✔ Show you a recurring theme

Take some time to explore the possibilities that surface. Whatever comes up is there for a reason, so follow it through by doing the following:

> ✔ Talk to a friend who knows something about the topic.
>
> ✔ Search the Web for more clues.
>
> ✔ Think back to the ideas you had ten years ago about the same topic.
>
> ✔ Enter your ideas into your journal for future reference.

Sometimes your visions tell you more about the essence of what you want than the literal expression of it. Sift through the layers to discover what idea, value, or desire is at the core of your picture.

Going on Vacation

As unbelievable as it seems, some of my clients have gotten their best career insights while away on vacation or upon their return.

Sometimes it's hard to fathom that anything productive can come from going on vacation, so I offer these examples from my clients and my own life as proof that wondrous shifts can and do happen when you get away:

- An afternoon journaling while sitting in a deck chair with her feet resting in the waves of the Pacific gave one client a picture of how to restructure her work to be more stimulating and satisfying.

- A cross-country drive resulted in one client moving out of state to a quieter, more rural community.

- A retreat in a cozy cabin brought me an idea that served as a catalyst to start my business.

If you can swing it, get away for at least two nights by yourself and allow yourself to do whatever you are called to while you are away.

Something happens when you get out of the daily grind and away from your usual surroundings. You find new parts of yourself as you move about unhindered by how you are "supposed" to be according to those who are usually around you. You do the following:

- Take risks

- Try new things

- Experiment with how you present yourself to others

- Have the experience of conquering your fears, doubts, and discomfort

And as a result, you can feel freer than you've felt in years.

If your trip doesn't provide an insight, don't despair. Some of the most startling and memorable insights occur as you come back home. During your reentry, you have a great opportunity to see your life from a new vantage point as you overlay your vacation perspective on your everyday reality. In that moment, you may realize with a jolt that you can no longer put up with your crazy schedule, your obnoxious boss, or your unbearable workload.

By being a bit detached from your life, you can more easily sense what isn't in alignment with your needs. Don't disregard the messages that your body and emotions send you as you reenter your life; they remind you of your truth. Listen and act accordingly.

If you can't find a way to get out of town, unplug for a while by taking a shower, going for a walk, curling up with a good book, or going for a drive. Find ways to give your mind a chance to get away.

Projecting into the Future of Your Current Career

If you feel that you need to jolt yourself out of a pessimistic downward spiral, think about what your life would be like if you did absolutely nothing about your career. Fast forward five years and ask yourself the following questions:

- ✔ What are you doing in your career?
- ✔ Who are you working with?
- ✔ How is your health?
- ✔ How is your attitude?
- ✔ What's your family life like?
- ✔ What about your social life?

For some of my clients, projecting into the future provided the catalyst to move them into taking action and pursuing their dreams. Even if you can't put all your dreams into action, implementing even some of them takes you further, much further in some cases, than doing nothing.

If you catch yourself wondering whether you are too old to change your career, remember that in five years, you will be five years older whether you do something to change your life now or not. So why not take advantage of those years and expand your life by finding more joy, passion, and excitement than you have now?

Just for inspiration, check out what these folks have accomplished in their later years:

- ✔ **Age 52:** Ray Kroc began franchising McDonald's restaurants.
- ✔ **Age 71:** Coco Chanel designed the suit she's best known for — after coming out of retirement!
- ✔ **Age 77:** John Glenn returned to space.
- ✔ **Age 78:** Grandma Moses started painting.
- ✔ **Age 80:** Goethe finished writing *Faust*.
- ✔ **Age 90:** Grandmother, Elizabeth Eichelbaum, received her Ph.D. in Art Therapy.
- ✔ **Age 100:** Amos Alonzo Stagg continued to coach football.

Deciding How to Celebrate

You embark on a huge undertaking when changing careers: facing the unknown on a daily basis; experiencing frequent shifts in your work life and your personal life; sensing deep changes within yourself.

To help you keep at least one eye on the prize, your new career, take a moment to think about how you want to celebrate your successful career change when the time comes.

Start by brainstorming your ideal celebration. Be extravagant and state exactly what you would like, including the following:

- **What you want to do:** Have a party, take a trip, or go out to dinner, for example.

- **Whom you want to invite:** For example, just yourself, your partner, members of your family, or your friends.

- **Where you want to celebrate:** Which could be at home, in a restaurant, at a local venue, out of the country, or someplace else that has special meaning to you.

Okay, so maybe having dinner in Paris or a taking a week's vacation in Tahiti is beyond your reach. Don't fret. Take a moment to get a sense of the essence of your dream picture. Discover the feeling that you want with your celebration. Then put on your thinking cap to find a creative, more realistic way of bringing this feeling into play. Your final picture may or may not match your original one, but that's okay. Your goal is to experience the feeling that matches your initial desire.

During your career change, keep your celebration alive by creating a symbol of your celebration — a photograph of where you plan to visit, some glitter to remind you of the party ahead, a match box from the restaurant you've chosen for your celebration — and placing it where you can see it regularly. You may put it in a desk drawer at work, on your medicine cabinet, on your dash board, or in your wallet.

Use the inherent excitement and fulfillment of your celebration to fuel you to move forward and achieve your goals.

Talking with People Who Love Their Work

You are probably not particularly happy with your current career. If you complain frequently about your work, you can easily take that attitude with you to your next career. Instead, before you start your new career, prime the pump and prepare yourself to love your new job.

Without any role models, you may find it hard to imagine having a career you like, let alone love! Keep your eye out for people who obviously love what they do. It doesn't matter what job they hold, just that they enjoy their work. Talk with them to get a sense of what it's like to live life when you have a terrific career. Ask them the following questions:

- What do you love about your job?

- How do you feel when you wake up to go to work?

- Is there anything you don't like about your work? How do you deal with those things and still stay so positive?

- What's the best thing about your job?

- Was there ever a time when you didn't like your work? What did you do to change that?

After you get a sense of what it's like to love your career, start to foster that feeling of success and happiness in yourself. Begin to take notice of what it feels like when you enjoy something, anything. Don't be picky at first. You may find that you enjoy the following:

- Something related to your work, a hobby, or a social event

- A task that takes just five minutes or less to perform

- Something that you rarely do in the course of your life

No matter what you find you enjoy, notice the feeling you have. Then practice recreating that feeling wherever and whenever you can. Discover what choices you can make to bring that sense of enjoyment into your life on a more regular basis.

Although it's unlikely you can grow to love your current career at this point, it may brighten your life to see that one or two tasks in your current life add a bit of joy to your day. The better your outlook on life in general, the easier your career change can be.

Buddying Up

Changing careers is a major life transition. In addition to changing your job, you may change your identity, your social system, and your home life to some degree. During this time, you may feel confusion, a sense of chaos, and angst about not knowing where you are headed.

In all likelihood, you may hesitate to share your thoughts and fears with the following people:

- **Your colleagues at work:** Because you may need to keep your career moves confidential.

- **Your friends:** Because they are sick of hearing about it already.

- **Your family members:** Because the changes you are contemplating may make them feel uncomfortable and uncertain themselves.

The best person to support you is someone who is also in the process of changing careers. Because you both face the same issues, you are in a perfect position to inspire, support, and advise each other in ways that others can't because they aren't living the experience.

As a team, you can do the following:

- Share resources

- Brainstorm additional contacts

- Scout out leads for each other

- Role play calls, interviews, or offer negotiations

- Plot your next moves

- Celebrate your successes

After you locate a buddy, think about the ways you can interact to help each other most. For example, you may want to do the following:

- Contact each other as needed when one or the other of you thinks to call.

- Schedule a weekly call or time for coffee.

- Exchange daily e-mails.

- Arrange a combination of all of these options.

Keep your ears open. Ask the people around you if they know of anyone else who is contemplating or making a career change. After you make contact with someone you feel comfortable with, play with the format of your interaction until you find one that works for both of you.

Index

• *Numbers & Symbols* •

2young2retire.com, 87
100 Best Companies to Work For list, 52

• *A* •

AAERT. *See* American Association of
    Electronic Reporters and Transcribers
AANC. *See* American Association of
    Nutritional Consultants
ABA. *See* American Bar Association
ABF. *See* American Beekeeping
    Federation, The
About.com, 225, 263
academia, 51
accounting, 142–143
ACDA. *See* American Choral Directors
    Association, The
ACF. *See* American Culinary Federation
ACNM. *See* American College of
    Nurse-Midwives
ACS. *See* American Chemical Society
ACSM. *See* American Congress on Surveying
    & Mapping
acting, 192–193
ADD. *See* Adult Attention Deficit Disorder
ADHA. *See* American Dental Hygienists'
    Association
Adult Attention Deficit Disorder (ADD), 305
Advanced Placement (AP) examination, 264
aeronautical engineering, 141
AES. *See* Audio Engineering Society
AFM. *See* American Federation of Musicians
AFPA. *See* American Fitness Professional &
    Associates
AFT. *See* American Federation of Teachers
AHTA. *See* American Horticultural Therapy
    Association
AIAA. *See* American Institute of Aeronautics
    and Astronautics
AIBS. *See* American Institute of Biological
    Sciences
AICPA. *See* American Institute of Certified
    Public Accountants

AIMR. *See* Association for Investment
    Management and Research
AIP. *See* American Institute of Physics
Air Line Pilots Association International
    (ALPA), 181
Air and Waste Management Association
    (AMWA), 219
airplanes, working from, 16
ALA. *See* American Library Association
ALCA. *See* Associated Landscape Contractors
    of America
ALPA. *See* Air Line Pilots Association
    International
alternative medicine, 156–157
AMA. *See* American Management Association;
    American Marketing Association
American Association of Electronic Reporters
    and Transcribers (AAERT), 121
American Association of Nutritional
    Consultants (AANC), 157
American Bar Association (ABA), 125
American Beekeeping Federation, The
    (ABF), 214
American Chemical Society (ACS), 133
American Choral Directors Association, The
    (ACDA), 198
American College of Nurse-Midwives
    (ACNM), 157
American Congress on Surveying & Mapping
    (ACSM), 179
American Counseling Association, 159
American Culinary Federation (ACF), 189
American Dental Hygienists' Association
    (ADHA), 186
American Federation of Musicians (AFM), 197
American Federation of Police (AFP), 168
American Federation of Teachers (AFT), 123
American Fitness Professional & Associates
    (AFPA), 191
American Foreign Service, 128
American Guild of Musical Artists, 203
American Horticultural Therapy Association
    (AHTA), 209
American Hotel & Motel Association
    (AHMA), 163

American Institute of Aeronautics and Astronautics (AIAA), 141
American Institute of Architects, 176
American Institute of Biological Sciences (AIBS), 131
American Institute of Certified Public Accountants (AICPA), 143
American Institute of Chemical Engineers, 141
American Institute of Physics (AIP), 135
American League of Lobbyists, 128
American Library Association (ALA), 119
American Management Association (AMA), 167
American Marketing Association (AMA), 115, 126
American Massage Therapy Association, 188
American Mathematical Society (AMS), 134
American Meteorological Society, 218
American Music Therapy Association, 199
American Nurses Association, 155
American Planning Association (APA), 180
American Purchasing Society, 149
American Society of Appraisers, 146
American Society of Association Executives, 227
American Society of Civil Engineers (ASCE), 136
American Society of Composers, Authors, and Publishers (ASCAP), 198
American Society for Horticulture Science (ASHS), 207
American Society of Interior Designers (ASID), 178
American Society of Journalists and Authors (ASJA), 115
American Society of Landscape Architects (ASLA), 208
American Society of Limnology and Oceanography (ASLO), 216
American Society of Mechanical Engineering International (ASME), 137
American Society of Music Copyists (ASMC), 198
American Society of Travel Agents (ASTA), 163
American Statistical Association, 134
American Translators Association (ATA), 120
American Veterinary Medical Association, 213
America's Career InfoNet, 228

America's Learning Exchange, 264
AMHA. *See* American Hotel & Motel Association
AMS. *See* American Mathematical Society
AMWA. *See* Air and Waste Management Association
Anderson, Sherry Ruth, 34
angel investors, 287
animal care, 212
animals, working with, 210–214
anorexia, 305
AP. *See* Advanced Placement examination
APA. *See* American Planning Association
AFP. *See* American Federation of Police
appraising, 146
apprenticeships, 259
architecture, 176
art, 169–174
ASCAP. *See* American Society of Composers, Authors, and Publishers
ASCE. *See* American Society of Civil Engineers
ASHS. *See* American Society for Horticulture Science
Asia, 140
ASID. *See* American Society of Interior Designers
ASJA. *See* American Society of Journalists and Authors
ASLA. *See* American Society of Landscape Architects
ASLO. *See* American Society of Limnology and Oceanography
ASMC. *See* American Society of Music Copyists
ASME. *See* American Society of Mechanical Engineering International
assistants, virtual, 65, 151
AssistU.com, 151
Associated Landscape Contractors of America (ALCA), 209
Association for Investment Management and Research (AIMR), 146
Association for Non-Traditional Students in Higher Education, 268
associations, professional, 227
ASTA. *See* American Society of Travel Agents
ATA. *See* American Translators Association
BATF. *See* Bureau of Alcohol, Tobacco, and Firearms
Atlanta, 140
Audio Engineering Society (AES), 200

• *B* •

Back to College, Resources for the Re-Entry Student, 268
balancing careers and family, 14
banks, 143
Basic Books, 78
beaches, working from, 16
beekeeping, 214
benefits, determining requirements for, 60
Beverage World, 118
Biggest Employers, List of, 52
biology, 130–131
bonuses, 62
bookstores, 310–311
Boston, 140
Botanical Society of America, 207
botany, 206–207
breeding, 214
Bridges, William, 107
broadcasters, 122
buddy system, 318
Bureau of Alcohol, Tobacco, and Firearms (BATF), 167
Bureau of Diplomatic Security, 167
Bureau of Labor Statistics, 226
business cards, 242
business plans, creating, 291
Business Plans For Dummies, 291
businesses, starting. *See* starting a business
buying, 149

• *C* •

Cabinet Makers Association, The, 186
career paths, progressions of, 11–12
career changes. *See* changing careers
Career Zone, 225
careers. *See* changing careers
  accounting, 142–143
  acting, 192–193
  animal care, 212
  animal training, 211
  appraising, 146
  architecture, 176
  art, 169–174
  beekeeping, 214
  biology, 130–131
  botany, 206–207
  brainstorming, 96–101
  breeding, 214
  buying, 149
  changing. *See* changing careers
  chemistry, 132–133
  childcare, 159–160
  coaching, 160, 190–191, 204
  collecting, 148–149
  composite, 107
  computer science, 135–141
  construction, 176–177, 189–190
  cosmetology, 175
  counseling, 158–159
  culinary work, 188–189
  dancing, 193–194
  dentistry, 185–186
  drawing conclusions from your research of, 245
  ecology, 216–217
  editing, 117–118
  employee support, 165–166
  engineering, 135–141
  entomology, 214
  environmental, 215–219
  equipment repair, 187
  estimated number of during a lifetime, 11
  event planning, 147–148
  expanding horizons, 106–107
  exploring in bookstores, 310–311
  fashion design, 174–175
  finance, 145–146
  finding most intriguing, 101–103
  firefighting, 191
  foleying, 201
  food science, 209
  foreign service, 128
  forestry, 209–210
  gathering information about, 223–233
  graphic design, 170–171
  health care, 154–157
  horticulture, 207
  hospitality, 163
  image consulting, 175
  interior design, 177–178
  investigating, 150
  investing, 144–145
  jewelry work, 184–185
  journalism, music, 201
  landscape design, 208
  law, 124–125
  law enforcement, 167–168
  librarians, 118–119

careers *(continued)*
linguistics, 120
live performances, 199–200
loan officers, 143
lobbying, 128
management, 166–167, 201
managing businesses, 166–167
marketing, 115, 125–126
mathematics, 133–134
medicine, 130–131, 213
message therapy, 188
metal working, 184
meteorologists, 217–218
money management, 144
music, 195–204
musical instrument repair, 188
newscasters, 122
observing environment of, 239–245
observing lifestyle of, 240
observing someone at work in, 238
ombudsman, 128
personal and professional coaching, 160
photography, 171–172
physics, 134–135
piloting, 180–181
producing, 201–202
professional organizing, 151
professional speakers, 124
project management, 151
projecting future of, 315
public relations, 126–127
recording, 200–201
recreation, 161–162
relocations, 151
reporters, 122
sales, 115, 127, 201
scanning newspapers for, 309–310
soil science, 209
staffing, 164–165
success in, definition of, 13–15
surveying, 178–179
tailoring, 186
taking classes related to, 236–237
teachers, 123
therapy, music, 197–199
training, 190–191
transcriptionists, 120–121
transitioning into, 253–254, 307
translators, 119–120
travel, 162–163
trying lifestyle of, 237–238

undertaking, 160
urban planning, 179–180
veterinary medicine, 213
virtual assistants, 151
waste management, 218–219
wildlife management, 213–214
woodworking, 186
writing, 112–116
zoology, 210–211
cars, working from, 16
celebrations, successful career changes, 316
Center for Community Futures, The, 291
Chain Leader, 118
Chamber of Commerce, 292
Chanel, Coco, 315
changing careers
acting on plans for, 306–307
allowing time for thinking deeply about, 301–302
attending professional association meetings, 241–242
choosing companies where you want to work, 50–59
choosing industries of interest, 90
choosing topics of interest, 82–89
clarifying goals, 262–263
committing to, 299–300
creating buddy system, 318
creating distance from current situation, 302–303
deciding how to celebrate after, 316
deciding what matters most, 28
defining success, 21
determining most important needs, 40–41
effects of location on career options, 35–36
employment contract options, 48–49
evaluating how you live, 20
evaluating state of health, 32–33
evaluating your personality, 18–19, 305
expansion of choices, 12–13
favorite tools, equipment, and raw materials, 89
feeling at home in, 283–284
finding emotional support during, 300–301
finding open doors, 305–306
following up on leads, 275–279
getting a degree, 262–269
getting out of ruts, 303–305
giving notice at current job, 282–283
ideal work schedules, 45–48
identifying values, 32

imagining working in new job, 237
impacts of family on your work, 37–40
income and benefit requirements, 60
inspiring yourself during, 309–318
joining online communities, 243–244
keeping sanity during, 73, 299–307
launching searches, 272–275
listening to inner cravings, 27–28
motivating yourself, 309–318
planning for, 306–307
preferences in coworker characteristics, 63–67
projecting future of current career, 315
pursuing hobbies and interests, 33, 35
rating current work arrangement, 21–26
receiving job offers, 281–283
receiving some experience in, 244–245
releasing old strategies and answers about, 303–305
resolving conflicts about, 247–254
subscribing to newsletters, 243
taking vacations from, 70, 72, 313–314
talking to people who love their jobs, 317
transitioning into, 253–254, 307
trying lifestyle of, 237–238
uncovering and rediscovering skills, 77–82
understanding your personality and temperament, 30–31
Charleston Regional Business Journal, 118
checklists for career changers
  brainstorming new career possibilities, 96–101
  building profile of ideal work situation, 68
  characteristics of coworkers, 63–67
  characteristics of favorite clients and customers, 91
  choosing companies where you want to work, 50–59
  choosing industries of interest, 90
  choosing topics of interest, 82–89
  deciding what matters most, 28
  defining success, 21
  employment contract options, 48–49
  evaluating work options where you live, 35–36
  examining work you do now, 26–27
  favorite tools, equipment, and raw materials, 89
  hobbies and interests, 33, 35
  how you live, 20
  how you work, 22

ideal work schedules, 45–48
identifying values, 32
impacts of family on your work, 37–40
intriguing career ideas, 101–103
listening to inner cravings, 27–28
listing most important needs, 40–41
Multiple Intelligence profile, 78–80
pay and benefits, 22–23
payment options and benefits, 60–63
personality and temperament, 30–31
recording hottest passions and interests, 92–93
state of health, 32–33
uncovering and rediscovering skills, 77–82
what makes work meaningful, 92
where you work, 23–24
who and how you are, 18–19
who you work with, 24–25
chemical engineering, 141
chemistry, 132–133
childcare, 63, 159–160
children, effects of on career options, 37
choosing careers. *See* changing careers
Cinema Audio Society, The, 201
civil engineering, 136
classes, 236–237, 259
clients, characteristics of, 91
co-workers, characteristics of, 63–67
coaching, 160, 190–191, 204
collecting, 148–149
colleges. *See* schools
Collegiate.net, 263
Columbia Books Inc., 227
commissions, 62
commitments to career changes, 299–300
community service, 14, 63
commuting, reimbursement for, 63
companies. *See* starting a business
  career paths in, 11–12
  choosing where you want to work, 50–59
  cultures of, 53–54
  dress codes in, 58–59
  Fortune's lists of the best and biggest, 52
  giving notice at, 282–283
  lifetime employment with, 10–11
  locations of, 56–57
  observing culture of during interviews, 278
  purpose of, 54–55
  reach of, 54–55
  training financed by, 260–261
  transfers within, 70

companies *(continued)*
  types of, 51–52
  virtual, 16
  work areas in, 57–58
  working on-site, 15–16
  working on the road for, 14, 38, 56, 59
compensation. *See* benefits; salaries
competition, checking on, 289
Complementary Alternative Medical
    Association, 157
composite careers, 107
composing, 198
computer consulting, 141
computer engineering, 139–140
computer science, 135–141
Conari Press, 301
concierge services, 63
conducting, 198
conferences, 261
conflicts over changing careers, resolving,
    247–254
construction, 176–177, 189–190
consultants, 49, 64–65, 141
contacts, how to make, 231–233
contract employees, 49, 65
contracts with employers, 48–49
Cool Careers For Dummies, 226
copying music, 198
Cornell University's Career Zone, 225
corporations, 292
cosmetology, 175
cost of living, effects of on career options, 36
Council of Fashion Designers of America, 175
counseling, 158–159
courses. *See* classes
cravings, listening to, 27–28
credits, converting experience into, 264
culinary work, 188–189
Cultural Creatives subgroup, 34
*Cultural Creatives, The: How 50 Million People
    are Changing the World*, 34
cultural subgroups, 34
cultures of companies, 53–54
customers, 91, 289
Customs, 167

Dallas, 140
dancing, 193–194
data dumps, 311–312
daycare. *See* childcare
DEA. *See* Drug Enforcement Association
deal-breakers, 280–281
degrees, receiving from schools, 262–269
dental insurance, 63
dentistry, 185–186
Denver, 140
Dictionary of Occupational Titles, The, 226
Directory of Associations, 227
distance, creating from current situation,
    302–303
distance learning, 264
Distance Learning Online For Dummies, 263
domain names, 293
downshifting positions, 12, 70
dress codes, 58–59
Drug Enforcement Association (DEA), 167

• E •

e-mail, 242, 274
e-zines, 243
Ecological Society of America (ESA), 217
ecology, 216–217
economy, effects of on work options, 35–36
editing careers, 117–118
Editorial Freelancers Association (EFA), 118
editorial writing, 114–115
educational institutions, 51
EFA. *See* Editorial Freelancers Association
Eichelbaum, Elizabeth, 315
elder care, 63
electrical engineering, 137–138
Electronics Technician Association (ETA), 187
emotional support during career changes,
    300–301
employee assistance programs, 63
Employee Relocation Council (ERC), 151
employee support, 165–166
employment, lifetime for same company, 10–11
employment contracts, 48–49
Employment Training Administration, 226
Encyclopedia of Associations, 227

Encyclopedia of Careers and Vocational Guidance, The, 226
engineering, 135–141
engineering technology, 141
Enneagram, 31
Entomological Society of America, 214
entomology, 214
environmental careers, 215–219
equipment, favorites to work with, 89
equipment repair, 187
ERC. *See* Employee Relocation Council
ESA. *See* Ecological Society of America
ETA. *See* Electronics Technician Association
evaluations. *See* checklists
event planning, 147–148
examinations, converting work experience into credits through, 264
Executive Council on Foreign Diplomacy, 128
executives, careers for, 166–167
Exit Stage Right, 87
expense accounts, 63
eye care insurance, 63

● **F** ●

Falkenstein, Lynda, 289
families, 14–15, 37–40
family-owned companies, 51
fashion design, 174–175
Faust, 315
fax, sending resumes by, 274
Federal Bureau of Investigation (FBI), 167
finance, 145–146
financial aid for college, 266–267
Financial Management Association International (FMA), 144
financial resources, 301
finding jobs. *See* changing careers
firefighting, 191
flex-time, 16, 47
FMA. *See* Financial Management Association International
foleying, 201
food science, 209
foreign service, 128
forestry, 209–210
Fortune magazine, 52
Frames of Mind: The Theory of Multiple Intelligences, 78

Free Scholarship Search Web site, 267
freelance writers, 116
freelancers, 49, 65
friends, getting career ideas from, 104
full-time employment, 49
funding for businesses, 287
future of current career, thinking about, 315

● **G** ●

GAG. *See* Graphic Artist Guild
Gale Group, 227
Gardner, Howard, 78
Geographic Information System (GIS), 178
Geological Society of America, 216
geologists, 215–216
Germany, 140
GIS. *See* Geographic Information System
Glenn, 315
Global Positioning System (GPS), 178
Goethe, 315
government agencies, 51
GPS. *See* Global Positioning System
Graduate Record Exam (GRE), 264
Grandma Moses, 315
grandparents, effects of on career options, 37
Graphic Artist Guild (GAG), 171
graphic design, 170–171
GRE. *See* Graduate Record Exam
Great Voice, 204
Gulf Mariner, 118
Guterman, Mark, 32

● **H** ●

hands, working with, 186–189
headhunters, 273
health, evaluating state of, 32–33
health care, 154–157
health clubs, 63
Highly Sensitive Person Web site, 305
hobbies
ability to explore, 14
pursuit of, 33, 35
holistic medicine, 156–157
home-based companies, 51
horticultural therapy, 209
horticulture, 207
hospitality, 163

hotelling, office, 56
hotels, working from, 16
HotJobs.com, 275
hourly wages, 62
Human Genome Project, 130
human resources, 164–166

• *I* •

IAFF. *See* International Association of
    Firefighters
ICCA. *See* Independent Computer Consultants
    Association
identities, business, 292–293
IEEE. *See* Institute of Electrical and
    Electronics Engineers
IFT. *See* Institute of Food Technologist
image consulting, 175
Immigration and Naturalization Service
    (INS), 167
incomes, determining requirements for, 60
Independent Computer Consultants
    Association (ICCA), 141
industrial engineering, 138–139
industries, 90
industry profiles, 224–226
informal training, 258–259
informational interviews, 232–233
inner cravings, listening to, 27–28
INS. *See* Immigration and Naturalization
    Service
inspiration, keeping alive during career
    changes, 309–318
Institute of Electrical and Electronic
    Engineering Computing Society, 140
Institute of Electrical and Electronics
    Engineers (IEEE), 138, 141
Institute of Food Technologist (IFT), 209
Institute of Industrial Engineers, 139
instruments, playing, 196–197
insurance, 63
interests, pursuit of, 33, 35
interior design, 177–178
International Association of Firefighters
    (IAFF), 191
International Association of Fish and Wildlife
    Agencies, 214
International Coach Federation, 160
International Crime Scene Investigators
    Association, 150
International Ombudsman Institute, 128

Internet, posting resumes on, 274. *See also*
    Web sites
Internet access, 36
interviews, 232–233, 276–279
investigating, 150
investing, 144–145
investors, angel, 287
Ireland, 140

• *J* •

Jewelers of America, 185
jewelry work, 184–185
JG Ferguson Publishing Company, 226
job searches
    acting on plans for, 306–307
    allowing time for thinking deeply about,
        301–302
    attending professional association
        meetings, 241–242
    choosing companies where you want to
        work, 50–59
    choosing industries of interest, 90
    choosing topics of interest, 82–89
    clarifying goals, 262–263
    committing to, 299–300
    creating buddy system, 318
    creating distance from current situation,
        302–303
    deciding how to celebrate after, 316
    deciding what matters most, 28
    defining success, 21
    determining most important needs, 40–41
    effects of location on career options, 35–36
    employment contract options, 48–49
    evaluating how you live, 20
    evaluating state of health, 32–33
    evaluating your personality, 18–19, 305
    expansion of choices, 12–13
    favorite tools, equipment, and raw
        materials, 89
    feeling at home in, 283–284
    finding emotional support during, 300–301
    finding open doors, 305–306
    following up on leads, 275–279
    getting a degree, 262–269
    getting out of ruts, 303–305
    giving notice at current job, 282–283
    ideal work schedules, 45–48
    identifying values, 32
    imagining working in new job, 237

impacts of family on your work, 37–40
income and benefit requirements, 60
inspiring yourself during, 309–318
joining online communities, 243–244
keeping sanity during, 73, 299–307
launching searches, 272–275
listening to inner cravings, 27–28
motivating yourself, 309–318
narrowing focus of, 13
planning for, 306–307
preferences in coworker characteristics, 63–67
projecting future of current career, 315
pursuing hobbies and interests, 33, 35
rating current work arrangement, 21–26
receiving job offers, 281–283
receiving some experience in, 244–245
releasing old strategies and answers about, 303–305
resolving conflicts about, 247–254
skills for. *See* skills
subscribing to newsletters, 243
taking vacations from, 70, 72, 313–314
talking to people who love their jobs, 317
transitioning into, 253–254, 307
trying lifestyle of, 237–238
uncovering and rediscovering skills, 77–82
understanding your personality and temperament, 30–31
job sharing, 49
Job-hunt.org, 275
jobs
    accepting new job in the same field, 72
    converting experience into college credits, 264
    downshifting, 12, 70
    examining work you do now, 26–27
    finding project related to, 260
    flex-time, 16, 47
    following up on leads, 275–279
    full-time, 49
    giving notice at, 282–283
    imagining working in, 237
    keeping sanity without, 73
    launching searches for, 272–275
    observing environment of, 239–249
    observing lifestyle of, 240
    observing someone at work in, 238
    on-site, 15–16
    part-time, 49, 261

rating current arrangement, 21–26
    receiving offers for, 281–283
    receiving training at, 259–260
    recommended length for staying in, 10
    reinventing, 70
    renegotiating responsibilities, 70
    satellite offices, 15
    short-term, 261–262
    stepping-stone, 72
    success in, definition of, 13–15
    talking to people who love, 317
    telecommuting, 15, 56
    with temporary agencies, 71–72
    temporary. *See* short-term jobs
    toxic environments, 25
    transfers within companies, 70
    in unrelated fields, 71
    working on the road, 14, 38, 56, 59
JobShift: How to Prosper in a Workplace Without Jobs, 107
JobSleuth.com, 275
journalism, music, 201
journals, 311–312

• K •

Kaplan, 267
Karp, Terry, 32
Kennedy, Joyce Lain, 273
Kiersey Character Type Sorter, 31
Kroc, Ray, 315

• L •

landscape design, 208
landscaping, 209
lateral moves, 12
law, 124–125
law enforcement, 167–168
leads, following up on, 275–279
leaves of absence, 70
librarians, 118–119
life insurance, 63
lifestyles, 14–15, 18–20, 237–238
linguistics, 120
Linguistics Society of America, 120
live performances, 199–200
loan officers, careers for, 143
lobbying, 128

locations
   effects of on work options, 35–36
   finding for thinking deeply about career
      changes, 201
   for gaining new skills, 257–258
   scouting for starting businesses, 290
long-term disability, 63
lunches, inviting people to, 242

• *M* •

McDonald's, 315
Make Your Site Sell, 292
management, 166–167, 201
managers, characteristics of, 65–67
managing time, 73
marketing, 115, 125–126, 293–294
mathematics, 133–134
mechanical engineering, 136–137
medical insurance, 63
medicine, 130–131, 213
Meeting Professionals International, 148
meetings, professional associations, 241–241
message therapy, 188
metal working, 184
meteorologists, 217–218
micro businesses, 52, 291
mid-size companies, 52
midwifery, 157
Minneapolis, 140
minorities, expanded career choices for, 13
modems, 36
Moderns subgroup, 34
Mom Goes Back to School, 268
money management, 144
Monster.com, 244, 275
mortgages, 143
motivation, keeping alive during career
      changes, 309–318
MTNA. *See* Music Teachers National
      Association
Multiple Intelligence profile, 78–80
music, 195–204
Music Critics Association, 201
music journalism, 201
Music Teachers National Association
      (MTNA), 197
music therapy, 197–199
musical instrument repair, 188

• *N* •

NAB. *See* National Association of
      Broadcasters
NAEYC. *See* National Association for
      Education of Young Children
NAHB. *See* National Association of
      Home Builders
NAMB. *See* National Association of Mortgage
      Brokers
nameprotect.com, 293
names, choosing for businesses, 293
NAPFA. *See* National Association of Personal
      Financial Advisors
NAPO. *See* National Association of
      Professional Organizers
NARM. *See* National Association of Recording
      Merchandisers
NASD. *See* National Society of Security
      Dealers
NASP. *See* National Association of Sales
      Professionals
National Academy of Recording Arts and
      Sciences, 202
National Artists Equity Association, 174
National Association for Education of Young
      Children (NAEYC), 160
National Association of Broadcasters
      (NAB), 122
National Association of Home Builders
      (NAHB), 177
National Association of Milliners,
      Dressmakers, and Tailors, 186
National Association of Mortgage Brokers
      (NAMB), 143
National Association of Personal Financial
      Advisors (NAPFA), 146
National Association of Professional
      Organizers (NAPO), 151
National Association of Recording
      Merchandisers (NARM), 201
National Association of Sales Professionals
      (NASP), 127
National Conference of Personal Managers
      (NCOPM), 201
National Dance Association, 194
National Dog Grooming Association of
      America, 212
National Electrical Contractors Association
      (NECA), 190

National Funeral Directors Association, 160
National Institute for Certification in Engineering Technologies (NICET), 141
National Institute for Metalworking Skills (NIMS), 184
National Pet Dealers and Breeders Association, 214
National Recreation and Parks Association (NRPA), 162
National Rehabilitation Association, 156
National Society of Security Dealers (NASD), 145
National Speakers Association (NSA), 124
National Trade & Professional Associations Directory, 227
National Weather Service, 217
National Writers Union (NWU), 116
NCOPM. *See* National Conference of Personal Managers
NECA. *See* National Electrical Contractors Association
Network Solutions, 293
networking, 273–274, 283
New York City, 140
newscasters, 122
newsletters, subscribing to, 243
newspapers, 309–310
NICET. *See* National Institute for Certification in Engineering Technologies
Niche Press, 289
Nichecraft: Using Your Specialness to Focus Your Business, Corner Your Market and Make Customer Seek You Out, 289
niches, defining for businesses, 288–289
NIMS. *See* National Institute for Metalworking Skills
North Carolina, 140
not-for-profit companies, 51
notices, giving at current job, 282–283
NRPA. *See* National Recreation and Parks Association
NSA. *See* National Speakers Association
nursing, 154–155
nutrition, 157
NWU. *See* National Writers Union

• O •

objectivity in informational interviews, 233
Occupational Outlook Handbook, 225–226
offers, receiving for jobs, 281–283

office hotelling, 56
ombudsmen, 128
online career profiles, 224–226
online communities, becoming member of, 243–244
online courses, 259
online job searches, 274–275
opinions, writing, 114–115
organizing, 151

• P •

painting, 172
panic, avoiding while not working, 73
parents, effects of on career options, 37
parking, reimbursement for, 63
part-time employment, 49, 261
partner-owned companies, 51
partners
 effects of on career options, 37
 spending more time with, 14
partnerships, 52, 292
Peace Corps, 303
performances, live, 199–200
Perseus Books, 107
personal coaching, 160
personality, evaluating, 30–31, 305
Peterson, Steven D., 291
pets, effects of career options on, 39
phased-out retirement, 49
Phoenix University, 264
phones. *See* telephones
photography, 171–172
physics, 134–135
Piano Technicians Guild (PTG), 188
piloting, 180–181
plants, working with, 206–210
PMI. *See* Project Management Institute
portfolios, 264
PPA. *See* Professional Photographers of America
pre-IPOs, 51
precision work, 183–186
Princeton Review, 225
privately-held companies, 51
producing, 201–202
products, defining for businesses, 288–289
professional associations, 227, 241–242
professional coaching, 160
Professional Handlers' Association, The, 212
professional organizing, 151

Professional Photographers of America (PPA), 172
profiles, online career and industry, 224–226
profit sharing, 62
project management, 151
Project Management Institute (PMI), 151
PRSA. *See* Public Relations Society of America
psychology, 158–159
PTG. *See* Piano Technicians Guild
public companies, 51
public relations, 126–127
Public Relations Society of America (PRSA), 127

quality of life. *See* lifestyles
questions
asking about careers, 229–230
asking during interviews, 277–278

• R •

raw materials, favorites to work with, 89
Ray, Paul H., 34
recording, 200–201
recreation, 161–162
recruiters, 273–274
Recruiters Network, 164
Regents College Examinations, 264
rehabilitation, 155–156
relocations, 151
reporters, 122
reporting careers, 113–114
Research Triangle, 140
resumes, 272–274
Resumes For Dummies, 273
retirement, 49, 63
retreats, 70
RileyGuide.com, 275
Room For Older College Students, A., 268
royalties, 62
Runner's Gazette, 118
ruts, getting out of, 303–305

• S •

sabbaticals, 73
SAG. *See* Screen Actors Guild
salaries, 62, 228

salary.com, 228
sales, 115, 127, 201
San Francisco, 140
sanity, keeping during career changes, 73, 299–307
satellite offices, 15, 56
SBA. *See* Small Business Administration
scanned resumes, 274
schedules, work, 45–48
Scholarships 2001, 267
schools, 14, 51, 262–269
SCORE. *See* Service Corps of Retired Executives
Screen Actors Guild (SAG), 193
searching for jobs. *See* changing careers
Season of Change, The, 301
Secret Service, 167
selecting careers. *See* changing careers
self employment, 49
Service Corps of Retired Executives (SCORE), 291
services, defining for businesses, 288–289
severance packages, 63
sheilaellison.com, 87
short-term disability, 63
short-term jobs, 261–262
SHRM. *See* Society for Human Resource Management
SICB. *See* Society for Integrative and Comparative Biology
Silicon Valley, 140
singing, 202–203
sites. *See* Web sites
sizes of companies, 50, 52
skills
deciding best learning method for, 256–258
deciding what's needed to improve, 255–256
gaining on the job, 259–260
receiving informal training, 258–259
uncovering and rediscovering, 77–82
Small Business Administration (SBA), 287, 291–293
Small Business Development Centers, 291
small businesses, 52
Society of American Archivists, 149
Society of American Foresters, 210
Society for Human Resource Management (SHRM), 166
Society for Integrative and Comparative Biology (SICB), 211
Society of Professional Audio Recording Services (SPARS), 201

Society for Technical Communication (STC), 113
software engineering, 140–141
soil science, 209
Soil Science Society of America, 209
sole proprietors, 52–53, 292
solutions, conflicts over changing careers, 247–254
SPARS. *See* Society of Professional Audio Recording Services
speakers, 124
staffing, 164–165
Stagg, Amos Alonzo, 315
start-ups, 51
starting a business
  acquiring technical knowledge for, 286
  checking out competition, 289
  choosing names for, 293
  creating a business identity, 292–293
  creating a business plan, 291
  defining products and services, 288–289
  easing into, 290
  establishing work spaces, 293
  exploring funding options, 287
  feeling at home in, 294–296
  getting emotional support, 288
  looking at key personality traits, 285–286
  marketing strategies, 293–294
  receiving basic skills to operate, 286–287
  scouting location options, 290
  staying focused in, 296
  structuring, 292
  talking to potential customers, 289
STC. *See* Society for Technical Communication
stepping-stone jobs, 72
Stevenson, Nancy, 263
stock options, 62
subgroups, cultural, 34
subscriptions to newsletters, 243
Success Anorexia Web site, 305
success in careers, 13–15, 21
support networks, effects of career options on, 39
surveying, 178–179

• T •

tailoring, 186
teachers, 123
teaching, 197

TECEP. *See* Thomas Edison College Examination Program
technical writing, 112–113
telecommuting, 15, 56
telecourses, 259
telephones, 36
temperament, evaluating, 30–31
temporary agencies, 71–72
temporary employees, 49, 65
temporary jobs. *See* short-term jobs
therapy
  horticultural, 209
  music, 197–199
Thomas Edison College Examination Program (TECEP), 264
Tiffany, Paul, 291
time, managing wisely, 73
tools, favorites to work with, 89
Topica, 244
topics of interest, choosing, 82–89
toxic environments, 25
trade-offs, 280–281
trademarks, 293
Traditionals subgroup, 34
training
  careers in, 190–191, 211
  deciding best method for, 256–258
  deciding what's needed, 255–256
  informal, 258–259
  receiving on the job, 259–260
transcriptionists, 120–121
transitions into new careers, 253–254, 307
translators, 119–120
travel
  careers in, 162–163
  effects of on career options, 36
  working on the road, 14, 38, 56, 59
treats, 71

• U •

undertaking, 160
United States Department of Labor, 11
United States Open University, 264
United States Secret Service, 167
universities. *See* schools
urban planning, 179–180
U.S. Department of Labor, 226

• V •

vacations, 70, 72, 313–314
values, identifying, 32
VASTA. *See* Voice and Speech Trainers Association
vendors, 65
venture capital firms, 287
veterinary medicine, 213
virtual assistants, 65, 151
virtual companies, 16, 56
voice coaching, 204
Voice and Speech Trainers Association (VASTA), 204
voiceovers, 203–204
volunteering to gain skills, 259
Votech Education, 226

• W •

wages. *See* salaries
walks, inviting people on, 242
waste management, 218–219
weather, effects of on work options, 35
weather forecasters, 217–218
Web sites
  2young2retire.com, 87
  About.com, 225
  Adult Attention Deficit Disorder (ADD), 305
  Air Line Pilots Association International (ALPA), 181
  Air and Waste Management Association (AMWA), 219
  American Association of Electronic Reporters and Transcribers (AAERT), 121
  American Association of Nutritional Consultants (AANC), 157
  American Bar Association (ABA), 125
  American Beekeeping Federation, The (ABF), 214
  American Chemical Society (ACS), 133
  American Choral Directors Association, The (ACDA), 198
  American College of Nurse-Midwives (ACNM), 157
  American Congress on Surveying & Mapping (ACSM), 179
  American Culinary Federation (ACF), 189

  American Dental Hygienists' Association (ADHA), 186
  American Federation of Musicians (AFM), 197
  American Federation of Police (AFP), 168
  American Federation of Teachers (AFT), 123
  American Fitness Professional & Associates (AFPA), 191
  American Horticultural Therapy Association (AHTA), 209
  American Hotel & Motel Association (AHMA), 163
  American Institute of Certified Public Accountants (AICPA), 143
  American Institute of Aeronautics and Astronautics (AIAA), 141
  American Institute of Architects, 176
  American Institute of Biological Sciences (AIBS), 131
  American Institute of Chemical Engineers, 141
  American Institute of Physics (AIP), 135
  American League of Lobbyists, 128
  American Library Association (ALA), 119
  American Management Association (AMA), 167
  American Marketing Association (AMA), 115
  American Massage Therapy Association, 188
  American Mathematical Society (AMS), 134
  American Meteorological Society, 218
  American Music Therapy Association, 199
  American Nurses Association, 155
  American Planning Association (APA), 180
  American Purchasing Society, 149
  American Society of Appraisers, 146
  American Society of Association Executives, 227
  American Society of Civil Engineers (ASCE), 136
  American Society of Composers, Authors, and Publishers (ASCAP), 198
  American Society for Horticulture Science (ASHS), 207
  American Society of Interior Designers (ASID), 178
  American Society of Journalists and Authors (ASJA), 115
  American Society of Landscape Architects (ASLA), 208

American Society of Limnology and Oceanography (ASLO), 216

American Society of Mechanical Engineering International (ASME), 137

American Society of Music Copyists (ASMC), 198

American Society of Travel Agents (ASTA), 163

American Statistical Association, 134

American Translators Association (ATA), 120

America's Career InfoNet, 228

America's Learning Exchange, 264

AssistU.com, 151

Associated Landscape Contractors of America (ALCA), 209

Association for Investment Management and Research (AIMR), 146

Association for Non-Traditional Students in Higher Education, 268

Audio Engineering Society (AES), 200

Back to College, Resources for the Re-Entry Student, 268

Botanical Society of America, 207

Cabinet Makers Association, The, 186

Center for Community Futures, The, 291

Cinema Audio Society, The, 201

college information, 263

Complementary Alternative Medical Association, 157

Cornell University's Career Zone, 225

Cultural Creatives, 34

Dictionary of Occupational Titles, The, 226

Directory of Associations, 227

Ecological Society of America (ESA), 217

Editorial Freelancers Association (EFA), 118

Electronics Technician Association (ETA), 187

Employee Relocation Council (ERC), 151

Encyclopedia of Associations, 227

Encyclopedia of Careers and Vocational Guidance, The, 226

Enneagram, 31

Entomological Society of America, 214

Exit Stage Right, 87

Falkenstein, Lynda, 289

Financial Management Association International (FMA), 144

Fortune's 100 Best Companies to Work For and Biggest Employers lists, 52

Free Scholarship Search, 267

Geological Society of America, 216

Graphic Artist Guild (GAG), 171

Great Voice, 204

Highly Sensitive Person, 305

Independent Computer Consultants Association (ICCA), 141

Institute of Electrical and Electronic Engineering Computing Society, 140

Institute of Electrical and Electronics Engineers (IEEE), 138

Institute of Food Technologist (IFT), 209

Institute of Industrial Engineers, 139

International Association of Firefighters (IAFF), 191

International Association of Fish and Wildlife Agencies, 214

International Coach Federation, 160

International Ombudsman Institute, 128

Jewelers of America, 185

job searches, 275

Kiersay Character Type Sorter, 31

Linguistics Society of America, 120

Make Your Site Sell, 292

Meeting Professionals International, 148

Mom Goes Back to School, 268

Monster.com, 244, 275

Music Critics Association, 201

Music Teachers National Association (MTNA), 197

nameprotect.com, 293

National Artists Equity Association, 174

National Association of Broadcasters (NAB), 122

National Association for Education of Young Children (NAEYC), 160

National Association of Home Builders (NAHB), 177

National Association of Mortgage Brokers (NAMB), 143

National Association of Personal Financial Advisors (NAPFA), 146

National Association of Professional Organizers (NAPO), 151

National Association of Recording Merchandisers (NARM), 201

National Association of Sales Professionals (NASP), 127

National Conference of Personal Managers (NCOPM), 201

Web sites *(continued)*
National Dance Association, 194
National Dog Grooming Association of
America, 212
National Electrical Contractors Association
(NECA), 190
National Institute for Certification in
Engineering Technologies (NICET), 141
National Institute for Metalworking Skills
(NIMS), 184
National Recreation and Parks Association
(NRPA), 162
National Rehabilitation Association, 156
National Society of Security Dealers
(NASD), 145
National Speakers Association (NSA), 124
*National Trade & Professional Associations
Directory,* 227
National Writers Union (NWU), 116
Network Solutions, 293
Occupational Outlook Handbook, 225–226
Phoenix University, 264
Piano Technicians Guild (PTG), 188
portfolio reviews, 264
Princeton Review, 225
Professional Handlers' Association, The, 212
Professional Photographers of America
(PPA), 172
Project Management Institute (PMI), 151
Public Relations Society of America
(PRSA), 127
Recruiters Network, 164
Room For Older College Students, A., 268
salary.com, 228
Screen Actors Guild (SAG), 193
Service Corps of Retired Executives
(SCORE), 291
sheilaellison.com, 87
Small Business Administration (SBA), 287
Small Business Development Centers, 291

Society of American Archivists, 149
Society of American Foresters, 210
Society for Human Resource Management
(SHRM), 166
Society for Integrative and Comparative
Biology (SICB), 211
Society of Professional Audio Recording
Services (SPARS), 201
Society for Technical Communication
(STC), 113
Soil Science Society of America, 209
Success Anorexia, 305
Topica, 244
United States Open University, 264
virtual assistant information, 65
Voice and Speech Trainers Association
(VASTA), 204
Votech Education, 226
Wetfeet.com, 225, 244
Work Options, 44
Yahoo! Groups, 244
Web-based companies, 51
Wetfeet.com, 225, 244
wildlife management, 213–214
women, expanded career choices for, 13
woodworking, 186
work areas, 57–58
Work Options Web site, 44
work. *See* jobs
writing careers, 112–116

• Y •

Yahoo! Groups, 244

• Z •

zoology, 210–211

Notes

Notes